W9-DGK-093

SECRETS OF ENTERTAINING
FROM AMERICA'S BEST INNKEEPERS

7

SECRETS OF ENTERTAINING
FROM AMERICA'S BEST INNKEEPERS

by
Gail Greco
illustrations by Lynne M. Kopcik

THE GLOBE PEQUOT PRESS CHESTER, CONNECTICUT

All inns in this book were included on the sole basis of owners' and managers' responses during interviews and to questionnaires. No one paid or was paid to have an inn featured.

Library of Congress Cataloging-in-Publication Data
Greco, Gail.
    Secrets of entertaining from America's best innkeepers / by Gail Greco.—1st ed.
        p.   cm.
    Includes index.
    ISBN (invalid) 0-86106-533-9
    1. Entertaining.   I. Title.
TX731.G688   1989
642'.4—dc20   89-11905
                                                      CIP

Cover: The Inn at Wethersfield, Wethersfield, Vermont
Cover Design: Barbara Marks

Manfactured in the United States of America
First Edition/First Printing

For the Heritage Inn,
whose cheerful lantern was a welcoming sight
on a lonely autumn night
in the heart of the Catskill Mountains

Contents

Preface   1

Host Appeal   5
  Preparing Your Home for Guests   7
  Preparing the Guest Room   8
  Preparing the Guest Bathroom   13
  Scent-sational Ideas for Guests   16
  Preparing Yourself for Guests   18
  Greeting and Hosting Guests   19
  The Goodbyes   22

Cooking and Entertaining   24
  Kitchen Tips   26
  Entertaining Preparations   27
  Setting the Table   28
  Serving   38
  Entertaining Etiquette   41
  Garnishes   41
  Coffee Perks   45
  Wine Wisdom   46
  Picnics   47
  Breakfast   48
  Appetizers, Snacks, and Beverages   70
  Entrees and Side Dishes   86
  Desserts and Other Sweets   93

Taking Tea **102**
  Making Tea 104
  Serving Tea 107
  Theme Teas 110
  Beverages 113
  Scones, Tea Cakes, Breads, and Muffins 117
  Pies, Cakes, and Sweets 130
  Sandwiches and Other Nonsweets 138

Hosting a Holiday, a Party, or a Theme Dinner **144**
  Tips for All Holidays 145
  Valentine's Day 146
  Saint Patrick's Day 147
  Easter 147
  Memorial Day 150
  Independence Day 150
  Halloween 150
  Thanksgiving 151
  Christmas 153
  New Year's Eve 161
  Special-Occasion Parties 162

Restoration and Home Improvements **168**
  Shopping for an Old Home 170
  Restoration Basics 175
  Bathroom Restoration and Renovation 182
  Kitchen Renovation 184
  House Exterior 187

Decorating and You **189**
  Decorating Basics 191
  Painting 197
  Wallcoverings 199
  Stenciling 201
  Window Treatments 206
  Decorating with Sheets 208
  Lighting 210
  Decorating Hints for All Rooms 212
  Floor Decor 219
  Decorating with Collections 219
  Wall Hangings 221

Antiques and Collectibles   **227**
  Using Your Antiques   228
  Buying and Caring for Antiques   247

Cut Flowers, Plants, and Gardens   **252**
  Flowers   253
  Indoor Plants   256
  Gardening   257

Fireside Tips   **265**
  Starting a Fire   266
  Fireplace Decor   269
  Fireside Entertainment   270

Household Hints   **275**
  Making Housekeeping Easier   276
  Cleaning   277
  Homemaking Improvements   288
  Creative Housekeeping   289
  Furniture   290
  Laundry Care   292
  Bedding Control   294
  Front-Porch Philosophy   296

Appendix   **305**

Index   **325**

Preface

It was nighttime, and we were lost. As our tiny sports car negotiated the treacherous mountain road, our predicament seemed as chilling as the blustery fall air. To the left of the roadway, the landscape fell away into a ravine just beyond the narrow strip of blacktop. A thick, shadowy forest jutted up from the valley floor below and towered above us. To the right, a broad, rocky mountain face caressed the roadway.

Somewhere in this seemingly endless mountain range, I shivered at the prospect of passing the night beside the lonely two-lane highway—wedged against a car door with no pillow to buoy either cheek or sinking spirit. My husband and I had been driving for hours. We were listless and in need of a good meal, and our energy was ebbing as the night grew older. Suddenly, a glow of light over a nearby rise signaled hope and awakened our senses.

We followed the beam with anticipation and found an antique lantern hanging from a restored and freshly painted milk wagon. A sign read, FINE FOOD AND LODGING. An inviting two-story farmhouse stood before us. We knocked heartily on the beckoning front door. A smiling innkeeper ushered us into what we would later describe as something out of a storybook. An abundance of flickering candles coaxed the romantic atmosphere. A mélange of welcoming cooking aromas floated through the entryway. That we had never been in a country inn before and did not know what to expect was no problem; the innkeeper came to our rescue and squired us toward our room. As we followed him up the staircase, we could hear the fire's embers crackling above quiet conversations and eclipsing the gentle clinking of china in the dining room.

Our room was decorated circa 1890; our bath down the hall was pleasant. As we freshened up for dinner, we wondered what other surprises awaited us down and around the Victorian staircase.

In the dining room, plush Queen Anne chairs comforted us at our elegant table. A panoply of gourmet dishes were soon placed before us. We savored each bite, taking a long, much needed respite before retiring. The evening was over too soon. Back in our room, we climbed into a delightfully squeaky antique bed with a firm mattress and a down comforter. Only the light from the sign on the front lawn was visible against the quiet horizon as we turned down the lamp in our room. We reflected—something wonderful had begun!

Our inaugural stay at a country inn came in the early 1980s, just when inn-going started to become popular in America. Since then, we have visited scores of inns, taking home more than just fond memories. Innkeepers, with their vast and unique sense of personal style, have taught us plenty. Our take-home luggage has consisted of not only our personal belongings, but also ideas we have bagged from the things innkeepers do so well: hosting, home decorating, cooking, renovating, and, most importantly, sharing themselves with their guests. Even though we do not run an inn, we found their ideas and their spirit to be applicable in our own home.

Secrets of Entertaining from America's Best Innkeepers emerged out of my fervent desire to bring these ideas into your home, too. You do not have to live in a sprawling Victorian or a historic farmhouse to offer your guests the best you have. As Jane Austen wrote in her classic novel *Persuasion:* "They all went indoors with their new friends, and found rooms so small as none but those who invite from the heart could think capable of accommodating so many."

Austen reminds us that hospitality comes from within and can be found anyplace where the host is a willing one—regardless of the size or splendor of the abode. So whether you live in a large house or a small apartment, the innkeepers' tips will help you make your home more inviting for yourself as well as your guests. Your parties, dinners, and holiday gatherings will get an extra boost. You will learn how to save time and money setting up and keeping house. You will learn how to hold an afternoon tea, maybe even host a friendly ghost. And you will be filled with sage advice embodied in the innkeepers' philosophies.

Not only will you find out how to live better in the present, but the innkeepers will teach you how to enjoy a touch of the past through antiques or a restoration project. Many of them have put all of their efforts and money into saving homes doomed for the wrecker's ball. In so doing, they have revived old-fashioned life-styles and an enchanting milieu that we also want to reclaim. In their own homes, they have given us the chance to experience Colonial splendor, Early American rural life, Victorian opulence, and farmhouse and country comforts as they help to preserve the architectural heritage of this country.

We cannot all buy the sprawling mansion of our dreams. But we can capture the ambience of a well-appointed inn by following this recipe: Take the innkeepers' ideas and mix them with a generous portion of yourself. A true country home, like a fine inn, is one created out of the owner's individual personality.

These tips were not dreamed up in a boardroom or other think tank. Ideas flowed in generously from innkeepers, who sometimes offered more than one approach to the same situation, to suit the many and varying needs of readers. These are all tried-and-true hints.

This book will be a timeless home reference. It may also supplement your guidebooks and brochures for travel planning. If what you read about an inn appeals to you, call the inn. As Sandra Cartwright-Brown of Conyers House in Sperryville, Virginia, says, "Call and have a chat with the innkeepers. If you enjoy your first telephone conversation with them, you'll enjoy the inn."

And be sure to save that brochure from your first visit to an inn. You may want to frame it, just as my husband and I framed the one from that unexpected discovery in the mountains so many inns ago.

A special thank you to: my dear friend Nancy Thompson Smolak for the many hours she spent in helping to prepare this book; Cary Hull for her careful, professional editing and ideas and Sally McMillan for her enthusiasm and support; Joy Bagley for her time; librarian Eric Weiskopf for his research assistance; the innkeepers who somehow found the time to participate in this project; and to my husband, Tom Bagley, for his unselfish teamwork and enthusiasm for staying at a fine inn and enjoying it with me.

Host Appeal

Preparing a Warmer Welcome

Whenever you invite someone for dinner or an extended visit, you like to roll out the red carpet. In other words, you want to make your guests' visits memorable.

Incidentally, this hospitable expression has firm roots. Red carpets really were unfurled for kings and other nobility during public and private appearances. The practice is still carried out today among the world's remaining royal families. And figuratively speaking, a different type of red carpet is turned out today in American homes—a carpet of hospitality. Someone is hosting someone else every minute of every day from the most humble to the grandest of households.

Colloquially, the old catchphrase means we want the best for our visitors, who deserve nothing less. But you need not do palatial curtsies to make someone's stay a regal one. Stylish slumber is often created by the littlest touches that make a guest's stay special.

The innkeepers know this well, and they supply their home and guest rooms with the most thoughtful touches. At the Rosewood Inn in Corning, New York, for example, innkeepers Dick and Winnie Peer keep a flashlight on bedstands for guests' use when padding down the hall to a shared bathroom in the middle of the night. Not all houses have private baths in guest rooms, so a flashlight seems an appropriate aid for those who are not familiar with your home.

Flashlights are also in use at The Fairhaven Inn in Bath, Maine. Sallie and George Pollard make sure there is one outside the front door so that guests staying out late can find their way back to their room. What a good idea. I wish we had thought of that at our house when we were teenagers. A front-door light was left on. But inside, we groped around in the dark, not turning on lights for fear of waking someone who would notice curfew had passed!

Another thoughtful but less pragmatic nicety at inns has become a tradition—mints on the pillow at turn-down time, or fruit, as they do at O'Duach'ain Country Inn in Bigfork, Montana. "Fresh fruit in season," says innkeeper Tom Doohan, "makes a neat pillow surprise." Guests often find baskets of toiletries in their room. At The Governor's Inn in Ludlow, Vermont, the Butler's Basket contains such trial-sized goodies as toothpaste, shampoo, deodorant, cough drops, razor, soap, mending kit, chewing gum, and lip balm.

There is great reward in making the traveler feel comfortable and right at home. Staging rooms for guests is the innkeepers' specialty. You hear them offer this sentiment repeatedly, "We want guests to feel as though no one has ever stayed in this room before."

Innkeepers know how to serve and entertain guests and how the host can be a part of the fun. Some inns even go to the length of greeting guests in costume. At The Doubleday Inn in Gettysburg, Pennsylvania, innkeepers Joan and Sal Chandon and hostess Olga Krossick sometimes greet guests in Civil War period garb. Explains Joan, "They (visitors) may be met by a soldier or lady of the house. That's when they cross the bridge through time and enjoy nineteenth-century hospitality."

You may not go to these great lengths to entertain your guests, but such ideas instill a sense of escapism, which is possibly the best gift you can offer your own house guests.

Dorry Norris, owner of Sage Cottage in Trumansburg, New York, does this little bit that makes for an escapist's dream reception: "Huge bunches of aromatic herbs are tucked in every corner of the house. When guests arrive, they smell thyme, woodruff, marjoram, oregano, and scented geraniums permeating the house, and always the smell of baking bread," says Dorry. Ah, that "always the smell of baking bread" goes right to the senses and evokes images of simpler times. Just the thought of it, and you want to run right over to Dorry's and bask in the pleasure of smell alone.

Once you get into the habit of preparing for your guests in the spirit of the innkeepers, you will wonder why you didn't think of these niceties before—and not only for guests, but for your family and for yourself. It's really not hard to do. As Adella and Bob Schulz of Sweet Adeline's in Salida, Colorado, put it, "There aren't too many secrets to innkeeping or hosting your own guests at home. Just open your heart, and the rest will take care of itself."

 # Preparing Your Home for Guests

I (Lisa) clean every day. Otherwise it gets out of hand. Dust and vacuum in the morning, and the rest of the day will be free. If someone calls unexpectedly, you don't have to worry about rushing around picking up things.

> Lisa and Daniel Hileman,
> Countryside B&B, Summit Point,
> West Virginia

An antique child's chalkboard is used to post the day's weather forecast for our guests when they come to breakfast. It's a nice touch for house guests who are likely to ask about the weather when they sit down to breakfast.

> Bev Davis and Rick Litchfield,
> Captain Lord Mansion,
> Kennebunkport, Maine

Bird feeders just outside the breakfast window provide natural enjoyment for our guests. But we enhance the fun by leaving a bird-identifying book on each table. What a conversation starter!

> Betty and Ed Dinwiddie, Trillium
> House, Nellysford, Virginia

Parasols by the door encourage guests to take a stroll around the sun-drenched farm.

> Mary and Ray Nichols, Hannah
> Marie Country Inn, Spencer, Iowa

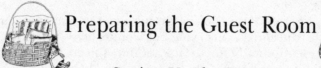

Preparing the Guest Room

Setting Up the Room

When setting up a guest room, imagine that you are the guest and try to provide everything that you can for your comfort or pleasure. This will give you hints of what might be needed. For example, I like to read in bed, so I always provide good reading lights and two extra pillows on the bed.

> Betty York, Four Chimneys,
> Nantucket, Massachusetts

Spend one night in your guest room to determine if the furniture is placed in the best arrangement. This offers clues to any missing amenities.

Familiarize your guests with their accommodations, and define the space available for their use. This also gives you some much-needed privacy during their stay.

> Debbie McCord, Shellmont B&B,
> Atlanta, Georgia

Bev utilized her sewing talents to make Do Not Disturb signs in counted cross-stitch for each guest room.

> Bev Davis and Rick Litchfield,
> Captain Lord Mansion,
> Kennebunkport, Maine

Tasteful signs in the room, with instructions such as "Remove quilts and shams before retiring," help guests feel more comfortable about what is expected and also put you at ease, knowing that your things are well taken care of. Our signs are quality, artistic directives on wood plaques.

> Stuart W. Smith, Churchtown Inn,
> Churchtown, Pennsylvania

We have a welcoming letter in the room. Perhaps in your home there can be a scaled-down version, handwritten to explain some unusual things. If you have a hard time finding the bathroom light switch because the switch is in an unusual place, your guests might too. Make them aware of this nuance. You might personalize the note with the guests' names and put it on the dresser. Other things you can explain are what bathroom they may use, where to put their used towels, and what other niceties you have for them in their room and throughout the house.

> Joanne and George Hardy, Hill
> Farm Inn, Arlington, Vermont

We always have a small, nonglaring light on in the hallways, drawing room, parlor, and each bedroom and bathroom. A dark inn or home has no sense of welcome. Yes, we have high electric bills. But when you are welcoming guests, lights spell warmth to those who are visiting. The same goes in your own home if you have guests coming over.

> Linda and Rob Castagna, Chestnut
> Hill on the Delaware, Milford,
> New Jersey

An attractive clothes tree in a guest bedroom provides added space for clothing, especially if you have limited or no closet space.

> Lois and Paul Dansereau, Silas
> Griffith Inn, Danby, Vermont

Bedding for the Guest Room

Good mattresses are a must. Although all of our beds are antiques, we make sure the mattresses are firm. And we use only English cotton-flannel sheets for warmth and cozy comfort.

> Meri and Mike Hern, Hilltop Inn,
> Sugar Hill, New Hampshire

We make up all of our beds in the twenty-eight rooms with designer ruffled sheets. As a result, we have to launder them ourselves. Commercial launderers won't touch them. But we aren't dissuaded. The extra effort and time is worth it to us, and it will be for your own house guests too. We want our guests to experience an elegant home and our hospitality, right down to the sheets.

> Merrily and Max Comins, Kedron
> Valley Inn, South Woodstock,
> Vermont

For marvelous bedding, ironed sheets are a must. Sorry, there's just no comparison, no matter how wrinkle-free the sheets are that come out of the dryer.

> Roberta Pieczenik, Captain Dexter
> House, Vineyard Haven,
> Massachusetts

If you require extra beds but don't have the space, any bed with legs and a clearance of 14 inches can house a pop-up trundle bed with a good innerspring mattress, versus the foam mattress on a rollaway.

> Louise, Pat, and Bumpy Walter,
> Grant Corner Inn, Santa Fe, New
> Mexico

Room Supplies

Keep a hamper in the guest room closet and explain to your guests that this is where they can put their wet towels. It answers a dilemma for them, and it almost ensures that a wet towel won't be hung over your antique headboard or dresser to dry.

> Frank and Honesty Buczek,
> Thompson Park House, Owego,
> New York

A pincushion with pins, safety pins, and one or two needles plus thread in your guest room allows guests to make emergency repairs to clothing while they are away from home.

> Marjorie and John Pratt, Inn on
> Cove Hill, Rockport, Massachusetts

A stuffed toy and some books placed on a child's bed prior to arrival can go a long way to making a strange place seem much more secure and inviting.

> Meri and Mike Hern, Hilltop Inn,
> Sugar Hill, New Hampshire

Keep a supply of easy-to-read books and magazines in a guest room, keeping the male species in mind by getting current magazines men might like, such as *Smithsonian* and *Time.*

> Hettie and Joe Hawvermale,
> Folkestone B&B, Berkeley Springs,
> West Virginia

Guests on vacation may not want to read a book that will take them a long time to get through. I leave a copy of *Tales for Travellers* in each bedroom. The book contains short stories by famous authors printed in a format like a folded road map.

> Catherine M. Clayton, manager,
> Balcony Downs, Glasgow, Virginia

We place books in guest rooms. If we know a guest's particular interest, we try to find a book about that subject. This may be easier for homeowners who know most of their overnight guests.

We also have small book lights available, so guests can read comfortably in bed without disturbing their partners.

> Robin and Bill Branigan, Roaring
> Lion, Waldoboro, Maine

You can buy old books cheaply at flea markets and garage sales. They're nice to keep around. If guests become interested in one, you can tell them (as we do) that they can take it home.

> Catherine and Jim Bartaglia,
> Summerland Inn, Summerland,
> California

We leave bookmarks on nightstands in our guest rooms.

> Mary Lee and James Papa, Shire
> Inn, Chelsea, Vermont

We have a hot water bottle hanging in each guest room to help bones and muscles relax.

> Tony Clark, Blueberry Hill,
> Goshen, Vermont

We place flannel nightshirts in the rooms for our guests to use while they are with us. Even if they don't wear them, people are touched by the gesture. Chances are they don't wear nightshirts at home, so if they do try one on, it's usually good for some laughs and a snugly night's sleep to boot.

Roberta Crane and Wayne Braffman, Tyler Hill B&B, Tyler Hill, Pennsylvania

We provide guest rooms with small portable ironing boards. This prevents anyone from ironing on the bed or dresser. An ironing board and iron in the closet of your own guest room at home will prevent your having to lug out the household ironing board for a guest and taking time to set it up while you're in the middle of fixing a lavish dinner.

Iris and Bill Simantel, Hearthstone Inn, Eureka Springs, Arkansas

Padded hangers are placed in each closet.

Ruth and Cliff Manchester, Bramble Inn, Brewster, Massachusetts

Author's Tip: Padded hangers are great for protecting clothing, especially a garment's shape. Coordinate them with colors in the room. Sew a label containing your name on each hanger. This will remind guests that the hangers are your property. If by accident one is taken home, it's a nice souvenir, reminding them to visit you again.

Put a glass and a carafe of ice water by your guest's bed to quench a midnight thirst. Place them on a tray with a cloth napkin.

Susan Hannah, Winters Creek Inn, Carson City, Nevada

An alarm clock in a guest room allows a good night's sleep without the worry of oversleeping.

Phyllis Niemi-Peacock and Bud Peacock, Palmer House, Falmouth, Massachusetts

Ceiling fans that light are in each guest room. For your own home, they'll provide a pleasant and romantic setting as well as good ventilation.

> Sallie and Welling Clark, Holden
> House, Colorado Springs, Colorado

To make our guests feel welcome, we have sparkling water and chocolates in the room. We also put extra blankets and pillows in the closets.

> Carolyn and Jeff Rawes, Ash Mill
> Farm, Holicong, Pennsylvania

To make guests feel more at home, I go up to their room at night with a small basket containing home-baked goodies.

> Gail Istler, Locust Hill, Morrow,
> Ohio

When we prepare a room for a guest, the crisp linens are turned down to create a welcoming sight to the eye.

> Linda Kaat, Sweetwater Farm, Glen
> Mills, Pennsylvania

I make large stuffed lambs with woven hats and scarves. One sits on each guest bed to welcome guests. Some say it helps them not miss their pets so much.

> Linda and Mike Levitt, Six Water
> Street B&B, Sandwich,
> Massachusetts

 ## Preparing the Guest Bathroom

To put it simply: The bathrooms must sparkle.

> Jan and Gene Kuehn, Victorian
> B&B, Avoca, Iowa

A pillow for the tub adds to a luxurious bath for you or your guests.

> Mary and Ray Nichols, Hannah
> Marie Country Inn, Spencer, Iowa

Tiny paper cups in the bathroom are sanitary and practical.

> Frank and Honesty Buczek,
> Thompson Park House, Owego,
> New York

Fancy bathroom soaps are fine for the ladies, but make sure you also have a man's soap in the bathroom.

> Hettie and Joe Hawvermale,
> Folkestone B&B, Berkeley Springs,
> West Virginia

Peg rails, similar to those the Shakers used, are in our bathrooms and guest rooms. The racks are handy catchalls for your house guests and for your own family. You can buy them or have a local craftsman or carpenter design one to fit the length of one wall or to wrap around the entire room.

> Doris and Jerry Bartlett, Two
> Brooks, Shandaken, New York

Small baskets lined with material that matches the guest room colors contain extra soap and shampoo.

> Bonnie and Bill Webb, Inn on
> Golden Pond, Holderness, New
> Hampshire

When you have guests, it's nice to leave small sizes of toiletries in a basket in case they have forgotten something. We leave such things as shampoo, hairspray, and even bubble bath.

> Marjorie and Bob Daly, Freedom
> House, Freedom, New Hampshire

Custom-crafted, stained-glass nightlights are in each bath for our guests' convenience.

> Bev Davis and Rick Litchfield,
> Captain Lord Mansion,
> Kennebunkport, Maine

Towels

Big towels of the bath sheet kind are very important for guests. There's nothing worse than offering guests towels that do not wrap all the way around them.

Evelyn Chester, Cobb's Cove,
Barnstable Village, Massachusetts

Extra towels are made accessible to guests. They are in an armoire in the hallway. Tell your guests where your extra towels are, just in case they need one.

Sally and Ken McWilliams, Main
Street B&B, Madison, Indiana

Author's Tip: We have towel racks on the back of the guest room door. One rack holds clean towels, and a double hook, close to the top of the door, gives guests a place to dry the towels. We always leave clean towels in the room, so that when company is coming, it's one less matter we have to take care of to prepare for their visit.

Towels are placed in decorative baskets in each room. The guest may then use the basket to carry toiletries to the bathroom.

Karen and Ken West, Benner
House, Weston, Missouri

Terry cloth bathrobes are provided for guests in case they didn't bring their own. This adds a touch of luxury and is worth the extra laundering.

Nan and Ian Aitchison, Over Look
Inn, Eastham, Massachusetts

Scent-sational Ideas for Guests

Each of our female guests receives a small bag of homemade sachet. You can do this for your own house guests. Here's what you need:

3   ounces lavender flowers
1   ounce powdered orrisroot
4   drops lavender oil

Mix the ingredients together in a bowl and place them in a sealed container for at least two weeks. Fill small bags (you can make your own fabric bags) and tie with a bow.

Added bonus: After the lavender has dried, the stems are used to make incense sticks. Here's how: Soak stems in a mixture of one tablespoon of saltpeter and one cup of water for thirty minutes. Dry completely. Light a couple of the stems in rooms that need refreshing. They will smolder long enough to perfume a room. You can wave them around the room or stand them in a glass and watch them smolder. Don't leave them unattended.

> Helen and Gene Kirby, Horatio
> Johnson House, Belfast, Maine

Sew up a small, thin, cloth bag. Fill it with rosemary, mint, or lavender and add one teaspoon of crushed cinnamon stick. Attach it to a hanger and place in a closet. It makes a spicy moth bag.

Pierce the skin of a lemon or orange with a meat skewer, making several holes close together. Push whole cloves into the fruit to make a pomander. Then place it in a closet or a drawer.

Make an herb cushion by cutting muslin to desired size and sewing up three sides. Fill with crushed herbs such as peppermint, sage, lavender, and lemon balm. Sew up the fourth side to close.

Eucalyptus makes a pleasant scent in the house. At our inn, we have bunches of it in the hallways.

> Sallie and George Pollard,
> Fairhaven Inn, Bath, Maine

A bowl of honeysuckle in a bedroom with the door shut will emit a wonderful fragrance when guests enter the room.

> Catherine M. Clayton, manager,
> Balcony Downs, Glasgow, Virginia

A handful of dried fresh lavender under the mattress pad sweetens the guest's bed.

> Robin Brooks, Robins Nest, San
> Andreas, California

In early times, beds were often musty smelling. So early settlers sweetened their nocturnal comforter with scented sleep bags. Today, I put the practice to use for the sheer enjoyment of guests. Here's how to make a sleep bag:

    3   cups dried rose petals
    1   cup spearmint leaves
    1   tablespoon powdered cloves

Mix the ingredients; you will have enough for many bags. Place a few handfuls of the mixture into a tiny muslin bag. If you sew up your own bag, stencil over it for design. Place on a bedroom pillow.

> Daisy Morden, Victorian House, St.
> Augustine, Florida

In the winter, we put cinnamon sticks in a teakettle filled with warm water. It smells just wonderful throughout the house.

> Penny and Chip Kessler, Mill Farm
> Inn, Tryon, North Carolina

Apples, cinnamon, and cloves boiled in a medium-size saucepan of water will fill the house with an inviting aroma. Later, the apples can be made into applesauce by removing the cloves and mashing the apples with a potato masher.

> Britt House Staff, San Diego,
> California

To provide a wonderful scent in the inn during the winter, we offer hot spiced cider in the evening. We take a bottle of apple juice, two pureed apples, cinnamon, and nutmeg, and simmer for a few minutes. The aroma spreads everywhere.

> Phyllis Niemi-Peacock and Bud Peacock, Palmer House, Falmouth, Massachusetts

A good way to have a nice scent in a room is to place a light-bulb ring around one of the bulbs in each room and put several drops of scented oil on the ring. As the bulb heats the oil, it fills the air with aroma. Light-bulb rings are available in home improvement stores.

> Roberta Pieceznik, Captain Dexter House, Vineyard Haven, Massachusetts

Potpourri in your rooms lends a pleasant, welcoming odor to your home. We've used antique porcelain cups to hold potpourri.

> Andy and Tommie Duncan, Arcady Down East, Blue Hill, Maine

Author's Tip: To dry flowers for potpourri, place petals or blossoms in a shallow box in a car trunk, where the heat will dry them and the darkness will help keep their color. In about a week, remove them and place them in a plastic bag. Mix the petals with spices and essential oils.

I save rose petals and put them in baskets with a few drops of rose oil. (Try a handful of rose petals in a bubble bath!)

> Ujjala Schwartz, Ujjala's B&B, New Paltz, New York

 ## Preparing Yourself for Guests

As host, make time for yourself. I (Deedy) get a good night's sleep and luxuriate in a whirlpool once each day. Then I'm refreshed. I love innkeeping and our guests. It's only work if you'd rather be doing something else.

Treat yourself as a guest in your own home. It works. Drag out your best things and use them often. If they break, they break. At least you had the pleasure of using them.

> Deedy and Charlie Marble,
> Governor's Inn, Ludlow, Vermont

Ministering to our guests is a sure cure for our blues or blahs. Need a pick-me-up? Have a guest to your home.

> Robin and Bill Branigan, Roaring
> Lion, Waldoboro, Maine

Hosting guests is hard work. But remember that when they arrive at your door, they are on a holiday, and that spirit is contagious. Sometimes the arrival of guests can turn around a day that had previously gone awry.

> Denise Anderson and David
> Karpinski, Quill and Quilt, Cannon
> Falls, Minnesota

Allowing myself (Ruth) extra time in the morning for hair and makeup, nice jewelry and something attractive to wear gives me a lift, even if all heck is breaking loose behind the scenes. And when things are running smoothly, it gives me that extra confidence to greet guests.

> Ruth and Cliff Manchester,
> Bramble Inn, Brewster,
> Massachusetts

It has often happened to me (Patricia) that I have just finished polishing my nails when a guest rings the doorbell. If this happens to you, or if you are in a hurry to go somewhere and can't wait any longer for your wet nails to dry, run them under cold water. They dry instantly. Then go answer the door or go paint the town.

> Patricia W. and Donald R. Cornish,
> Palmer Inn, Noank, Connecticut

 Greeting and Hosting Guests

Don't peer from behind the curtain. Rush out there and greet them before they reach the porch. You know you have been preparing for hours, so why act so surprised when your guests arrive? Why make them ring the bell and then count to ten before opening the door and ushering them in?

> Roberta Crane and Wayne Braffman, Tyler Hill B&B, Tyler Hill, Pennsylvania

We try to treat every guest who walks through our door as if he were the first we ever had. The most difficult part of innkeeping (or entertaining any guest) is staying fresh continuously. Be sure to greet your guests cheerfully, even if you're having a bad day.

> Bonnie and Bill Webb, Inn on Golden Pond, Holderness, New Hampshire

This sounds funny, but it's important to look presentable when guests arrive. It says you are ready for them. But don't let a guest arriving earlier than expected jostle you if you're not ready for them. An unprepared host will be an uncomfortable one. Excuse yourself and take time to get ready. Give them a drink and something to read and tell them you will be with them shortly. It's important that you are relaxed so that you can enjoy your visitors.

Overnight guests, especially those who have been traveling a long time, may not want to carry in their luggage right away. Encourage them to come on into the house first and settle down, freshen up, and then perhaps take a beverage in the parlor.

Finally, a memorable visit for your guests would be one in which you are giving them something different than they can get at home—a surprise around every corner. That's good to keep in mind when planning for company.

> Eva Mae and Frank Musgrave, Edge of Thyme, Candor, New York

We decorate with pineapples around the inn because they are the symbol of hospitality. We purposely named our inn after the famous fruit because we wanted to send the message that we are all about hospitality. Some people place fresh pineapples outside the front door. This tradition harkens back to the days of the traveling, early American sea captains. When they stopped at home before going on another journey, they first wanted time alone with their family. When that time had elapsed, fresh pineapples were placed in front of the house, signaling to neighbors that it was all right to visit. When you have guests coming, place a couple of pineapples outside your door or around the house and entertain them by relating the story of the tradition.

Suzi and Randy Leslie, Pineapple
Hill, New Hope, Pennsylvania

A scrapbook of things to do in the area is a handy item for your guests. Our guests enjoy knowing about the little out-of-the-way places to visit.

Adella and Bob Schulz, Sweet
Adeline's, Salida, Colorado

Author's Tip: Many times you're not sure what your own house-guests might like to do. A scrapbook would help them select attractions they want to see in your area.

We have an extensive inventory of brochures, articles, pamphlets, and maps to assist our guests. Chances are you, too, have a lot of travel information at home. We can't stress how efficient it is to keep this information in order. When you're ready to become guests somewhere else, you'll know where to begin looking to set up a travel agenda—especially should the opportunity to take a trip materialize unexpectedly. Indeed, file folders are one good way of keeping your information at hand.

Mariam and Charles Bechtel,
Bechtel Mansion Inn, East Berlin,
Pennsylvania

Complimentary port in a decanter is always in our Winston Churchill Library for a small after-dinner refreshment.

Nan and Ian Aitchison, Over Look
Inn, Eastham, Massachusetts

If you're entertaining guests at home, and they are celebrating an anniversary, birthday, or other special occasion, you may want to do what we do. Place wine and glasses in their room before arrival.

Joan E. Mason, Mason Cottage,
Cape May, New Jersey

A large basket of fresh apples sits in the lobby—fun, healthy, unexpected.

> Christi and Mark Carter, Carter
> House, Eureka, California

For honeymooners, we pin little brass bells—engraved with their wedding date—on the mattress.

> Robin Brooks, Robins Nest, San
> Andreas, California

In case a guest takes a fall and needs minor first aid involving ice, fill a balloon with water and then freeze it. This makes a neat and clean, hand-held ball to rub on an affected area. We're near a ski resort, and occasionally a guest returns to the inn needing such assistance.

> Ann and Clyne Long, Center Street
> Inn, Logan, Utah

 # The Goodbyes

We had note cards made from the line drawing of our inn. They make very inexpensive souvenirs for visitors.

> Iris and Bill Simantel, Hearthstone
> Inn, Eureka Springs, Arkansas

Author's Tip: Artists often offer to sketch private homes. Although you would probably like to have it done, the practical voice in you asks what in the world you will do with it. Well, have the sketches made into postcards. When your guests come to visit, offer them the postcards to send their relatives and friends back home. They will love them.

Inn guests sign out in our guest book and often leave comments about their visit along with their address. We use it for business purposes and as our own ledger. But it is a particularly good idea to have one in your own home. Have dinner and overnight guests sign your book. This gives you an automatic Christmas-card list. Also refer to the book when you're trying to remember when a guest last visited. A guest book can also thwart an embarrassing situation. If a friend brought a guest for dinner, you may have forgotten his or her name. Refer to the book and you will find the name that eluded you.

> Elizabeth Gundry Hooper, Corner
> Cupboard Inn, Rehoboth Beach,
> Delaware

After guests have gone, we send them a friendship card and enclose a sealed tea bag along with tea-making instructions. It's a reminder to them to relax with a cup of tea and remember the good times shared together. This is a nice thing to do for your own guests.

> Mary and Ray Nichols, Hannah
> Marie Country Inn, Spencer, Iowa

I make a collection of Pudding Creek Inn recipes on index cards and tie them with a ribbon. They are sold in our gift shop. You can do something similar for your family and friends. Wrap up the recipes you served for dinner or brunch and give them to your guests as they leave.

> Marilyn and Gene Gundersen,
> Pudding Creek Inn, Fort Bragg,
> California

Each of our repeat guests receives a platter of homemade chocolate chip cookies as a welcoming-back gift from us and our staff.

> Bev Davis and Rick Litchfield,
> Captain Lord Mansion,
> Kennebunkport, Maine

Cooking and Entertaining

Ideas from Chopping Block to Table

Whether it's breakfast, dinner, or a specially packed picnic lunch, meals at inns are almost always celebrated ones. Each innkeeper has his or her own way of preparing and presenting sumptuous creations. These edible bounties are not only palate pleasers but are often so eye-appealing that they paint their own still life on the table. The cry heard around the dining area goes something like, "This is as pretty as a picture. It looks too good to eat." It's no wonder the critics' applause is so uproarious. Many innkeepers are chefs or former chefs or culinary aficionados who excel in presenting food as an art form at their inn. And those who don't have a formal education in the art of cooking and preparing fine cuisine have learned quickly by doing, how to please their crowds, and they do this from sunrise to sunset.

For breakfast, for example, muffins are one of the most popular items at inns. Those plump, moist mounds of sweet bread that have been the subject of entire cookbooks are ubiquitous eye-openers on breakfast tables at inns across the country. There is clearly an undercurrent of muffin mania at bed-and-breakfasts and country inns, evidenced by the many innkeepers who could not wait to tell me about their muffin-making—and I had not even asked for it!

Getting muffins to look as good as they do at bakeries, restaurants, and your innkeeper's table is not as hard as I thought. Look for the innkeepers' tips on making muffins and their recipes in this chapter and the tea chapter.

Meals are announced at some inns by the sounding of a dinner bell or some other audible form of beckoning. A five-o'clock bell sounds at The Jabberwock in Monterey, California, signaling that aperitifs and hors d'oeuvres are being served on the veranda. At The Captain Lord Mansion in Kennebunkport, Maine, innkeeper Rick Litchfield calls guests by way of an antique music box. Daintily and cheerfully, tunes tinkle throughout the mansion at the drop of a coin into a metal encased disk player. Each morning a different concert of gently plucked notes beckons guests. Meanwhile, at The Captain Jefferd's Inn nearby, the clanking of a bell echoes throughout the old sea captain's mansion. Hungry patrons find their way to the dining room, aided by the aromas of a gourmet breakfast being stirred and sautéed in the neighboring kitchen, and by classical melodies musically setting the tone for another day of adventure and discovery.

Gathering for meals is delightfully ritualistic at some inns—sort of a culinary drama. Innkeepers often like to encourage mixing and mingling among guests, and mealtime presents the right opportunity for such socializing. Once the bell has sounded and everyone is standing behind a chair at Captain Jefferd's, the innkeepers announce each guest by name. Then the coffee is served. Strangers strike up conversations immediately.

Novel table setting and serving ideas abound at inns. Antique china and sparkling crystal often accent place settings. Mel and Jean Hendrickson, former owners of The Middletown Springs Inn in Vermont, probably summed up what most innkeepers feel, when they said, "Running an inn gave us the chance to use all of the dishes and linens that were handed down through the family all these years."

The eclectic blend of an elegant but warm and unpretentious table works well at inns. It is not uncommon to find candles competing for illuminating rights with the early-morning sun, as candlelight breakfasts are popular at inns. The light reflects on silver tea sets at a table fit for ladies and gentlemen in formal evening attire—or so it would seem. But while kitted for royalty, the breakfast table usually enlists guests clad in casual garb, ready for a day of biking or sightseeing, perhaps. Such finery mixed with such comfort is a hallmark of inn-going, and it begins with the innkeepers' keen attention to cooking and serving.

 Kitchen Tips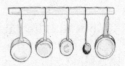

Organization is important in any size kitchen. No matter what its size, a kitchen is only a good one to work in if there is no mess. My country kitchen and dining room face each other, so I must keep my kitchen neat. Here are some suggestions for better preparation in your kitchen:

• Keep the cutting area in close proximity to sink and stove.
• Use separate drawers for cooking utensils, measuring spoons, cups, spatulas, and knives.
• Ceramic jars are always good for holding wooden spoons and other cooking implements. If there's no counter space, hang a deep basket on the wall near the stove for the utensils.
• To make your food preparation seem effortless, clean up after each dish you make. Never pile dishes in the sink.
• When following a recipe, put away your ingredients as you use them.
• Keep staples, such as baking supplies, together to cut down on unnecessary steps in the kitchen.

> Ujjala Schwartz, Ujjala's B&B, New Paltz, New York

We have no housekeeper, but we serve breakfast far away from the kitchen. Thus, when guests sit down with china, candlelight, soft music, and delicious food, they can't see the dirty pans, spilled flour, and opened juice containers that went into it all or hear us washing dishes and putting everything back in order.

> Linda and Mike Levitt, Six Water Street B&B, Sandwich, Massachusetts

If you have more than one cook using your kitchen, and that individual(s) is considerably taller or shorter than you are, you may develop back pain from the height of your baking counter. Make an adjustable baking center. Our baking counter was designed for me (Annie), and I am 5 feet tall. Our summer chef is 6 feet tall and nearly broke his back leaning over to knead dough on the low counter. We placed supports at two different heights on the ends of two cabinets (leaving about 4 feet between the two cabinets) and slid in a smooth-surfaced shelf. When I bake, I slide the shelf onto the lower supports. The shelf is easily removed to raise or clean.

Annie and Al Unrein, Glacier Bay
Country Inn, Gustavus, Alaska

If you're going to prepare something in the kitchen whereby your hands will become gooey, and there's no one in the house to answer the phone if it rings, place a medium-sized plastic bag beside the phone to slip over your hand before reaching for the receiver.

Debby and Hap Joy, The Decoy,
Strasburg, Pennsylvania

It's more efficient to store liners inside and at the bottom of the kitchen trash can. Remove the filled bag and you just slip up a liner.

Edna Colwell, manager, Clayton
Country Inn, Clayton, Oklahoma

 # Entertaining Preparations

When deciding on your menu, be sure to ask guests if they are allergic to any foods. Keep index cards on guests, noting these matters and also what you served them. The next time you have them, you will be assured you are not serving the same things.

Plan your menu one week in advance. Select items that can be made ahead. There are many gourmet dishes that can be pre-cooked and still give the illusion that you've cooked all day.

Eva Mae and Frank Musgrave,
Edge of Thyme, Candor, New York

Grocery shopping for a large crowd of household guests can be laborious and confusing. It's easy to forget items, even though they're on your shopping list. Although some of the food for the splendid breakfasts here comes from the farm where we raise chickens, keep bees, and harvest a large crop of raspberries, there is still plenty of supermarket shopping to do.

To make shopping more efficient, we prepared a list of all the things we normally purchase, putting them under subtitles like produce and dairy. Then we made fifty copies to be kept on file.

Before our grocery excursion, we fill one of these out, including cleaning items and odds and ends. Providing you don't leave the list home, it's a big help and saves time, because you aren't writing everything down each week.

Amy Donohoe, manager, Barley
Sheaf Farm, Holicong, Pennsylvania

Setting the Table

Centerpieces

Your table can set the mood. An old-fashioned atmosphere can be created by placing antique greeting cards as the centerpieces, flanking them with oranges studded with whole cloves and scattering them with dried rose petals. Another attractive and useful centerpiece is a bowl full of fruit on top of a pretty doily. Then, depending on the season, I scatter flower petals around the bowl and on the doily and intermingle satin ribbons with the petals.

Marjorie Bush, Bluff Creek Inn,
Chaska, Minnesota

An array of glass candlesticks of differing heights makes an interesting centerpiece. Add spring flowers, fall foliage, or Christmas greenery.

Rebecca E. Shipman, Inn at
Buckeystown, Buckeystown,
Maryland

The four seasons are celebrated in a hearty and earthy style on our dining-room table. Small potted plants, such as ivy or violets, flank the rim of an antique washbowl. Inside the bowl is a potted plant, changed according to the time of year: poinsettia for Christmas, tulips or daffodils in the spring, and fresh flowers from the garden during the summer and fall.

Carolyn and Jeff Rawes, Ash Mill
Farm, Holicong, Pennsylvania

Centerpieces consist of plants that grow in our area, including hedge apples, horse chestnuts (buckeyes), and pinecones with fir and boxwood greenery in the fall; peonies, lilacs, and roses in the spring. A simple bowl of nuts in their shells with a nutcracker makes a good decoration and keeps guests occupied.

Ripley Hotch and Owen Sullivan,
Boydville The Inn at Martinsburg,
Martinsburg, West Virginia

A lovely centerpiece that matches the theme of your dinner or party can be suspended over the dining-room table. This will provide more room on the table and won't be in anyone's way. Suspend the centerpiece from the ceiling using clear fishing line.

Jan and Gene Kuehn, Victorian
B&B, Avoca, Iowa

Author's Tip: Centerpieces give the table a focal point. However, there is nothing worse than a centerpiece that blocks the line of view between people sitting across from one another. In addition to the Kuehns' solution, you can also choose to place the centerpiece at one of the corners of the table, if it is too tall and cumbersome for the center.

Make your entire dining table a centerpiece! Have a piece of glass cut to your table size. During foliage season, place drifts of colored leaves under the glass. Develop your own themes: woodland garden, colonial garden, herb garden. Press plants all summer, then use them under glass all winter. (Use blotting paper between the table and plants with succulent foliage or flowers.)

Kate Kerivan, Bungay Jar, Easton,
New Hampshire

Pinecones and greens, miniature pumpkins, a large wicker basket full of freshly dug moss, and violets announce the various seasons when I place them on the table as centerpieces.

Dorry Norris, Sage Cottage,
Trumansburg, New York

We try to use everything fresh at hand for centerpieces. My favorite is persimmons stacked on a cake pedestal. The effect is a delight to the eye. You can stack almost any fruit or vegetable and add a little greenery or other garnish.

> Mitzi and Lew Jones, Old Pioneer
> Garden, Unionville, Nevada

If you do use fresh flowers for a centerpiece, use floral preservative in the water (available at florist-supply places). Also, soda water instead of tap water seems to help flowers last longer, due to the carbon dioxide in the water. (See more on this subject in the garden chapter.)

> Planaria Price and Murray Burns,
> Eastlake Inn, Los Angeles,
> California

To add color to fresh-flower arrangements, fill a clear vase with complementary food coloring.

> Mary and George Heim, Garnet
> Hill Lodge, North River, New York

Colorful marble chips in the bottom of a vase hold fresh flowers nicely for a centerpiece. We like to use compotes for our vases.

> Loretta and Ed Friihauf, Reluctant
> Panther, Manchester, Vermont

Candles

Lighting is a main ingredient of a good table setting. Lighting your dining area with plenty of candles and kerosene lamps really adds to the atmosphere. You might get your guests involved in lighting the candles. That's a nice way to make them feel a part of your entertaining.

> Marjorie Bush, Bluff Creek Inn,
> Chaska, Minnesota

Although they are more expensive, it's best to buy dripless candles. They won't mess your candle holders or tablecloth, and besides, they last longer than nondripless.

If your conventional candles drip, remove wax from candle holders by putting them in the refrigerator to cool. Then carefully remove the wax with your fingernails. Wash off the residue with hot, soapy water.

Ann and Jim Carver, Beal House,
Littleton, New Hampshire

Votive candles burning on the table and in different parts of the house are an elegant welcome for dinner guests. Put several along the mantel, along windowsills, above doorsills, on plate rails, and on the counter in the powder room. Be sure to place them safely and away from fabrics and other flammables. They give even an informal beach house that inviting glow of formality.

Beverly and Ray Compton, Spring
Bank Inn, Frederick, Maryland

All of our rooms have candles in them. Since we use so many of them, we have found that using household emergency utility candles works well. They are less expensive than decorator candles and look just as good on the table or anywhere. They usually can be found in any grocery or hardware store.

Pam Stewart, manager, Little River
Inn, Aldie, Virginia

Author's Tip: To curb candle drippings and keep candles from burning too quickly: Keep candles away from house ducts or vents and drafts. And cut down excess wicks, or they will tend to droop and burn the sides of the candles.

Place Cards

Since we seat our guests at large harvest tables for breakfast, we put name cards out. Then the guests have an assigned seat and don't feel awkward deciding where to sit. This is a good idea for your own guests, even those you know well.

Amy Donohoe, manager, Barley
Sheaf Farm, Holicong, Pennsylvania

Porcelain place cards work well, as you can write on them with felt-tip pens and clean them off with water. Determining the evening's seating arrangement is a daily job. One night, a large group of local residents came for dinner. We put names of famous people (presidents, movie stars, athletes, etc.) on the place cards. Everyone got to pick who they wanted to be for the evening. Pope John Paul and Muammar Gaddafi had a rousing conversation. The ladies had a good time deciding who looked most like Dolly Parton or Princess Diana (or wished she did).

Annie and Al Unrein, Glacier Bay
Country Inn, Gustavus, Alaska

Author's Tip: For an interesting place card, arrange a small bunch of dried flowers that coordinate with your table-setting colors and tie it with a bow. Slip in a color-coordinated card with the guest's name. The bouquet goes home with the guest. Flowering herbs also work nicely.

You can use seashells as place cards. Write the name of your guest on the shell and set it down beside the fork or at the bottom of a long-stemmed glass.

Jackie and Lee Morrison, Laurel
Hill Plantation, McClellanville,
South Carolina

Tablecloths

Some bolt fabrics make beautiful tablecloths. I cut to shape and hem polyester/cotton/rayon–blend fabric in beautiful plaids (60 inches wide). The tablecloths wash beautifully and need little ironing. We often serve fresh steamed crab with lots of melted butter for dinner. After an entire season of use, the tablecloths show no stains and still look great!

Annie and Al Unrein, Glacier Bay
Country Inn, Gustavus, Alaska

If you use an old quilt to cover a buffet table, spray on a protective fabric coating to guard against any spills. Usually, you won't have much of a problem with food spills. But beware of dripping candles. They will stain the quilt.

Mary Louise and Ron Thorburn,
Inn at Weathersfield, Weathersfield,
Vermont

Author's Tip: Many times you shy away from buying an antique or other tablecloth you really like, because it isn't large enough for your table. But you don't have to cover the entire top if you are only serving four people. Try turning the tablecloth until you get a corner at each of the four place settings. This provides the right coverage and still shows off the wood of the table.

I have a smaller lace tablecloth over the bottom one, tied on the ends with a ribbon and a flower stuck through the ribbon. It's a pretty effect. Any tablecloth that hangs well over the table can be gathered at the four corners and tied with a pretty ribbon. It looks nice and stays out of your guest's way.

> Patricia Parks, Eton House,
> Fayetteville, Arkansas

If you have round tablecloths and no round table, use them on your large, rectangular dining-room table over rectangular cloths. We even use a card-table or luncheon cloth as an accent for the center of the table.

> Jan and Gene Kuehn, Victorian
> B&B, Avoca, Iowa

Sheets, plain or printed, make excellent tablecloths. Drape one or two together, and top with a lace cloth to make a very romantic table.

> Phyllis Niemi-Peacock and Bud
> Peacock, Palmer House, Falmouth,
> Massachusetts

We have cut down on our linen-storage problem by putting as many as four tablecloths on the table at once. The bulk serves as padding as well as keeping them from getting creased in folds in a drawer.

> Jan and Gene Kuehn, Victorian
> B&B, Avoca, Iowa

Place Mats

Place mats are better to use if there are only two guests at the table. Our table is meant to seat eight, and using two place mats provides a more intimate feeling than would be possible with a large expanse of, say, white linen.

> Marian and Don Harvey, White
> House, Goliad, Texas

My place mats are made of the dining-room wallpaper. You can buy plastic covers just for making your own place mats. Cut the wallpaper to size and insert.

> Patricia Parks, Eton House,
> Fayetteville, Arkansas

To add color to the table and cut down on laundering, place a paper-lace place mat over a solid-colored, ruffled fabric place mat. For example, a cranberry-colored fabric mat is topped with a white paper mat and a colorful, kelly green cloth napkin. The paper keeps the mat clean.

> Linda and Rob Castagna, Chestnut
> Hill on the Delaware, Milford, New
> Jersey

Author's Tip: I enjoy buying linen towels with a design printed on them, especially as souvenirs from places I've visited. When you have enough of them, use them as place mats. Iron them flat and place them two-thirds on the table and the other one-third off the table. They look attractive and will instigate conversation if they are all from different places. For example, one of mine is from Williamsburg, Virginia. There are dates on the cloth and sketches of some of the buildings at Williamsburg. It's always an eye-catcher that prompts guests to get into a discussion of travel.

Have a glass top made for your dining-room table. Place lace doilies underneath as place mats. Your dishes go directly onto the glass. The cleanup is easy, and the table stays in good shape.

> Rosemary Kip, Widow Kip's, Mt.
> Jackson, Virginia

Mirrored place mats help the table sparkle. Also, mirrors, especially those with unusual frames, can be very showy serving platters, particularly for a buffet. Nice for fruits, cheeses, desserts.

Phyllis Niemi-Peacock and Bud
Peacock, Palmer House, Falmouth,
Massachusetts

We use finger towels for place mats and napkins. They launder easily and come in an array of colors to coordinate with your decor.

Elaine and Ray Grandmaison,
Captain Stannard House,
Westbrook, Connecticut

Fingerbowls

Author's Tip: The use of fingerbowls is a charming custom that makes a great deal of sense for today. Why not keep small bowls of water on your table? Traditionally, these bowls were filled with tepid water and set before each guest just before dessert. I think the bowls can be placed on the table at the beginning of the meal and used by dinner guests to clean their hands between courses. You can add a slice of lemon to the bowl for color and added cleanliness. It can be placed on a flat plate on a doily, with a fresh napkin beside it. The hostess should quickly use the fingerbowl first, in case a guest is unfamiliar or uncomfortable with the procedure.

Napkins and Napkin Rings

Author's Tip: Did early man wipe his mouth with animal skin, his hand, or a dried leaf? We may never know for sure. However, we have traced the use of napkins to early Rome, when guests even brought their own wiping cloths to a friend's feast. Sometimes, they carried leftover vittles home, wrapped in the cloth. During the Middle Ages, only the aristocracy used napkins. And it is believed to be during this era that finer napkins were made for dining and wiping. Noblemen wore large collars, so the napkins were tied around their necks to shield the ruffles. This was a difficult maneuver, as the ruche was quite cumbersome. Hence, we get the expression, "to make both ends meet." Fancy napkin folding in geometric shapes began to take place, and by the 1600s it became an art form. The rich competed for the best napkin displays.

An easy cloth-napkin design is to fold the napkin once, then make 1½-inch accordian folds. Pull it through a napkin ring for a nice fan shape.

Barbara and Lyle Wolf, Greenhurst
Inn, Bethel, Vermont

We use richly colored washcloths and brightly striped dishcloths for breakfast napkins. Guests enjoy the creative use of these cloths and find them more absorbent. They also launder better than regular fabric napkins.

Elaine Schnitzer, Summerport B&B,
Schroon Lake, New York

Most of us think of cloth napkins as a lot of work these days, and so we tend to use paper ones most of the time. But cloth napkins can be so inexpensive and easy to launder that you can use them daily. Here at the inn, we make our own (15-by-18-inches with a very small, rolled hem) from a cotton/polyester blend, so they can be easily washed, dried, and folded. They really do dress up a table and are very little work.

Joanne and George Hardy, Hill
Farm Inn, Arlington, Vermont

I have a collection of more than 200 antique handkerchiefs. The beautiful colors and embroidery on these inspired me to use them as napkins. They look beautiful on the table, and I'm making good use of antiques that otherwise might sit in a trunk somewhere and turn yellow.

Daisy Morden, Victorian House, St.
Augustine, Florida

A quick and easy way to set a place for breakfast with a cloth napkin is to tuck the napkin through the handle of a coffee mug and fluff it out.

Chris and Jill Raggio, Ilverthorpe
Cottage, Narragansett, Rhode
Island

Napkin rings initially had a utilitarian rather than decorative purpose. The napkins were large and required intricate laundry care. So they were used for more than one meal. The ring was inscribed with the regular user's name. Ring and napkin were put aside until they were used by the same person at the next meal.

Sandra Cartwright-Brown, Conyers
House, Sperryville, Virginia

We use napkin rings that I (Jackie) tole paint. Each ring has a distinguishing design. Guests store their napkin in their ring and use it for a couple of breakfasts. This saves on laundry and napkin wear and tear, and it keeps a tradition going. You can do the same in your own home. If you don't paint, use some other identifying method. Being able to hold onto a cloth napkin that is hardly soiled may encourage more people to use them more often.

Jackie and Lee Morrison, Laurel
Hill Plantation, McClellanville,
South Carolina

Napkins are in rings on our table. We arrange the napkin so the top of it fluffs out around the base of the goblet.

Mary Lou and Ross Overcash, Red
House, Lincolnville Beach, Maine

Cookie cutters make wonderful rings for thinner napkins.

Karen and Ken West, Benner
House, Weston, Missouri

Author's Tip: Having a party for youngsters or children in their early teens? Set the table with paper napkins fed through a medium-to-large, hard and edible pretzel. This may be the introduction to napkin rings for some of your young party-goers.

Small wicker mats make very nice napkin holders. Double the mats and sew them together at the tops. Weave lace through the wicker, and trim with a bow.

Audrey Nichols, Heritage Inn,
Salmon, Idaho

Cloth napkins are a must—even for breakfast!

Betty Lee Maxcy, Covered Bridge
Inn, Ephrata, Pennsylvania

Serving

Don't be afraid to let your imagination run wild when thinking about ways to dress a table. I love using extraordinary containers for serving and display. For example, I have a few fan-shaped vases. I don't use them just for flowers. I put sauces into them. They look pretty on the table, encourage conversation, and work really well for pouring.

An antique tin, opened to show any inside labeling on the lid, also makes a wonderful container. Place a colorful napkin inside the tin, and add fresh-baked muffins or cookies. Top with a piece of baby's breath.

Unmatched china and crystal that you can buy inexpensively from garage sales provide an interesting array at the table.

Marjorie Bush, Bluff Creek Inn,
Chaska, Minnesota

Author's Tip: Old or new eggcups can serve as decorative and conversational pieces while holding table necessities, including pats of butter and toothpicks.

Make use of seashells by using them as servers on a table where seafood is being served. You can even clean them in the dishwasher. We live on the coast and can gather large clam or scallop shells (4 or 5 inches in size). If such shells are unavailable to you, they can be purchased at the store.

Jackie and Lee Morrison, Laurel
Hill Plantation, McClellanville,
South Carolina

We use marble and terra-cotta tile samples to keep trays of food warm on the serving table. They can be heated in the oven while the food bakes, then placed on top of hot pads under trays. They continue to keep food warm for about one hour.

> Mary Louise and Conley Weaver, Red Castle Inn, Nevada City, California

Children's plastic pails make excellent ice buckets for porch or patio tables. The shovels are novel servers.

> Phyllis Niemi-Peacock and Bud Peacock, Palmer House, Falmouth, Massachusetts

Silver goblets for orange juice seem to keep the juice colder and make the entire table sparkle. Unexpected and elegant, they make everyone feel special. And why not? If you've got them, use them for heaven's sake.

> Roberta Crane and Wayne Braffman, Tyler Hill B&B, Tyler Hill, Pennsylvania

Halved coconuts make interesting ice cream dishes for any informal summer luau.

> Mary Lee and James Papa, Shire Inn, Chelsea, Vermont

Frequently during the summer, we serve chilled soups in frosted sherbet glasses. It's always a big hit.

> Jan and Gene Kuehn, Victorian B&B, Avoca, Iowa

Clay flowerpots rubbed with oil and lined with aluminum foil make great containers for chicken pot pie. Fill the pot with the hot pie filling, top with a circle of pastry (fluting the edges), and bake. Serve in the plant pot.

> Annie and Al Unrein, Glacier Bay Country Inn, Gustavus, Alaska

Our entire meal-serving philosophy is to treat our cookery as art, from plate presentation to table setting and right down to the flower we set upon each guest's dinner napkin.

> Tony Clark, Blueberry Hill, Goshen, Vermont

We use clear glass dishes in our place settings. They make very pleasing settings, whatever your color of napkins or tablecloths. You can place a doily or even a pressed leaf or dried flower underneath the clear dish.

Nancy and Dave Phillips, Hamilton House, Decatur, Illinois

Use 12-inch serving plates as the underlining to your entree dish.

Sandra Cartwright-Brown, Conyers House, Sperryville, Virginia

Wicker baskets can become colorful servers for muffins or rolls if you add a fabric liner of washable material.

Audrey Nichols, Heritage Inn, Salmon, Idaho

Fresh herbs in clay pots, baskets of dried herbs, and an assortment of calico napkins and interesting place mats help keep me from getting bored when I set the table every morning.

Dorry Norris, Sage Cottage, Trumansburg, New York

If you need more room at the table after you've used your leaf extensions, go to the lumberyard and have a rectangular piece of plywood cut at least half again as long as your table. Place a protective cloth over your table, and put the plywood on top. Decorate with a tablecloth. This is great to keep handy, especially for parties and holidays when you have large groups. Store the plywood in a dry place to prevent warping.

Doris and Jerry Bartlett, Two Brooks, Shandaken, New York

Author's Tip: An attractive and interesting way to get more serving space is to use a stepladder. Place an opened one adjacent to the table. Pretty plates and bowls can be placed on each rung. Paint the ladder. Stencil it. Do whatever pleases your taste to make the ladder complement your decor and style. It is prettiest when each rung has something on it. Decorate with green plants or flowers if you have the space.

Entertaining Etiquette

Don't let your guests know how hard you've worked to set the beautiful table or cook the wonderful meal. All of this will be obvious. There is nothing worse than a hostess who complains about the toil.

When introducing your guests at a dinner party, we suggest you don't bother with last names. Take your time with the introduction, so that the guests clearly hear each name. They may remember names better that way. Also, if you know the person's interests or occupation, mention that too. Then there won't be any problem with getting a conversation going. When planning who to invite to your party, especially a small dinner get-together, carefully select guests who are compatible.

And consider that when it's time to pour the coffee, whether for breakfast, lunch, or dessert, it's a nice touch to have the man of the house do the honors.

Eva Mae and Frank Musgrave,
Edge of Thyme, Candor, New York

Guests at Ash Mill Farm have plenty of lighthearted conversation between courses. Everyone gets chatting once the innkeepers begin asking where everyone went for dinner the night before.

If you have a dinner party with people who don't know each other, a good way to break the ice is to start talking about some good places where you have dined.

Carolyn and Jeff Rawes, Ash Mill
Farm, Holicong, Pennsylvania

 # Garnishes

Use that zucchini that grew into a monster overnight to make a Viking ship for your veggie salad. Cut the zucchini in half lengthwise. Scoop out enough insides to make room for the salad. A bamboo skewer makes a good mast. Decorate a paper sail to fit the occasion. Tongue depressors make great oars, with a little bit of unskilled whittling.

Robin Brooks, Robins Nest, San
Andreas, California

For our salads, we use cookie cutters to cut out hearts from turnips. Just add them to the bowl.

Libby and Jim Hopkins, Old Broad
Bay Inn, Waldoboro, Maine

Our garnishes include a tomato rose on the side of Spanish scrambled eggs to add the *olé*. We make tomato roses two ways. Either take a cherry tomato, cut off the stem top, and then make two interesting cuts almost all the way through. Then turn it upside down and spread it out to look like petals. Or peel the skin from a tomato in a continuous circle, and roll it up like a rose.

The Aztec mushroom is made by taking a medium-to-large mushroom cap and starting in the center with the tip of a sharp knife and making little indentations in the mushroom as you work around in circles. We use it on our quiche. It also looks good on top of a steak.

Mary and Gary Riley, Williams
House, Hot Springs, Arkansas

I (Planaria) often use Swiss chard to line trays of food instead of doilies.

I buy a huge purple or savoy cabbage, pull out the center, and pour dip into the cabbage cavity. Sometimes I stand a large basket on one end and prop the cabbage up next to it for a dramatic effect. Then I fill the area in with raw vegetables to dip, including radishes and baby ears of corn (from a can).

Planaria Price and Murray Burns,
Eastlake Inn, Los Angeles,
California

We make floral arrangements out of vegetables. This is a skillful art. For help on how to make such arrangements, there are two books I recommend: *Edible Art*, by David and Paul Larousse, and *Garnishes and Decorating*, by Rudolph Beller (Van Nostrand Reinhold, P.O. Box 668, Florence, KY 41022–9979). Another publication for less-advanced cooks and food artists is *Garnishes Made*

Easy, by Miriam B. Loo (Current Inc., Colorado Springs, CO 80941).

> Kay Easton, activity director,
> Middlebury Inn, Middlebury,
> Vermont

No entree or bread will be ignored by your guests when it is presented with a special touch. Any type of garnish will give your dish pizzazz. When accenting with flowers, it's nice to tell your guests what the flowers are, and of course, which ones are edible.

> Chris and Jill Raggio, Ilverthorpe
> Cottage, Narragansett, Rhode
> Island

Fresh fruits and flowers are my kind of garnishes. Also, golden oregano with nasturtiums, dwarf sage with calendulas, and borage with purple basil all give lift to summer palates. In winter, thyme is useful with grapes and oranges.

> Dorry Norris, Sage Cottage,
> Trumansburg, New York

When pansies are in season, we place one flower on each guest's morning melon. It adds wonderful color and a delicate touch.

> Mimi and Jim Agard, Brafferton
> Inn, Gettysburg, Pennsylvania

A nice idea for ice water on the table: Place one edible flower in each ice-cube pocket before freezing. When the cubes are frozen, place several in a glass and pour in the water. Bring to the table to the oohs and ahhs of your guests.

> Sandy and Dave Granger, 1830 Inn
> on the Green, Weston, Vermont

If you want to put flower garnishes on your guests' plates, but they are not in abundance, take a few petals instead of the entire flower. Make sure you know your flowers. Some of them, such as lilies of the valley and begonias, are poisonous.

> Ujjala Schwartz, Ujjala's B&B, New
> Paltz, New York

Many types of edible flowers can be used as garnishes. Here are a few: mustard flower, chrysanthemum, honeysuckle, tulip, squash blossom, rose, fennel, chive, gladiola, forget-me-not, day lilies, and jasmine.

> Deedy and Charlie Marble,
> Governor's Inn, Ludlow, Vermont

While flowers make great garnishes, this is a reminder to watch for creepie-crawlies hidden between petals and leaves. Wash your flowers very well.

> Sandra Cartwright-Brown, Conyers
> House, Sperryville, Virginia

Everyone knows parsley makes a great garnish. But fresh parsley is great on breakfast dishes, not just at dinner. We have a window box of the herb growing outside the kitchen door, providing us with a steady supply of parsley all summer. We freeze our fall crop to be used in our dishes all winter.

> Phyllis Niemi-Peacock and Bud
> Peacock, Palmer House, Falmouth,
> Massachusetts

Herbs make great garnishes. You can put them on butter pats or on the main course.

> Eva Mae and Frank Musgrave,
> Edge of Thyme, Candor, New York

Garnishings don't have to be exotic or elaborate to make an eye-appealing dish. A simple slice of orange on a plate of French toast or a strawberry on celery leaves brightens the morning and shouts in its sunny voice you care enough to try.

> Roberta Crane and Wayne
> Braffman, Tyler Hill B&B, Tyler
> Hill, Pennsylvania

This is a cute garnish that can be added to a fruit tray or decorative centerpiece. It's a mouse made from a pear: Slice a pear in half lengthwise so that it lies flat, leaving the stem intact. Add two whole cloves for eyes. From the sliced-off section, cut two small pieces for ears. Carve a small hole above the clove, and attach each ear with a toothpick. Add a toothpick as a tail, covering it with a fresh chive stem.

> Chris and Jill Raggio, Ilverthorpe
> Cottage, Narragansett, Rhode
> Island

Strawberries—cut into thin slices and fanned out on a plate—make an easy and pretty food topping.

> Judy and Jack McMahon, Inn at
> Starlight Lake, Starlight,
> Pennsylvania

 # Coffee Perks

Scents of cinnamon drift through the house when the coffee brews at Ash Mill Farm. One-quarter of a teaspoon of the spice is added to a ten-quart pot of coffee. This gives the coffee a nice flavor and cuts down on the bitterness. All our guests think the coffee is a special blend. Add your own amount of cinnamon, according to taste.

> Carolyn and Jeff Rawes, Ash Mill
> Farm, Holicong, Pennsylvania

Dried orange peel takes away bitterness in coffee.

> Ripley Hotch and Owen Sullivan,
> Boydville The Inn at Martinsburg,
> Martinsburg, West Virginia

In Sandwich, we're lucky enough to have a natural spring that gives us wonderfully clean drinking water. We use this water in coffee makers. Not only does the coffee taste better, but the coffee maker remains clean without much mineral deposit. The same can be accomplished with bottled spring water.

> Linda and Mike Levitt, Six Water
> Street B&B, Sandwich,
> Massachusetts

One of our best investments was the purchase of insulated coffee servers. They keep the beverage piping hot, and guests may serve themselves when they get up earlier than breakfast time. Shop around for decorative servers with a push-button top. Don't buy a server you must unscrew in order to pour. This type can lose heat as you pour.

> Karen and Ken West, Benner
> House, Weston, Missouri

 # Wine Wisdom

Being in the wine country, we have found the absolute best way to chill champagne (especially if you're in a hurry): Add water to the ice in an ice bucket. Then submerge the bottle three-fourths of the way into the bucket. You'll have ice cold bubbly in just 15 minutes.

> Carol and Jim Beazley, Beazley
> House, Napa, California

Up here in Vermont, we have lots of snow, so we use some of it in ice buckets for chilling wine and champagne. The snow does a better job of cooling and looks much nicer than ice.

> Rosemary and Ed McDowell, Tulip
> Tree Inn, Chittenden, Vermont

The 1819 Red Brick Inn houses a small winery in the basement, where the innkeepers make a sparkling wine for sale to guests and passersby. Inn rooms are named after wine varieties. For example, the Bordeaux Room has a carpet in a color reminiscent of the essence of that type of wine, stenciling of grapes as a border along the walls, a grapevine wreath, and posters by local artists of area vineyards.

Innkeeper Raymond Spencer is a winemaker and also bottles and sells water from a natural spring next to the inn. He believes that wine serving shouldn't be stuffy. No one should feel intimidated. He offers these tips on wine for your own entertaining.

Ideally, wine should be stored in a room that is at fifty to sixty degrees. At home, this is not always possible. Besides, there is a misconception about wine storage. The point is not so much the lower temperature, but to store wine where the temperature is consistent. This means it can be a closet in a modern, ranch-style home, as long as the closet does not reach temperatures of ninety degrees in the summer and sixty in the winter. The fluctuation of temperatures can cause a cloudiness of the wine. Or if the wine is kept too cold, it can develop nitrate crystals.

If you're just starting to try wines, I recommend finding a local wine merchant. Ask him for a recommendation, but don't buy anything expensive yet. Wait until you try his suggestion. If you don't like his choice, find another wine merchant.

Head out to a winery to sample a number of wines. Here, too, you can examine the cleanliness of the preparation rooms. Sanitation is important.

The older a wine is, the longer it should be opened prior to serving. Think of it as a room closed up for twenty years. Open the bottle and let it breathe to freshen it up—an hour or so, on average.

I don't feel that too much ceremony should accompany the serving of wine. You don't want to inhibit your dinner guests who may not know much about wines. Instead, help your guests enjoy it just as much as they will enjoy your food. When the wine is first opened, someone should smell it and taste it for obvious off characteristics of flavor or aroma.

It is better to serve red wine in a glass with a wide-mouthed bowl, since red wine releases more aroma. White wines can be poured into a tulip glass that has a large bowl at the bottom and a narrower mouth, so that you can capture and concentrate the aroma. Champagne needs to be served in fluted glasses, contrary to the traditional wide and not very deep glasses. The narrow glasses allow for the vision of stringy bubbles that will last longer.

Raymond Spencer, 1819 Red Brick
Inn, Dundee, New York

 Picnics

For something different, pack a picnic breakfast for your guests. Our picnic hamper often includes French toast in pottery dishes to keep it warm on the way to a nearby park. Padded place mats further protect the food from getting cold. A thermos is filled with coffee.

Pat Hardy, Glenborough Inn, Santa
Barbara, California

Gourmet picnics are prepared for guests upon request at The Governor's Inn. Here's what we put into our picnic hampers. You can do something similar for yours. We fill a wooden basket with an elegant four-course meal. A detailed menu of what's inside is handwritten. There are linen napkins and silverware tied with ribbon. One hamper might start picnickers with a chilled *potage* of fresh tomato-and-lemon cream and nut bread with cream cheese. A sandwich of smoked baby clams with cucumbers and dill dressing might follow, all topped off with a pleasing bottle of French wine.

We offer the inn's collection of recipes for our guests. They can prepare some of the dishes at home and make up their own picnic baskets, so that they can remember a special day in Vermont. The linen, wine glasses, and basket are for guests to keep.

Deedy and Charlie Marble,
Governor's Inn, Ludlow, Vermont

 Breakfast

Overripe pears, peaches, apples, kiwis, strawberries, and other overripe fruits can be placed in a blender with ice, milk, and fruit juice to make a delicious and nourishing drink. Here's one example of a favorite beverage.

GRANT CORNER INN ORANGE FRAPPÉ

4	cups freshly squeezed orange juice
	Juice of 1 lemon
1	large banana
6	strawberries, fresh or frozen
¼	cup whipping cream
6	ice cubes
	Fresh mint leaves for garnish

Blend all the ingredients but the mint on high for 1 minute. Serve in frosted, stemmed goblets, garnished with fresh mint. Yield: 6 servings.

Grant Corner Inn Breakfast and
Brunch Cookbook, Santa Fe, New
Mexico

I make all our morning juice, including apple, grape, and tomato juice. Good culinary shops sell automatic juicers for fifty dollars and up. You don't need an expensive one. You can freeze or can some of the juices. I use empty plastic, one-liter bottles to freeze the juice.

Robin Brooks, Robins Nest, San
Andreas, California

To keep our juice cold throughout breakfast, we place juice containers inside a freezer's ice-storage bucket. On either side of the containers, we insert small, rigid freeze packs like those used for picnics. They keep the juice cold and eliminate wetness and inconvenience for guests.

Bonnie and Bill Webb, Inn on
Golden Pond, Holderness, New
Hampshire

Author's Tip: A nice breakfast or brunch beverage we make at our house is Cranberry Juice Sparkler. Mix two-thirds cranberry juice to one-third club soda. Add ice and serve immediately. The color is great on the table. Match it with cranberry napkins or place mats.

HOT CURRIED FRUIT

1   16-ounce can pears
1   16-ounce can peaches
1   16-ounce can pineapple chunks
1   16-ounce can pitted sweet cherries

⅓   cup packed brown sugar
4   tablespoons butter, melted
1½   teaspoons curry powder

Preheat oven to 325 degrees. Drain fruit and place in a buttered 2-quart casserole. Mix brown sugar, butter, and curry powder. Pour mixture over fruit. Bake for 30 minutes. Yield: 12–14 servings.

The Summer Cottage Inn Cookbook,
Cape May, New Jersey

When fresh fruit is in abundance, I combine fruits such as black raspberries with nectarine chunks and blueberries, and stir in blueberry, raspberry, or vanilla yogurt for a breakfast, snack, or lunch dish.

I also provide a special breakfast treat on warm summer mornings by serving frozen fruit salad, a nice make-ahead dish. Line muffin tins with paper muffin cups. Fill with fruit and freeze. When frozen, remove from muffin tins and store in plastic bags. Serve frozen.

Debby and Hap Joy, The Decoy,
Strasburg, Pennsylvania

Fruit is often the garnish or topping to a dish, but fruit can also be topped. Toppings can include toasted coconut, almonds, or kiwi. And big, red ripe strawberries can go over the rim of your guest's juice glass.

Linda and Mike Levitt, Six Water
Street B&B, Sandwich,
Massachusetts

The addition of a paper doily underneath a fruit cup makes it special.

Karen and Ken West, Benner
House, Weston, Missouri

To freeze berries, place them on a flat cookie sheet. Freeze and then place in plastic bags. Label each bag.

Alan Stott, Hannah's House, Pigeon
Forge, Tennessee

Pineapple is an acid fruit. Place chunks of it into a fresh fruit mixture, and it will prevent the other fruits from turning brown. To cut a pineapple, first twist the top off. Cut the fruit in half lengthwise, and then quarter each half. Remove the middle core. Cut away from the skin into chunks, and place the chunks back on the skin for serving.

Denise and Clark Champion,
Haikuleana, Haiku, Hawaii

Mix fresh fruits for a colorful effect. For instance, on a plate, we have a slice of cantaloupe and then a prune, and then another slice of melon, and so on.

Bonnie and Bill Webb, Inn on
Golden Pond, Holderness, New
Hampshire

BREAKFAST PARFAIT

Fill parfait glass in this order:

2–3	tablespoons granola
2–3	tablespoons flavored yogurt
2–3	tablespoons fresh fruit of the season

Repeat, ending with fresh fruit at the top of the glass.

Churchtown Inn, Churchtown,
Pennsylvania

HOMEMADE GRANOLA

3	cups old-fashioned rolled oats
1	cup chopped walnuts
1	cup wheat germ
¼	cup brown sugar
¼	cup whole wheat flour
¼	cup honey
¼	cup molasses
½	cup vegetable oil

¼   cup water
1   tablespoon vanilla extract
1   cup raisins
1   cup shredded coconut

Preheat oven to 325 degrees. Combine all the ingredients with the exception of the raisins and coconut. Spread on a well-greased baking sheet. Bake for 30 minutes, or until browned, stirring occasionally. Remove from oven. Add raisins and coconut. The granola crisps as it cools. Yield: 6–8 servings.

Captain's House, Chatham,
Massachusetts

SKYLINE APPLE MUFFINS

This is the absolute favorite recipe at The Lord Proprietors' Inn.

1½   cups firmly packed brown sugar
⅔   cup oil
1   egg
1   cup buttermilk
1   teaspoon salt
1   teaspoon baking soda
1   teaspoon vanilla extract
2   cups flour
1½   cups chopped Granny Smith apples
½   cup chopped nuts

Preheat oven to 350 degrees. Mix together brown sugar, oil, and egg. In a two-cup measure, mix the buttermilk, salt, baking soda, and vanilla. Stir. Mix thoroughly into egg mixture. Add the flour all at once, and fold in the apples and nuts. Pour into greased muffin cups. Bake for 30 minutes. Yield: 12 muffins.

Lord Proprietors' Inn, Edenton,
North Carolina

BALI H'AI MUFFINS

2½   cups unprocessed bran
1⅓   cups whole wheat (or white) flour
2½   teaspoons baking soda
½   teaspoon salt
1   cup raisins
1   cup shredded coconut
2   eggs
½   cup buttermilk
½   cup vegetable oil
1   cup mashed ripe bananas
½   cup honey

Preheat oven to 375 degrees. Combine bran, flour, soda, salt, raisins, and coconut. In another bowl, beat eggs, then add remaining ingredients. Combine the two mixtures until blended. Spoon into greased muffin cups. Bake for 20–25 minutes. Yield: 18–24 muffins.

> Forsyth Park Inn, Savannah,
> Georgia

PINEAPPLE MUFFINS

½   cup butter
2   eggs
1⅛   cups sugar
3   cups flour
3   teaspoons baking powder
½   teaspoon salt
     Pinch baking soda
1   cup milk
1   teaspoon vanilla extract
1   16–ounce can crushed pineapple

Preheat oven to 400 degrees. Cream together butter, eggs, and sugar. Combine dry ingredients in a separate bowl. Add vanilla to milk. Add flour mixture to the butter mixture, alternately with the milk. Add pineapple. Spoon into muffin tins. Bake for 15–20 minutes. Yield: 18–24 muffins.

Forsyth Park Inn, Savannah,
Georgia

MORNING GLORY MUFFINS

2   cups flour
1¼   cups sugar
2   teaspoons baking soda
2   teaspoons cinnamon
3   eggs, beaten
1   cup vegetable oil
2   teaspoons vanilla extract
2   cups grated carrots
1   apple, grated
½   cup raisins
½   cup chopped pecans
½   cup shredded coconut

Preheat oven to 375 degrees. Grease muffin cups and areas between cups. In a large bowl, mix first 4 ingredients. Set aside. In a small bowl, mix together eggs, oil, and vanilla. Add to flour mixture. Stir until moist. Fold in carrots, apple, raisins, pecans, and coconut. Spoon into the muffin cups, filling each one to the rim. Bake for 25 minutes. Yield: 12 muffins.

Partridge Brook Inn,
Westmoreland, New Hampshire

BANANA-NUT MUFFINS

½   cup oil
1   cup sugar
2   eggs
3   ripe bananas
2   cups flour
1   teaspoon baking soda
½   teaspoon baking powder

½   teaspoon salt
3   tablespoons buttermilk
1   teaspoon vanilla extract
¾–1   cup chopped pecans or walnuts

Preheat oven to 350 degrees. Grease 15 muffin cups. Mix oil, sugar, eggs, and bananas in food processor. Add the remaining ingredients except nuts. Mix well. Add nuts. Fill muffin cups two-thirds full. Bake 30 minutes.

Boydville The Inn at Martinsburg,
Martinsburg, West Virginia

QUICK MUFFIN MIX

This mix keeps for six weeks in the refrigerator. It's nice to have it made up in advance and then bake the muffins when you're ready. There's nothing better in the morning than muffins cooking in the oven. Mix together 4 beaten eggs, 2 cups sugar, 1 cup salad oil, 1 quart buttermilk, 5 teaspoons baking soda, 2 teaspoons salt, 5 cups flour, and 1 15-ounce box raisin bran cereal. Add to this mix whatever you like, such as nuts, coconut, or fruits. Refrigerate. Take out the amount you need when ready to bake. Bake muffins in a 400-degree oven for 20–25 minutes.

Folkestone B&B, Berkeley Springs,
West Virginia

COFFEE MUG BREAD

A favorite with our guests is breakfast in a coffee mug. Grease the inside of a coffee mug, preferably one with a pedestal base. Partially thaw a loaf of frozen bread dough. Cut the loaf in half crosswise. Then divide each half into 4 strips. Roll each strip between the palms of your hand, and then dredge it in a mixture of cinnamon sugar and chopped walnuts. Twist 2 strips together, divide in half, and place in a spiral fashion into 2 mugs. Let the dough rise until double in bulk. The dough will extend beyond the top of the mug and resemble a swirl of whipped cream topping. Bake about 15 minutes in a 350-degree oven. Garnish with a cinnamon stick, and serve immediately, right in the mug!

Ilverthorpe Cottage, Narragansett,
Rhode Island

We cook batches of banana-nut muffins and freeze them in plastic bags. When ready to serve, put them right from the bag into a basket lined with a cloth napkin and zap them for 2 minutes in the microwave. They're just like fresh.

Ripley Hotch and Owen Sullivan,
Boydville The Inn at Martinsburg,
Martinsburg, West Virginia

Leave out milk or water in muffin recipes, and substitute a flavorful and moist applesauce.

Debby and Hap Joy, The Decoy,
Strasburg, Pennsylvania

We make great use of the freezer. Many doughs can be frozen raw and baked fresh in the morning. We do this with several yeast coffee cakes, muffins, and breads.

Barbara and Carl Beehner, Steele
Homestead Inn, Antrim, New
Hampshire

Since it's difficult enough for a hostess to have company—expected or otherwise—anything that can be done in advance eases the stress of entertaining. We manage to serve home-baked goodies—even on short notice—by employing our muffin trick. Here's how to make muffins in advance, so they will still taste as though you just made them.

Grease your muffin cups (we use the very tiny ones, but this works with any size) with a nonstick spray. Make muffin batter, one batch at a time. Fill each muffin cup half full, and immediately place the pan in the freezer. Caution: Do not allow the batter to begin to rise before you pop the pan into the freezer. The dough must be allowed to rise in the oven, only.

When the muffin batter is frozen, pop the muffins out of the pan and place in a plastic bag, marking the bag with the type of muffin. Repeat until you have several different muffins, such as cranberry, blueberry, date, lemon, and pumpkin.

Store the plastic bags in the freezer until you're ready to serve. Simply prepare the muffin cups again, pop the frozen muffins back into them, and bake at 350 degrees for about 25 minutes for smaller muffins, and 35 minutes for larger muffins.

Deedy and Charlie Marble,
Governor's Inn, Ludlow, Vermont

Do prepare muffins ahead of time, and freeze the batter. When ready to bake, take them directly from the freezer to the oven. Bake frozen and uncovered 5 minutes longer than the recipe indicates. This yields a far superior muffin than if you were to freeze the cooked muffins.

Sally and Ken McWilliams, Main
Street B&B, Madison, Indiana

If you don't feel like making muffins and you have overripe bananas, throw whole bunches into the freezer for later. They turn black and are mushy when you defrost them. But that makes them easier to use when you do make muffins or quick bread.

Ripley Hotch and Owen Sullivan,
Boydville The Inn at Martinsburg,
Martinsburg, West Virginia

Popovers at breakfast are a tradition at the Beal House. Guests exclaim how they have never seen such large, puffy popovers (known as Yorkshire Pudding in England). Here's how to make your popovers burst with pride:
First, make your batter the night before. Leave the batter to rest at room temperature (near a cooler place in very hot weather). In the morning, preheat the oven to 400 degrees. Place the popover pan into the oven for 15 minutes. Remove the pan and spray cooking oil into each cup. Whisk the batter slightly and pour, filling each cup to the brim. Cook for 45 minutes. Make sure the oven is at 400 degrees. Use an inexpensive thermometer to test that your oven temperature is accurate. This is very important.

Ann and Jim Carver, Beal House,
Littleton, New Hampshire

Author's Tip: During the Victorian era (1837–1901), muffins were sold in the streets by vendors, who carried trays of them around their necks, ringing a handbell to attract attention to their tasty treats.

If we have fruit that is overly ripe, rather than throw it out, we puree it, add softened butter and confectioner's sugar, and blend well. We then have fruit butter to serve with muffins in the morning. These butters can be frozen for up to one month.

Phyllis Niemi-Peacock and Bud
Peacock, Palmer House, Falmouth,
Massachusetts

We make our own butter because it's healthier, plus we enjoy keeping the old method alive. We can make certain that there are no chemicals or additives in our butter by churning our own. Churned butter is lighter and sweeter, and we don't add any salt. Sometimes, we add herbs or a fruity liqueur.

You can buy wooden or pottery churns, new or antique. If you buy an old wooden one, here's one way to clean it before using: Clean with a mixture of water, detergent, and baking soda. Wash well. Then fill the churn with fresh water and keep rinsing it well. Let sit one-half hour to dry.

We prefer a table-top or hand-held churn, typical of those used in an eighteenth-century kitchen. Ours is a red-glazed pottery churn. The best way to churn butter is with heavy cream that comes directly from a farm that has been authorized by the health department to supply such cream. It is the cream skimmed off the top of raw milk. Using this, it takes only twenty minutes to get butter. You also can use goat's milk or heavy cream in churning butter. If you use regular milk, you'll wonder if it will ever churn; it takes much longer to work.

Leave the cream out on the counter the night before, preferably near a window where it can be kept cool. The cream will thicken in a cool area. Next morning, pour the cream into the churn. Place the churn between your legs (if it's a hand-held one), and use an upward motion to make your butter.

Mary Louise and Ron Thorburn,
Inn at Weathersfield, Weathersfield,
Vermont

Use small candy molds to make interestingly shaped butter pats. I make them ahead and freeze them until needed.

Daisy Morden, Victorian House, St.
Augustine, Florida

Butter can take on all kinds of shapes when you press cookie cutters into very cold amounts.

Marjorie Bush, Bluff Creek Inn, Chaska, Minnesota

This is good at breakfast or brunch. Microwave unsalted butter until softened. Mix in brown sugar and cinnamon to taste. Using a pastry tube with a star tip, pipe into individual serving dishes. Chill until firm. Tastes good and looks attractive.

Merrily and Max Comins, Kedron Valley Inn, South Woodstock, Vermont

An easy and attractive effect is accomplished by cutting butter and making crisscrossing lines with a fork to resemble a pineapple's skin. It looks nice on the table.

Leftover butter pats from individual guest servings can be reused. Cover and cool leftover butter or margarine. When ready to reuse, heat container in warm water to soften butter. Use melon baller to reshape butter. Place on a dark-colored dish and cool before serving.

Betha and John Mueller, Wisconsin House, Hazel Green, Wisconsin

CHURCHTOWN INN'S APRICOT GLAZE FRENCH TOAST

4	eggs, beaten
½	cup heavy cream
¼	cup light cream
1	teaspoon vanilla extract
½	teaspoon cinnamon
12	¾-to-1-inch slices French bread
1	8-ounce package whipped cream cheese, softened
	Butter
12	ounces apricot preserves, heated
	Banana slices for garnish

Combine eggs, cream, vanilla, and cinnamon. Let stand. Spread cream cheese on 6 slices of bread, and put 1 slice on top of each one making a sandwich. Do not overfill near the edge of the bread. Dip sandwich into egg mixture for 10 minutes. Turn. Let stand another 10 minutes. Fry on a buttered grill at 250–300 degrees for about 5 minutes per side, or until golden brown. Pour heated preserves over the top of the sandwich. Garnish with banana slices. Yield: 6 sandwiches.

Churchtown Inn, Churchtown,
Pennsylvania

GENERAL'S TOAST

Cut a large slice of Italian bread and slit the center. Stuff it with fresh fruit. Make a dipping batter of egg, flour, brown sugar to taste, and milk. Dip the stuffed bread into the batter and then deep-fry. Cover with powdered sugar.

Doubleday Inn, Gettysburg,
Pennsylvania

BAKED FRENCH TOAST

No butter or syrup is needed for this moist and flavorful French toast. This is a make-ahead dish.

1	cup packed light or dark brown sugar
½	cup butter
2	tablespoons light or dark corn syrup
1	loaf French bread, cut in ¾-inch slices (estimate 2 slices per person, plus a few more for hearty eaters)
5	eggs
1½	cups milk
1	teaspoon vanilla extract

In a medium saucepan, over medium-low heat, mix and melt brown sugar, butter, and corn syrup. Meanwhile, spray a baking dish with nonstick vegetable oil. Pour the butter and sugar mixture into a 9-by-13-inch baking dish. In a blender, mix eggs, milk, and vanilla. Arrange bread slices in baking dish. Pour egg mixture over bread slices, not missing any areas, and using all of the mixture. The excess will be absorbed by the bread slices. Cover the baking dish and refrigerate overnight. The next morning, preheat oven to 350 degrees. Uncover the baking dish and bake for 30 minutes. Serve directly from the baking dish. Yield: about 8 servings.

Little River Inn, Aldie, Virginia

BAKED APPLE PANCAKES

4–5	red Delicious or Granny Smith apples, peeled, cored, and thinly sliced
½	stick unsalted butter
½	cup sugar
½	teaspoon cinnamon
6	eggs
1	cup flour
	Scant cup milk

Preheat oven to 375 degrees. In an 8-inch cast-iron skillet, melt butter. Sauté apples. Sprinkle with sugar and cinnamon. Cook until sugar is melted and apples have begun to soften. Mix together eggs, flour, and milk, and pour over apples. Bake for 20–30 minutes or until puffed and done in the center. Serve warm with maple syrup. Yield: at least 6 servings.

Bramble Inn, Brewster, Massachusetts

BANANA PANCAKES

This recipe yields a crepe-like pancake.

1½	cups flour
2	tablespoons sugar
2½	teaspoons baking powder
½	teaspoon salt

  2   eggs
1¼   cups milk
  3   tablespoons oil or melted butter
  2   medium-sized, overripe bananas, mashed

Mix together flour, sugar, baking powder, and salt. In another bowl, mix together eggs, milk, and oil or butter. Combine this with the dry ingredients. Add mashed bananas. Heat griddle and pour batter to desired pancake size. Yield: 4–6 servings.

Thomas Huckins House,
Barnstable, Massachusetts

Want to make pancakes lighter than air? Use low-fat milk instead of whole milk.

Mary Lee and James Papa, Shire
Inn, Chelsea, Vermont

Keep sourdough starter on hand to be added to prepared mixes or pancakes, waffles, and breads. It adds an interesting flavor.

Nancy Donaldson, Old Yacht Club
Inn, Santa Barbara, California

Located on the Gettysburg Battlefield, we try to put a little bit of the Civil War into everything we do, including our Blue-and-Gray Pancakes. To make your own Civil War pancakes, use a mix that requires water. Instead of the water, use the juice from a package of frozen blueberries. Then mix in the blueberries. The pancakes will have a blue/gray cast.

Joan and Sal Chandon, Doubleday
Inn, Gettysburg, Pennsylvania

Our favorite breakfast is blueberry pancakes. Jim fixes breakfast and likes to be prepared in advance. He makes his pancake mix ahead of time and preserves it in a crock. In the morning, he simply adds the wet ingredients—sort of an instant, homemade mix. You can keep your own pancake supply handy, too.

Glynrose and Jim Friedlander, Isaac
Randall House, Freeport, Maine

My favorite cooking shortcut is to eliminate separating the eggs when making a waffle recipe. Simply place the proper number of

whole eggs and milk into a bowl. Let your mixer run on high while
the rest of the ingredients are being prepared. By the time you're
ready to add the dry ingredients, the egg mixture is light and
fluffy.

> Betty Stewart, Sunning Hill,
> Pittsford, Vermont

Walnuts can top French toast and maple syrup.

Another syrup is made by mixing equal quantities of sugar and
apple cider. Boil 2 minutes. Add jam, such as raspberry, for color
and flavor. Pour over French toast.

> Faith and Charles Reynolds,
> Historic Merrell Tavern Inn, South
> Lee, Massachusetts

To soften hard brown sugar, put it in a pan with a little water and
heat gradually. Serve as syrup on pancakes or use as called for in
recipes.

> Shirley and Stephen Ramsey,
> Mayhurst B&B, Orange, Virginia

To make your own cinnamon sugar for French toast, toast,
muffins, coffee cakes, and much more: In a shaker or covered jar,
combine 2 tablespoons cinnamon and 1 cup of granulated sugar.
Shake well until blended.

> Libby and Jim Hopkins, Old Broad
> Bay Inn, Waldoboro, Maine

STU'S QUICK FRUIT CRISP

1	29-ounce can sliced peaches, apples, or pears, undrained
1	18½-ounce box yellow cake mix
½	cup melted butter
1	cup shredded coconut (optional)
1	cup chopped pecans
	Cinnamon to sprinkle on top
	Whipped cream

Preheat oven to 325 degrees. Place ingredients in the order listed (except the whipped cream) into a 9-by-13-inch ungreased baking dish. Bake approximately 50 minutes. Serve warm with a dash of whipped cream. Yield: 12 small servings.

Churchtown Inn, Churchtown,
Pennsylvania

GLAZED SAUSAGE AND APPLES

This is a nice side dish.

2	pounds precooked sausage links
⅓	cup water
¼	cup packed brown sugar
2	large tart apples, sliced
1	large onion, chopped

Brown sausages in large skillet. Remove sausages, drain on paper towels, and add remaining ingredients to same skillet. Cook 8 to 10 minutes until tender, then stir sausages into mixture, and continue cooking about 10 minutes longer. Yield: 6 servings.

The Summer Cottage Inn Cookbook,
Cape May, New Jersey

EASY SPUD BREAKFAST

Bake a potato. Slice it in half the long way. Scoop out some of the inside, and fill it with cooked scrambled eggs. Top with grated cheese. Heat in a microwave oven. Garnish with freshly chopped parsley and serve.

Pelham Inn, Philadelphia,
Pennsylvania

BREAKFAST EGG CASSEROLE

1	pound bulk breakfast sausage
4–5	slices of bread, cubed

⅓   pound mild cheddar cheese, cubed
6   eggs
2   cups milk
1   teaspoon salt (optional)
1   teaspoon dry mustard

Grease a 9-by-13-inch pan. In a medium skillet, brown sausage. Remove and drain. Place the bread cubes in pan, then add the sausage meat. Arrange cheese cubes over meat. In a small bowl, beat eggs, milk, salt, and mustard. Pour egg mixture over the cheese cubes. Refrigerate overnight. In the morning, preheat oven to 350 degrees. Bake the casserole for 45 minutes. Yield: about 8 servings.

Winters Creek Inn, Carson City, Nevada

BREAKFAST QUICHE

½   pound bulk breakfast sausage
3   eggs
½   cup milk
½   cup mayonnaise
1–2   cups grated cheese

Preheat oven to 325 degrees. Sauté sausage in skillet. Mix the other ingredients in a bowl. Add the drained sausage. Place all the ingredients in a pie pan and bake for 20 minutes. Yield: 6 servings.

Shaw House, Georgetown, South Carolina

SHAW HOUSE EGG FOR ONE

Slice miniature sausages or cocktail hot dogs in half, and sauté in butter in a skillet. Cover the bottom of a ramekin (or any individual baking dish) with the sausage or hot dogs. Spoon in 3 tablespoons of your favorite white sauce. Crack an egg on top.

Cover with grated cheese. Bake for 8 minutes in a 325-degree oven.

Shaw House, Georgetown, South Carolina

HAM AND CHEESE SANDWICH PUFF

1   cup ground ham
1   cup grated Swiss cheese
¼   cup mayonnaise
½   teaspoon prepared mustard
8   slices white sandwich bread
6   eggs
1¼   cups milk

The night before serving: Combine ham, cheese, mayonnaise, and mustard. Set aside. Toast bread. Divide ham mixture evenly on 4 slices of toast. Top with the 4 remaining slices. Cut each sandwich diagonally into 4 triangles. In a well-greased 9x6x2-inch casserole dish, stand each triangle upright on its outside edge, making 2 rows. Beat eggs and milk well, and pour mixture over the triangles in casserole. Cover and refrigerate overnight.

The next morning: Preheat oven to 325 degrees. Bake casserole, uncovered, for 35 minutes until set. Let stand 5–10 minutes before serving. Slice between sandwiches, and serve 3 or 4 triangles per person. Yield: 4–6 servings.

Boydville The Inn at Martinsburg, Martinsburg, West Virginia

CANADIAN-BACONED EGGS

Here is a recipe that is fun to make for a few or for several. Simply use an appropriate-sized baking dish for 2 or 20. Season and proportion according to your own taste and number to be served. Then it becomes your own recipe.

Eggs
Sliced Canadian bacon

Shredded Swiss cheese
Sour cream
Salt
White pepper
Paprika

Preheat oven to 325 degrees. Line baking dish with Canadian bacon. Spread cheese on top, creating a nest into which you place each egg. Cover each egg with sour cream. (Whip the sour cream lightly to help cover the egg more easily.) Sprinkle salt, pepper, and paprika over eggs. Bake approximately 20 minutes (varies with volume). Serve with a warm fruit or nut bread.

Manor House, Cape May, New Jersey

When a recipe calls for beating egg whites separately, the tiniest bit of yolk will keep them from whipping fully. The best way to remove a speck of yolk (or even a piece of eggshell) is to use another piece of eggshell to scoop it out.

Kathy Drew, Out-the-Inn-Door, Freeport, Maine

Egg whites cannot be frozen, but yolks can, if placed in a tightly sealed container.

Daun Martin, Britt House, San Diego, California

Our buffet breakfast table is set with an antique cloth. Small boxes of individual cereals are placed in a large basket for guests to help themselves. Egg frittatas or baked apple pancakes are served right out of large cast-iron pans.

Ruth and Cliff Manchester, Bramble Inn, Brewster, Massachusetts

Place eggs in the refrigerator with large ends up, as this keeps the yolks centered. Eggs will remain unspoiled in the refrigerator for up to one month. Since eggshells are porous, eggs may absorb odors from other foods in the refrigerator. Keep strong-smelling foods tightly covered and as far as possible from the eggs.

Daun Martin, Britt House, San Diego, California

It can be a pain to peel eggs when you're making deviled or hard-boiled eggs. Two tips: First, try to buy your eggs five or six days before you need them, especially farm-fresh eggs. Fresh eggs are very hard to peel. Second, put one-half cup of salt into the water with the eggs. Cook as you usually do. Then, place five or six eggs at a time into a colander and shake them rapidly while running under water. They peel themselves.

Debby and Hap Joy, The Decoy, Strasburg, Pennsylvania

Serve eggs scrambled, fried, or however, with sprigs of parsley, some mint, or chives cut finely with scissors.

Mrs. W. B. Nottingham, Tokfarm Inn, Rindge, New Hampshire

To save time, cook poached eggs in advance and refrigerate. They store beautifully and can be used in recipes or reheated.

Christi and Mark Carter, Carter House, Eureka, California

Serving a soft-boiled egg in an eggcup brings back Grandma's house or European travel memories. It makes a plain egg an event!

Lila and Rick Peiffer, Bluebelle House, Lake Arrowhead, California

We serve our eggs in glass hen dishes. The eggs keep warm, and the dishes really look great.

Ann and Jim Carver, Beal House, Littleton, New Hampshire

Seasoned salt is a must when serving eggs. It adds a wonderful secret flavor to them. Guests are always asking what we put in our eggs.

Debby and Hap Joy, The Decoy, Strasburg, Pennsylvania

Finger sausage tastes and looks better if you bake the links in the oven with water in the pan. They will cook thoroughly and be easier to chew. Bake about 40 minutes in a 400-degree oven.

Debby and Hap Joy, The Decoy,
Strasburg, Pennsylvania

CRAB BRUNCH SQUARES WITH RED-PEPPER CREAM SAUCE

4 eggs
2⅔ cups milk
¾ teaspoon Dijon-style mustard
6 ounces Brie, rind removed, cut in ¼-inch cubes
½ cup sliced black olives
1 small onion, finely chopped
2 tablespoons finely chopped parsley
1 teaspoon Worcestershire sauce
3½ cups cooked rice
1 pound fresh, frozen, or canned lump crabmeat, picked through for shells

Preheat oven to 325 degrees. In mixing bowl, beat eggs, milk, and mustard until blended. Stir in remaining ingredients except paprika. Pour into greased 9-by-13-inch baking pan. Bake for 40–45 minutes, or until knife inserted at center comes out clean. Serve with Red Pepper Cream Sauce.

RED PEPPER CREAM SAUCE:
4 tablespoons unsalted butter
1 large ripe red pepper, seeded and cut in ¼-inch dice
¼ cup thinly sliced green onion
¼ cup flour
¼ teaspoon salt
¼ teaspoon white pepper
1¾ cups milk
3 teaspoons lemon juice
Fresh snipped chives for garnish

Melt butter in small, heavy saucepan. Sauté red pepper and green onion for 2 minutes. Add flour and sauté on low heat 3 minutes. Blend in salt and pepper, then gradually whisk in milk and lemon juice. Cook for 1 minute, then transfer to blender container. Blend on high for 2 minutes, or until pepper and onion are pureed. Spoon over brunch squares and garnish with chives. Yield: 10 servings.

Grant Corner Inn Breakfast and Brunch Cookbook, Santa Fe, New Mexico

A pinch of freshly grated nutmeg takes the raw-tasting edge off of flour in cream sauces.

Tommie and Andy Duncan, Arcady Down East, Blue Hill, Maine

When measuring shortening, it is by far easiest to do it in cold water. For example, if you need ⅓ cup of shortening, put ⅔ cup of cold water in a one-cup measure. Then submerge shortening in the water until the water level reaches exactly 1 cup. Pour off the water, and you have the right amount of shortening, and it comes out of the cup easily.

Joanne and George Hardy, Hill Farm Inn, Arlington, Vermont

 Appetizers, Snacks, and Beverages

SESAME CHEESE STICKS

1	cup flour, sifted
½	teaspoon salt
½	teaspoon MSG
½	teaspoon ground ginger
1	cup grated sharp cheese
¼	cup toasted sesame seeds
1	egg yolk, beaten
⅓	cup butter, melted

1   tablespoon water
½   teaspoon Worcestershire sauce

Preheat oven to 350 degrees. Sift together dry ingredients. Stir in cheese and sesame seeds. Combine remaining ingredients, then add them to first mixture and stir to form a ball. Roll out on slightly floured board to ¼-inch thickness. Cut into 1-by-3-inch strips. Bake on ungreased baking sheet for 10–15 minutes. Yield: 4 dozen.

The Summer Cottage Inn Cookbook,
Cape May, New Jersey

TERIYAKI NUTS

2   cups mixed nuts
2   tablespoons butter
1   tablespoon soy sauce
½   teaspoon ground ginger
¼   teaspoon garlic salt
1   teaspoon lemon juice

Preheat oven to 325 degrees. Spread nuts on an ungreased, large baking sheet with raised sides. Roast nuts for 5 to 10 minutes, until lightly browned. Melt butter and stir in soy sauce, ginger, garlic salt, and lemon juice. Brush over nuts and roast 5 minutes longer.

The Summer Cottage Inn Cookbook,
Cape May, New Jersey

RED OR GREEN PEPPER JELLY

This is good with cream cheese and crackers.

1¼   cups seeded and finely chopped (in food processor) green or red bell peppers
1½   cups apple cider vinegar
6   cups sugar
1   bottle liquid pectin, such as Certo

Mix peppers, vinegar, and sugar in large stainless steel pan. Bring mixture to a boil. Add pectin. Then bring back to full rolling boil. Boil for exactly 1 minute. Remove from heat. Let stand for 3 minutes, then skim off foam. Ladle into sterilized jars. Seal and process in hot-water bath for 20 minutes. Yield: 6 half pints.

Grant Corner Inn Breakfast and Brunch Cookbook, Santa Fe, New Mexico

HOT ARTICHOKE DIP

1   12-ounce can artichokes, broken up (not marinated)
½   cup mayonnaise
1   2-ounce can chopped green chilies, drained
1   cup Parmesan cheese

Preheat oven to 350 degrees. Mix all ingredients and bake in a 4-cup shallow bowl for 15 minutes. Serve with crackers.

Glenborough Inn, Santa Barbara, California

BRIE AND BREAD

Scoop out the center of a round loaf of French bread. Put chunks of a wedge of Brie in it and warm in 350-degree oven until soft, about 5 minutes. Cut and serve.

Glenborough Inn, Santa Barbara, California

THE GOVERNOR'S INN MUSHROOM STRUDEL

This is our most-requested recipe.

6   cups minced mushrooms, caps and stems
1   teaspoon salt
¼   teaspoon curry powder

6   tablespoons sherry
4   tablespoons chopped shallots
4   tablespoons sweet butter
1   cup sour cream
1   cup plus 3 tablespoons dry bread crumbs
1   package frozen phyllo dough, thawed
½   cup sweet butter, melted
    Sour cream
    Fresh parsley

Sauté mushrooms with seasonings, sherry, and shallots in 4 tablespoons butter until mushrooms are wilted and liquid is gone (about 20 minutes on low heat). Cool. Add sour cream and 3 tablespoons dry bread crumbs. Refrigerate overnight.

Preheat oven to 375 degrees. Unwrap phyllo dough carefully. Place a sheet of dough on a large breadboard. Brush with melted butter and sprinkle with bread crumbs. Repeat until you have 4 layers. Spoon half the mushroom mixture onto the narrow end of the dough. Turn long sides of dough in about 1 inch to seal filling. Roll up dough like a jelly roll. Brush top of the roll with butter, and sprinkle with a few more crumbs. Place on a lightly greased cookie sheet. Score dough with a sharp knife for 8 equal slices. Make a second roll, using remaining mushroom filling. Bake for 40 minutes. Garnish with dollop of sour cream and chopped parsley. Serve hot. Yield: 16 slices.

The Governor's Inn Cookbook, Ludlow, Vermont

Fed up with your mushrooms getting brown before their time? Keep them in water, butter, and lemon juice for that whiter, brighter look.

Mary Lee and James Papa, Shire Inn, Chelsea, Vermont

MEATBALLS FOR A SANTA WATCH

On Christmas Eve, guests gather around the great fireplace to wait and watch for Santa. This is what we serve.

3   pounds ground beef
1½   cups cracker crumbs
3   eggs
½   cup minced onion
2   tablespoons chopped parsley
1   cup milk, scalded
     Salt and pepper to taste

Preheat oven to 350 degrees. Mix ingredients well and form into small, firm balls. Bake on a cookie sheet for 15 minutes. Drain well.

SAUCE:

¾   cup ketchup
½   cup water
¼   cup cider vinegar
¼   teaspoon black pepper
2   tablespoons brown sugar
1   tablespoon chopped onion
2   tablespoons Worcestershire sauce
1½   teaspoons salt
1   teaspoon dry mustard
6–10 drops hot sauce

Heat sauce ingredients together. Add meatballs. Transfer to a chafing dish and serve. Yield: about 150 meatballs.

The Governor's Inn Cookbook, Ludlow, Vermont

HOT RYES

1   cup finely grated Swiss cheese
¼   cup crumbled cooked bacon
1   4½-ounce can ripe olives, chopped
¼   cup minced green onions or chives
1   teaspoon Worcestershire sauce

¼ cup mayonnaise
Party rye bread

Preheat oven to 375 degrees. Mix first 6 ingredients together. Spread 1 tablespoon on each slice of bread. Bake for 10–15 minutes. May be frozen after baking and reheated. Yield: 36 servings.

Inn of the Arts, Las Cruces, New Mexico

GREEN CHILI PIE

18 eggs, beaten
1 pound Longhorn cheese, grated
1 pound whole green chilies
Garlic salt to taste

Preheat oven to 350 degrees. Butter all sides of 18x12x2½-inch baking dish. Place opened whole chilies on bottom. Sprinkle with garlic salt. Slowly pour eggs over green chilies. Sprinkle cheese on top. Bake for 40 minutes. Cut into 1½-inch squares. Yield: 20–25 servings.

Inn of the Arts, Las Cruces, New Mexico

Author's Tip: Wear rubber gloves when cutting chilies. The oils can burn your hands. Avoid cutting them on a wooden board, as the oils can transfer flavors to other foods.

SHRIMP APPETIZER

2 6½-ounce cans medium deveined shrimp, drained
2 8-ounce packages cream cheese
½ large onion, chopped
Juice of ½ lemon
Dash Worcestershire sauce

Preheat oven to 350 degrees. Mix ingredients. Pour into souffle dish and bake for 30 minutes. Serve with crackers.

Inn of the Arts, Las Cruces, New Mexico

MEXICAN ROLL-UPS

1   4-ounce can black olives, chopped
8   ounces cream cheese, softened
     Dash tabasco sauce
2   medium-size flour tortillas
     Medium-hot salsa

Fold olives into softened cream cheese. Add tabasco sauce. Mix. Divide the mixture in half. Fill each tortilla with half of the cream cheese filling. Roll the tortillas to form cylinders. Cut into ¾-inch slices. Hold each roll-up together with a decorative toothpick. Place salsa in a bowl as a dip for the roll-ups.

Locust Hill B&B, Morrow, Ohio

CLAM SPREAD

1   tablespoon light cream (add more if
         needed)
8   ounces cream cheese, softened
1   bunch green onions, chopped (tops too)
½   teaspoon garlic powder
2–3 grinds fresh black pepper
1   6½-ounce can chopped clams

Mix cream into cream cheese. Add onions, garlic powder, and pepper. Mix. Stir in clams. Chill at least 2 hours; best when chilled overnight. Serve with crackers or toast points.

Wanek's Lodge, Estes, Colorado

SHRIMP SPREAD

1   6- to 7-ounce can tiny shrimp, drained and
      mashed
1   teaspoon lemon juice
2   tablespoons mayonnaise
1   tablespoon grated onion
      Salt (optional)

Mix ingredients together, adding a dash of salt if desired. Chill,
then serve with crackers.

Graham's B&B, Sedona, Arizona

GREEK HUMMUS DIP

This is great with crackers or triangles of pita bread.

1   15½-ounce can garbanzo beans, drained
2   lemons, juiced
2   garlic cloves, pressed
½   cup tahini
      Olive oil
      Paprika
      Green or black Greek olives

In a blender, combine beans, lemon juice, garlic, and tahini. Add
more lemon juice, salt, or garlic to taste. Spread the dip on a plate,
dribble olive oil over it, sprinkle with paprika, and dot with green
or black Greek olives. Yield: 8–10 servings.

Eastlake Inn, Los Angeles,
California

SAUSAGE BISCUITS

1   pound bulk hot sausage
2   cups self-rising flour
½   cup shortening
⅔   cup milk

Preheat oven to 450 degrees. Place sausage in a bowl with flour. Cut in half the shortening into flour until lumps are pea-sized. Cut in the rest of the shortening until a cornmeal consistency. Add milk. Knead lightly on a floured board. Shape into small balls. Bake for 10 minutes, or until brown. Can be frozen after baking. Yield: about 24 biscuits.

Leftwich House, Graham, North Carolina

Our baked Montrachet goat cheese is served on a fresh grape leaf, or in the fall, a red or yellow maple leaf. Green grapes or sliced apple and homemade chutney accompany the cheese.

Ruth and Cliff Manchester, Bramble Inn, Brewster, Massachusetts

We boil down green apples to get the juice for pectin. Freeze the juice in ice-cube trays, store the solid cubes in plastic bags in the freezer, and use them as the pectin source when making jams and jellies. It's much cheaper than buying pectin.

Robin and Bill Branigan, Roaring Lion, Waldoboro, Maine

To keep cheese from drying out, dip a linen cloth or cheesecloth in wine. Squeeze out the excess wine and wrap the cheese in the cloth. The cheese is not only kept moist, but its flavor is improved.

Cliff House Staff, Cliff House B&B, Madison, Indiana

Cheese also can be kept fresh by covering it with a cloth moistened with vinegar.

Ruthmary Jordan, Pride House, Jefferson, Texas

A knife warmed under hot water makes cutting cheese or butter easier.

Beverly and Ray Compton, Spring Bank Inn, Frederick, Maryland

HOT BUTTERED WEDGWOOD

2   ounces almond liqueur
1   cup hot tea, cider, or apple juice
1   tablespoon whipped unsalted butter
    Twist of orange peel
1   cinnamon stick

Pour the almond liqueur into a mug. Fill with the hot tea, cider, or juice. Add the butter and orange peel. Garnish with a cinnamon stick. Yield: 1 serving.

Wedgwood Inn, New Hope,
Pennsylvania

HOT CIDER

1   gallon cider
3   sliced oranges
4   sticks cinnamon
2   teaspoons whole cloves in tea ball or
    cheesecloth bag

Simmer all the ingredients in heavy pot for at least 1 hour. Serve hot. Yield: about 24 cups.

Britt House, San Diego, California

KIM'S HOMEMADE COFFEE LIQUEUR

2   cups boiling water
2   ounces powdered instant coffee
3   cups sugar
1   fifth brandy or vodka
1   vanilla bean cut in sections

Pour boiling water over coffee. Stir to dissolve. Stir in sugar until dissolved. Cool. Add brandy or vodka. Pour into desired number of sterilized, dark-brown bottles. Add a section of vanilla bean to each bottle. Place each bottle in a brown bag. Store, for 1 month, shaking weekly. Yield: about 1 quart.

Britt House, San Diego, California

CRANBERRY CORDIAL

1   pound cranberries, washed and picked over
1   pound sugar
1   fifth of gin

Dry and punch a hole through each cranberry. In a half-gallon jar, place berries, sugar, and gin. Seal the jar, store it for 6 weeks, shaking it at least once a day. Strain and place in a nice decanter with a tight-fitting stopper.

Folkestone B&B, Berkeley Springs,
West Virginia

AMARETTO CORDIAL

6   cups sugar
1   quart water
3   ounces almond extract
2   quarts 100-proof vodka

Combine sugar and water. Bring to a boil and simmer for 5 minutes. Add almond extract and vodka. Store in a dark bottle. Yield: 18–20 servings.

Folkestone B&B, Berkeley Springs,
West Virginia

CHURCHTOWN INN'S FAVORITE WASSAIL

1   gallon apple juice
1   quart cranberry juice
1   cup sugar
3   cinnamon sticks

    1   tablespoon whole allspice
    3   small oranges studded with whole cloves
1½–2 cups dark rum

Combine ingredients. Heat gently. Simmer for ½ hour. Serve warm. Yield: 18–20 servings.

Churchtown Inn, Churchtown,
Pennsylvania

FIRESIDE QUENCHER

Although this is a great summer refresher, it can quench your thirst any time of the year. Fill a tall glass with ice. Add 2 healthy dashes of bitters and 1½–2 ounces of lime juice. Fill with sparkling mineral water. Add dark rum for a little kick.

Tulip Tree Inn, Chittenden,
Vermont

Fill a bundt pan with water and add fruit, tiny flowers, and greenery. Freeze. When ready for ice in the punch bowl, remove the bundt ice sculpture from the pan. (Dip the pan in hot water to help remove the sculpture.) This is beautiful when floating in the punch.

Joanne Parker, assistant manager,
Garnet Hill Lodge, North River,
New York

Having a brunch? Serve Blooming Bloody Marys with rose-shaped radishes or cauliflower-carnation swizzle sticks in lieu of the traditional celery stalk. Insert bamboo kabob-skewers through the base and up the center of scallions, allowing for a rigid stem and adjacent leaves. Stick radish roses or cauliflower-ettes on the ends of the stems to resemble flowers. Serve in drink glasses.

Beth and Franz Schober, Hopkins
Inn, New Preston, Connecticut

Mix equal parts lemonade and grape juice, and you have what tastes like a cranberry juice cocktail.

Barbara and Lyle Wolf, Greenhurst
Inn, Bethel, Vermont

WHITE GAZPACHO

One lovely inn and dinner guest shared this recipe with us. The topping of tomato, scallions, and cilantro looks beautiful on the white soup.

8	ounces cream cheese, softened
½	cup sour cream
1	cup light cream
1	cup double-strength chicken stock
1	cucumber, peeled and seeded
1	red onion, quartered
1	ripe avocado, peeled and quartered
1	bunch scallions (green ends off), sliced
1	green pepper, seeded and quartered
1	jalapeño pepper, seeded
½	cup finely minced cilantro leaves
1	clove garlic
1	ripe tomato, chopped
	Salt and white pepper to taste

Puree cream cheese and sour cream. Add light cream and chicken stock. In food processor, pulse cucumber, onion, avocado, peppers, and garlic until moderately diced. Add to cream mixture. Mix 1 tablespoon each of scallions and cilantro with the chopped tomato. Add remaining scallions and cilantro to soup. Allow soup to ripen in refrigerator for several hours. Serve chilled, garnished with tomato mixture. Yield: 6–8 servings.

Variation: Substitute lobster stock for chicken stock and add 1 cup finely diced lobster meat.

Bramble Inn, Brewster,
Massachusetts

DELICATE CREAM OF ARTICHOKE SOUP

2	8-ounce cans artichoke hearts, drained
1½	cups chicken broth (add more for thinner soup)
	Lemon juice to taste

2   cups light cream
     Shredded carrots for garnish

Combine artichoke hearts, broth, lemon juice, and cream in blender. Blend thoroughly. When ready to serve, heat gently and garnish with shredded carrots in the center. Yield: 8 servings.

Author

COUNTRY CORN BREAD

1½   cups cornmeal
½   cup flour
½   teaspoon baking soda
½   teaspoon salt
1   cup whole milk
2   large eggs, beaten
2   tablespoons vegetable oil
2   cups grated Vermont cheddar cheese
1   8-ounce can cream-style corn
1   pound lean, good-quality bacon, cooked, drained, and crumbled

Preheat oven to 350 degrees. Combine first 4 ingredients and mix well. Add milk, eggs, and vegetable oil, stirring well. Stir in remaining ingredients. Pour into a greased tube pan. Bake for 45 minutes, or until lightly browned. Cool for 10 minutes before removing from pan. Serve slightly warm. Yield: 6–8 servings.

The Governor's Inn Cookbook, Ludlow, Vermont

DILL AND CHEESE BREAD

1½   cups cottage cheese
¼   cup water
2   tablespoons sugar
2   tablespoons minced onion
1   tablespoon butter
3   teaspoons dill seeds

                1　teaspoon salt
                ¼　teaspoon baking soda
                1　egg
        2¼–2½　cups flour
                1　package yeast dissolved in ¼ cup warm
                    water
                    Softened butter

Heat cottage cheese to lukewarm in a pan, and then add ¼ cup water. Pour remaining ingredients, except softened yeast mixture and flour, into large bowl. Add softened yeast mixture. Then add flour to form a stiff dough, beating as flour is added. Cover dough. Let rise in warm place (85–90 degrees), until light and doubled in size, about 50–60 minutes. Stir down dough. Turn into greased, 8-inch round (1½–2 quart) casserole. Let rise in warm place until light, about 40 minutes. Bake at 350 degrees for 40–50 minutes, or until golden brown. Brush with softened butter. Yield: at least 6 servings.

Author

Soups are garnished with fresh snipped or chopped herbs or a chiffonade of basil or sorrel leaves. Make the chiffonade by rolling a stack of the herb leaves jelly-roll style and cutting it into thin slices.

Ruth and Cliff Manchester,
Bramble Inn, Brewster,
Massachusetts

Homemade bread that is baked in advance and frozen can taste as fresh as the day it was baked. Wrap the frozen loaf in tinfoil and heat in the oven one-half hour, and it seems as though newly baked.

Kathy and Helen Borgman,
Borgman's, Arrow Rock, Missouri

Top chilled summer soups with unsweetened whipped cream or fresh fruit. Contrasting-colored foods are attractive.

Ruth and Cliff Manchester,
Bramble Inn, Brewster,
Massachusetts

SALAD OF ENDIVE, RADICCHIO, AND GRAPEFRUIT WITH CITRUS VINAIGRETTE

Juice of 2 lemons
Juice of 1 lime
Juice of 1 pink grapefruit
Juice of 3 clementime or mandarine
    oranges
3 tablespoons honey
4 minced shallots
1 teaspoon fresh thyme
3 tablespoons raspberry vinegar
1 cup olive oil (half extra-virgin and half
    regular)
Belgian endive
Radicchio
Segments of pink grapefruit

Combine all juices. Check flavor; sweet tang is the desired taste. Whisk in honey in a steady stream. Add shallots, thyme, and vinegar. Add extra-virgin oil slowly, then add regular oil until the mixture has emulsified.

For each salad, arrange 3 endive leaves, 3 large radicchio leaves, and 3 to 5 grapefruit segments on a plate. Drizzle with vinaigrette. Serve immediately. Yield: about 8 servings.

Troutbeck Inn, Amenia, New York

Raspberry vinegar is great over salads, fruit, or pork, but it costs a fortune to buy. Here's how to make your own: To one quart of vinegar, add one pint of fresh raspberries. Bring to a boil. Lower heat and simmer for a few minutes. Cool. Strain into clean bottles. (Put some of the whole raspberries in the bottom.) Let stand a few months.

You can make herb vinegar the same way, substituting four ounces of tarragon, thyme, sage, marjoram, or dill.

Libby and Kim Hopkins, Old Broad
Bay Inn, Waldoboro, Maine

To dry large amounts of lettuce, place wet greens in a clean pillowcase, and put them in the washing machine on the spin cycle for one and a half to two minutes.

To revive wilted greens, douse them quickly in hot water, then in ice water with a little vinegar added.

Daun Martin, Britt House, San Diego, California

We use raw millet as seeds in our salads. People really enjoy it.

Ann Day Heinzerling, Knoll Farm Country Inn, Waitsfield, Vermont

Entrees and Side Dishes

STUFFED TENDERLOIN OF BEEF

1	trimmed tenderloin of beef (about 5 pounds)
6	slices bacon, chopped
1	large onion, chopped
2	cups herb-seasoned stuffing mix
1	3½-ounce package sliced pepperoni, minced
2	eggs, beaten
½	cup white wine or water
1–2	teaspoons minced garlic
	Freshly ground black pepper

Preheat oven to 400 degrees. In a skillet, sauté tenderloin with bacon and onion, browning on all sides. Cut lengthwise through the tenderloin to within ½-inch of the other side. Make two more cuts, one on either side of the first, being careful not to cut completely through to the other side. In a bowl, combine remaining ingredients to make the stuffing. Spoon stuffing mix into the openings. Fold the tenderloin in half. Tie securely with heavy string at 2–3-inch intervals. Place on a rack in a roasting pan and bake for 50 minutes for rare meat or 1 hour for medium. Let tenderloin rest for 5–10 minutes before slicing. Yield: 8–10 servings.

Trillium House, Nellysford, Virginia

STUFFED CORNISH GAME HENS WITH ORANGE SAUCE

4 Cornish hens, seasoned with salt and
   pepper inside and out
1¾ cups cooked white rice
½ cup chopped onions, sautéed
½ cup grated raw apple
½ cup raisins
¼ teaspoon poultry seasoning
   Melted butter

Preheat oven to 350 degrees. Mix rice, onions, apple, raisins, and poultry seasoning. Place ½ cup of stuffing into each hen cavity. Brush hens well with butter. Tie the legs together. Place hens, breast side up, in shallow roasting pan. Cover with foil and bake for 45–50 minutes. Uncover. Quickly brown under the broiler. Serve with Orange Sauce.

SAUCE:

1 6-ounce can frozen orange juice concentrate
1 cup light brown sugar
2 tablespoons butter

In small saucepan, cook sauce ingredients until thickened, stirring frequently. Serve warm. Yield: 4 servings.

Randolph House, Bryson City,
North Carolina

STUFFED BRACE OF QUAIL

8 quail
½ cup seedless white grapes
½ cup dried apricot halves
1 teaspoon tarragon
1 teaspoon chervil

Preheat oven to 350 degrees. Rinse quail and pat dry. Loosely stuff with fruit. Sprinkle liberally with herbs. Bake quail in a tightly covered pan for 1 hour. Yield: 4 servings.

Inn on the Common, Craftsbury, Vermont

GRAPEFRUIT SORBET

This pale-pink sorbet for cleaning the palate between courses was created especially for actors Paul Newman and Joanne Woodward when they visited The Governor's Inn.

    3   egg whites
    4   fresh grapefruit (or 2 16-ounce cans
             grapefruit sections in syrup)
    1   ounce white vermouth
    1   ounce grenadine syrup
    1½   cups simple syrup

In a mixing bowl, beat the egg whites until they are nicely stiff. Set aside. Place the grapefruit sections (with syrup, if canned), vermouth, grenadine, and simple syrup in a food processor with steel blades or in a blender. Mix. Fold in egg whites. Pour the mixture into an empty freezer container, and freeze until almost solid, about 3 hours. Pour the semisolid mixture back into the food processor or blender, and blend until all of the ice particles are finely granulated. Set the sorbet back into the freezer until ready to use. Serve in open-mouth champagne glasses. Yield: about 1 gallon.

Governor's Inn, Ludlow, Vermont

CHEF MICHAEL MYERS' PASTA PRIMAVERA

GARLIC BUTTER:
    ½   cup minced shallots
    ½   cup minced garlic
    ½   cup brandy
    ½   cup white wine

¼   cup cider vinegar
½   pound butter

In a skillet, reduce above ingredients except the butter to almost
dry. Place in a shallow pan in refrigerator to cool quickly. When
cooled, place in food processor and whip with butter. The mixture will have the consistency of butter. Reserve 2 tablespoons of
the butter; you may freeze the leftover butter and use it in many
different ways, including as a spread on bread or melted over
vegetables.

PASTA:
1   pound thin spaghetti, cooked and drained
2   cups julienne vegetables: carrots, zucchini,
        white turnips, broccoli, snow peas
2   tablespoons garlic butter
2   tablespoons white wine
¼   cup brandy
1   cup thickened chicken stock
1   cup heavy cream
    Grated smoked Gruyère cheese

In a skillet, sauté the vegetables in the 2 tablespoons of the garlic
butter until tender but crisp. Remove vegetables. Deglaze the pan
with the wine and brandy. Reduce sauce by one-half, and then
add chicken stock, heavy cream, and a liberal sprinkling of the
smoked Gruyère cheese. Cook mixture until heated through.
Add to the pasta and vegetables and serve. Yield: 4 servings.

Simmons' Way Village Inn,
Millerton, New York

You are better off working your own dough for homemade pasta
and then running the dough through a cutter than using a
machine that does it all. The key to good homemade pasta is
dough that hasn't toughened. You can feel the consistency when
you work it with your hands. If you run the machine too long, it's
too late. The dough will be tough. Whatever dough you make,
semolina is a more nutritional flour to use as the basis for your
pasta.

Michael Myers, chef, Simmons' Way
Village Inn, Millerton, New York

BABY ARTICHOKES WITH CRABMEAT RAVIGOTE

8   baby artichokes
8   lemons
1   cup Chablis
3   cups water
3   tablespoons butter
3   tablespoons flour
1   shallot, minced
1   tablespoon clarified butter
1   cup plus 3 tablespoons heavy cream
1   tablespoon chopped fresh French tarragon
1   pound snow crabmeat

Snip off points of artichokes and cut stems flush with bottoms. Remove rind from 2 lemons and reserve. Squeeze the 2 lemons and reserve their juice. Add rind to large saucepan along with 4 sliced lemons, Chablis, and 2 cups water. Add artichokes and poach them until the leaves can be pulled off easily. Drain. Combine reserved lemon juice and 1 cup cold water. Dip artichokes in this mixture, and cool. Open leaves, remove the choke with a spoon, and discard the choke. Dip artichokes in juice again.

To prepare ravigote sauce, melt butter and whisk in flour for the roux. Sauté shallot in clarified butter until translucent. Add 1 cup cream and heat to boiling. Stir in roux with a whisk. Squeeze remaining 2 lemons. Add juice, tarragon, and remaining cream. Cool. Combine sauce with crabmeat and stuff artichokes with mixture. Garnish with blanched purple or green kale and lemon twists, if desired. Yield: 8 servings.

Troutbeck Inn, Amenia, New York

BRAISED LEEKS, WILD MUSHROOMS, AND ROASTED RED PEPPERS

2   red bell peppers
¼   cup butter
1   leek, julienne

½ pound shiitake mushrooms, stems removed, sliced
¼ cup chicken stock

Seed peppers and roast in a shallow pan at 400 degrees for 30 minutes. Cool, then peel and julienne them. In a sauté pan, melt butter and add leek, peppers, and mushrooms. Sauté over medium heat for 2 minutes, then reduce heat and add stock. Cover and braise 10 minutes, until leeks are tender. Yield: 6 servings.

Vermont Marble Inn, Fairhaven, Vermont

BIRD'S NEST SIDE DISH

Skin and boil whole, small, new or red potatoes till tender. Meanwhile, sauté in butter julienned carrots and half as much sliced onion. When lightly browned, transfer onto a plate, forming the carrot and onion mixture into a bird's nest. Place three cooked potatoes on top. Sprinkle lightly with parsley flakes. This makes an attractive, conversational accompaniment to a chicken or steak dish.

Author

Author's Tip: Only a little pesto sauce is needed per serving of pasta. To make pesto ahead, freeze the sauce in an ice-cube tray. Cover the tray with freezer paper or layers of tinfoil. Remove a pesto cube as needed. You can do the same with other sauces, too.

To make a bouquet garni: Tie a bunch of preferably fresh herbs with cotton twine in cheesecloth. If you are using dried herbs, use half as much as you would with fresh herbs. Include in the bouquet: one bunch of Italian parsley and one of basil, plus one branch each of tarragon, winter savory, and oregano. This is only one combination, which is our favorite. You can make up your own, based on the fresh or dried herbs you have on hand.

Kate Kerivan, Bungay Jar, Easton, New Hampshire

Cut away the tough ends of broccoli stalks, and use them for soups.

Shirley and Stephen Ramsey,
Mayhurst B&B, Orange, Virginia

To tell if the soft-shell crabs you're buying are fresh, touch the leg of the crab and then your earlobe. If they are the same in softness, then you know the crabs are fresh.

Elizabeth Gundry Hooper, Corner
Cupboard Inn, Rehoboth, Delaware

Interested in a more salt-free diet? Add caraway seeds or garlic in your cooking, instead of salt.

Mary Lee and James Papa, Shire
Inn, Chelsea, Vermont

Author's Tip: Save the leaves of fresh radishes to add extra-peppery zing to any dish, including stir-fried vegetables.

To freeze fresh vegetables, blanch them in boiling water two to three minutes. Then run them under cold water to stop the cooking process. Place in plastic bags and freeze.

Pat and John Emerson, Emersons'
Guest House, Vergennes, Vermont

Keep onions in the refrigerator. They stay fresher longer.

Shirley and Stephen Ramsey,
Mayhurst B&B, Orange, Virginia

When cooking artichokes, add a tablespoon of lemon juice or vinegar, a pinch of oregano, and a tablespoon of oil to the water. This greatly enhances the flavor.

Daun Martin, Britt House, San
Diego, California

Don't consider serving fish only with lemon. Lime makes for a more colorful dish and adds just as nice a flavor. As garnish, cut lime slices about ½-inch thick. Then cut Vs out of the rind around the edges, leaving rind between each V, so that you have almost a pinwheel effect.

Elizabeth Gundry Hooper, Corner
Cupboard Inn, Rehoboth, Delaware

Tired of your lobster curling up while being boiled? Tie the tasty crustacean flat to a wooden board first, then cook.

Mary Lee and James Papa, Shire
Inn, Chelsea, Vermont

When planning a cookout menu of hamburgers and hot dogs, remember that there are some great hot dog types in the supermarket. Add half-smokes and kielbasa to the hot dog menu, as well as chili and sauerkraut.

Debby and Hap Joy, The Decoy,
Strasburg, Pennsylvania

Lemon yogurt is great as a topping for fish, and maple yogurt goes well over old-fashioned oatmeal.

Ann Day Heinzerling, Knoll Farm
Country Inn, Waitsfield, Vermont

Unfortunately, ginger root tends to get stringy. Thus it's difficult to grate finely when a recipe calls for the ingredient in nonsolid form. Our chef accidentally discovered that by freezing ginger you can grate it as finely as you do Parmesan cheese. Also, it can be frozen again with no harm to the flavor.

Jean and Dud Hendrick, Pilgrim's
Inn, Deer Isle, Maine

 Desserts and Other Sweets

WHITE CHOCOLATE COEUR À LA CRÈME

A gourmet dessert for a special night in front of the fireplace.

1	8-ounce package cream cheese, room temperature
1½	cups whipping cream
¾	cup powdered sugar, sifted
3	ounces white chocolate, melted and slightly cooled

1   12-ounce bag frozen unsweetened
     raspberries, thawed
⅓   cup sugar
1   8-ounce can unsweetened apricots, drained
     Amaretto liqueur
     fresh mint leaves

Line 6 ½-cup coeur à la crème molds with double thickness of dampened cheesecloth, extending beyond edges to enclose filling completely. Using an electric mixer, beat cream cheese with ¼ cup of the cream and the powdered sugar in a large bowl until fluffy. Add white chocolate and beat until smooth, about 2 minutes. In another bowl, whip 1 cup cream to stiff peaks. Gently fold whipped cream into cream cheese mixture. Spoon ½ cup cheese mixture into each prepared mold. Fold cheesecloth over tops. Place molds on a rack set over a pan. Refrigerate for at least 8 hours or overnight.

Drain raspberries, reserving juice. Puree berries with ⅓ cup sugar in processor. Press through fine sieve into a medium-size bowl to remove seeds. Add just enough reserved juice to thin puree to sauce consistency. Cover and refrigerate.

Puree apricots in food processor. Add amaretto to taste. Transfer to small bowl. Cover and refrigerate. (Sauces may be prepared 3 hours ahead.)

Whip remaining ¼ cup cream to stiff peaks. Spoon into pastry bag fitted with star tip. Pull back cheesecloth and invert a mold onto a large plate. Carefully remove cheesecloth. Pour 3 tablespoons raspberry sauce on left side of the plate. Spoon 1 tablespoon apricot sauce in center of raspberry sauce. Draw knife through center of apricot circle, forming heart pattern. Repeat with remaining molds and sauces. Pipe rosettes of cream onto each plate, and garnish with mint leaves. Yield: 6 servings.

Bramble Inn, Brewster,
Massachusetts

BENNER HOUSE BROWNIES

1¼   cups graham cracker crumbs
1   14-ounce can sweetened condensed milk

1   cup chocolate chips
¾   cup chopped walnuts
     Powdered sugar

Preheat oven to 325 degrees. Grease and flour 8-inch-square baking pan. Mix the ingredients and spread evenly in the pan. Bake approximately 25 minutes. Cut while still warm into 2-by-4-inch squares. Dust with powdered sugar before serving. Yield: 8 servings.

Benner House, Weston, Missouri

PRIZE-WINNING SPICE CAKE

2   cups flour
1   teaspoon cinnamon
1   teaspoon ground cloves
1   teaspoon allspice
½   teaspoon salt
1   teaspoon baking soda
2   teaspoons baking powder
2   eggs, beaten until lemon colored
1   cup sugar
2   tablespoons molasses (or brown sugar)
1   cup sour milk (mix 1 cup milk and 1
     tablespoon vinegar) or buttermilk
⅔   cup oil

Preheat oven to 375 degrees. Stir together flour, cinnamon, cloves, allspice, salt, baking soda, and baking powder. Set aside. Beat eggs and gradually add sugar and molasses. Beat well. Add dry ingredients to the egg mixture, alternately with the sour milk. Gently add the oil. Pour into 2 greased loaf pans, and bake for 25 minutes. Serve with a favorite cream-cheese topping. Yield: 2 loaves.

Britt House Cookbook, San Diego, California

COUPE TOBLERONE

Impromptu guests? Make sure you always have a stock of Toblerone bars in the cabinet. For each 3½-ounce bar, you will need
2 tablespoons of cream and 1 tablespoon of your favorite liqueur.
Melt chocolate over a low heat, and add cream and liqueur. Stir.
Pour the sauce over dishes of ice cream.

Having a buffet? Use the same formula with about 8 Toblerone
bars. Heat in and serve from a fondue pot with miniature, frozen
ice cream puffs and fondue forks in front of the fireplace.

Hopkins Inn, New Preston,
Connecticut

AMARETTO BREAD PUDDING

	Thin bread slices, buttered
3	eggs
2	egg yolks
½	cup sugar
	Pinch salt
1¼	cups milk
1½	cups heavy cream
1½	teaspoons vanilla
1½	teaspoons amaretto liqueur
⅛	teaspoon nutmeg
⅛	teaspoon cinnamon

Preheat oven to 325 degrees. Cover the bottom of a 9-by-13-inch
baking pan with the buttered bread. Mix together all the remaining ingredients. Pour mixture over the bread. Bake for 55 minutes. Cut into squares. Serve each piece with a dollop of whipped
cream and the desired amount of amaretto poured on top. Yield:
8–10 servings.

Academy Street B&B, Hawley,
Pennsylvania

CHOCOLATE BREAD PUDDING WITH BRANDIED APRICOTS AND PEARS

1	tablespoon butter
2	cups half-and-half
6	ounces semisweet chocolate chips
½	loaf day-old French bread, cut into ½-inch cubes
¾	cup brandy
⅓	cup chopped dried apricots
2	pears, peeled and sliced
1	cup heavy cream, whipped
3	large eggs
¾	cup sugar
1	teaspoon vanilla extract

Butter a 7-by-11-inch baking pan. In a saucepan, heat half-and-half. Remove, and stir in chocolate chips until smooth. Place bread cubes in a large bowl, stir in chocolate mixture, and let stand 45 minutes.

Heat brandy and apricots. Remove from heat and stir in pear slices. Cool and drain, adding some of the liquid to the whipped cream.

Whisk together eggs, sugar, and vanilla. Stir into chocolate-bread mixture along with the brandied fruit. Pour into prepared pan and bake 1 hour at 350 degrees. Serve warm with the brandied whipped cream. Yield: 10–12 servings.

Trillium House, Nellysford,
Virginia

EASTLAKE INN CHRISTMAS PLUM PUDDING

There are not and never have been plums in a plum pudding. So you won't find any in the plum pudding we serve guests during Thanksgiving and Christmas.

Note: Here is an optional step in making this pudding, which has become a tradition for us. At Halloween time, when we start to think about Christmas, we fill a pot (not aluminum) with one-half bottle of brandy and add to it the raisins, currants, and figs in the recipe below. We put the pot in the back of the refrigerator, where it sits until Christmas. In a pinch, the fruit can be marinated one week before the pudding is made.

1	pound raisins
1	pound currants
½	pound cut-up figs
2	cups finely chopped beef fat (about 1 pound, easily ordered from your neighborhood butcher or supermarket)
1	cup flour
1	grated nutmeg
1	tablespoon cinnamon
½	tablespoon mace
½	cup brown sugar
1	teaspoon salt
7	eggs, separated
¼	cup heavy cream
½	cup brandy plus more for flaming
3	cups grated stale bread

In a large bowl, mix the raisins, currants, figs, and finely chopped beef fat. (If the fruit has been marinated in brandy, strain the fruit and reserve the brandy.) Add ¼ cup flour and mix lightly. Put the remaining flour, spices, sugar, and salt in a sifter, hold it over the bowl, and sift over the fruit. Mix lightly. Then add 7 egg yolks, cream, ½ cup brandy, and bread. Mix lightly. Whip the 7 egg whites until stiff, and fold them lightly into the mixture. You can then pour the batter into a greased gallon mold or spring-form pan (which we use). Cover the mold tightly with aluminum foil. Place it on a rack in a big pot and steam it for 6 hours (no peeking). The pudding must be steamed slowly, so that the suet can melt and the flour can burst. It's worth the wait, and the entire house will smell delicious and festive.

For our guests, we usually place the pudding on a rounded dish, pour heated brandy on top, and then flame it. Or, you can serve the pudding with Hard Sauce:

HARD SAUCE:

2–5	tablespoons softened butter
1	cup sifted powdered sugar

½   teaspoon cinnamon
¼   teaspoon ground cloves
⅛   teaspoon salt
⅛   teaspoon lemon juice
1   teaspoon vanilla extract

Slowly add all of the ingredients to the butter. Blend until smooth. Refrigerate until ready to use. Yield: 20 servings.

Eastlake Inn, Los Angeles, California

TORTE TURNAROUND

Change that ordinary chocolate cake mix into an exciting torte. Buy a top-quality cake mix. Bake according to package directions. Split layers in half. Spread raspberry preserves between layers. Drizzle with raspberry liqueur. Assemble the torte, and pipe thick whipped cream as frosting. Decorate with raspberries and more drizzled liqueur.

Inn at Buckeystown, Buckeystown, Maryland

LEFTOVER PUDDING SURPRISE

We often have leftover pudding or custard and cookies or brownies. So we put some of the cookie or brownie into a ramekin, top it with the pudding or custard, and then add whipped cream with grated chocolate and nuts, or a chocolate topping plus whipped cream and nuts.

Britt House, San Diego, California

Orange flower water or rose water added to whipped cream adds an interesting flavor and smells great.

Rebecca E. Shipman, Inn at Buckeystown, Buckeystown, Maryland

Allspice makes a tasty addition to whipped cream.

> Mary Lee and James Papa, Shire
> Inn, Chelsea, Vermont

Pile on more and more apple slices when making apple pie. Stack them high so that when the apples cook down, you still have an impressive, old-fashioned pie.

> Sally and Ken McWilliams, Main
> Street B&B, Madison, Indiana

Here's a recipe on how to make your own vanilla: Place two to three pieces of vanilla bean in a small jar. Add some vodka. Let it stand for a few months. Replenish with vodka. Makes a great Christmas present.

> Libby and Jim Hopkins, Old Broad
> Bay Inn, Waldoboro, Maine

Make your own homemade chocolate mints. Crush peppermint candies into melted chocolate. Pour into candy molds and let harden.

> Emily Hunter, Briar Rose, Boulder,
> Colorado

When a recipe calls for melting chocolate chips, save time and energy by melting them in the microwave rather than on top of the range. Just watch carefully, because chocolate burns quickly. It only takes one minute or so. The chips will have a glossy, dark shine when they're ready.

> Annie and Al Unrein, Glacier Bay
> Country Inn, Gustavus, Alaska

Place a doily on top of chocolate cake. Sprinkle powdered sugar on top. Remove doily. Result: an easily decorated cake.

> Corky and Steve Garboski, Province
> Inn, Strafford, New Hampshire

To shave chocolate for decorating cakes or any dish, use a spackling knife.

> Penny Davidson and Barbara Ally,
> Fowler House, Moodus,
> Connecticut

Bay leaves coated with chocolate, chilled, and then peeled away, make lovely chocolate leaves for our Cappuccino Cheesecake or any special dessert.

Plastic catsup containers make great instruments for sauces. One of ours, for example, holds our chocolate sauce. It makes it easy to decorate desserts on top. One of the patterns we use is a spiderweb made by the squeeze of the plastic container.

Ruth and Cliff Manchester, The
Bramble Inn, Brewster,
Massachusetts

Taking Tea

"Good afternoon. One lump or two?"

When Martha Washington was a little girl, family acquaintances from the mother country would send a pound or two of tea to their colonial correspondents. What a treat it was! Tea was not abundant in America. Now, however, not only is tea ubiquitous in the United States, but the art of taking tea is slowly becoming a tradition. Although I have no facts to back this up, I believe that B&Bs and country inns are one of the largest groups responsible for the burgeoning of teatime here. Hundreds of inns are serving tea to thousands of guests. Once guests find what a lovely respite taking tea can be, they return home and hold their own teas, and some even open tearooms. So, while we've read about fanciful teas in Agatha Christie mysteries and other British novels, and we've heard about taking tea on the tennis lawn, inns are offering us many opportunities to actually participate in teatime as a nation.

When the Westminster chimes bong four times on the hour in this once-colonized country, some inns serve tea in the very British tradition. That means they reenact the gathering in the manner of Anna, seventh duchess of Bedford (1783–1857), who is said to be one of the creators of England's afternoon-tea respite. Although tea had been popular for centuries, Anna instituted teatime—a respite with tea and food. It is said that as summer wore on and the length of time between breakfast and dinner extended, Anna demanded that her servants prepare an afternoon snack with tea, the first time food and tea were shared together.

Meanwhile, high tea, an hour or two later, was held by peasant farmers across the land. Heartier foods were served with sweets so that the farmers could return to the fields for a few hours more until the sun went down.

At inns, high tea usually includes finger sandwiches and plenty of sweet comestibles, such as the teatime treats suggested in the recipe section of this chapter. But each inn has its own individual teatime techniques. At The Green Tree Inn in historic Elsah, Illinois, for example, white gloves are required for teatime. While not all inns have such formal teas, teatime is set aside for relaxation and socializing with a comforting beverage.

At The Summer Cottage in Cape May, New Jersey, tea is served at 4:00 P.M. Innkeeper Nancy Rishforth says, "No matter how hot, beautiful, and sunny the day, guests promptly remove themselves from the beach and other Cape May pursuits to a rocker, porch swing, or wicker chair on our shady wraparound veranda to await the arrival of our antique teacart. The cart is filled with homemade sweets and savories and our famous tea made with fresh mints (ten varieties of mint from our herb garden). When the weather is cool, tea is more formal with china, silver service, and crystal, all elegantly presented fireside."

A popular inn for taking tea in the Northeast is The Gingerbread House in West Harwich, Massachusetts. Innkeepers Jenny and Ken Hodkinson are transplanted Britishers who wanted to give Americans their tea experiences. Finger sandwiches and London-style scones are baked daily and served with authentic, clotted Devon cream imported from England. (Gourmet shops and some supermarket chains carry clotted cream.) The scones are served with tea and strawberry preserves between one and five o'clock. The Hodkinsons' secret to good tea is to bring water to a boil, warm the teapot, and always, "take the teapot to the kettle." Even on a warm day, The Gingerbread House dining room and Victorian gazebo are filled with "tea-totalers." Jenny says it's better to have a warm drink on a hot day. A cold one, she adds, may shock your system and can be unsettling. Her bottom-line lesson about tea is a soothing one; Jenny says, "Drinking a cup of tea puts everything right."

And when Mary Nichols at the Hannah Marie Country Inn in Spencer, Iowa, talks about tea, she likes to recall the words of Henry James: "There are few hours in life more agreeable than the hour dedicated to the ceremony known as afternoon tea." Mary offers her own reflection on the subject: "Tea-taking is refreshing and inspiring. Our worlds are so full and the tasks very demanding. But short, relaxing break-times are possible—and are a must."

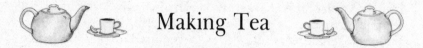

Making Tea

Fill your teakettle with cold water and bring it to a boil. Meanwhile, fill a thermal pot with hot tap water. When the water is just about to boil, pour out the tap water from your thermal pot and put in loose tea. (Don't use tea bags. The paper bags cut some of the characteristic edge from the tea by filtering out some of the tannin.)

Bring the warmed pot with the loose tea to the stove, and pour the boiling water over the leaves. Don't let the water boil long, for oxygen is lost from the water as it boils, and this affects the tea's flavor.

Cap the thermal pot and let it sit for five minutes. Meanwhile, heat your china teapot by filling it with hot tap water. (The best pot is called a Brown Betty, and the glaze looks like that on a bean pot. Iron is baked into the clay or the glaze, and this helps retain heat.) Pour the water out of the teapot, then strain the tea from the thermal pot, through a small mesh metal strainer, into the teapot.

> Daun Martin, Britt House, San Diego, California

Author's Tip: The general rule of measuring loose tea is to add one tablespoon per cup and one for the pot.

Aubrey Franklin, a nationally proclaimed tea ambassador, told us how to make the perfect cup:

The boiling and brewing are the important factors in the perfect cup. With so many world-famous blends available today, here is the correct tea drill:

1. Rinse the kettle of its contents and start with fresh, cold tap water.

2. The trick is to bring the water to its first rolling boil. Never overboil. Overboiling takes the oxygen out of the water, which in turn creates a flat beverage. Turn the heat down.

3. Take the teapot to the kettle, and rinse out the pot with the hot water from the kettle. Never take the kettle to the teapot, as you lose one degree of heat per second, and hot water for tea must be 212 degrees.

4. Use one tea bag or teaspoon of loose tea per cup. Leaves enter the warm pot, and the infusion starts as the leaves start to open up.

5. Pour hot water gently over the leaves. (Never bruise the leaves.)

6. Allow the tea to brew for a minimum of three to five minutes, according to the blend of tea and how you like your tea.

> Mary and Ray Nichols, Hannah
> Marie Country Inn, Spencer, Iowa

Place six regular tea bags in the filter basket of your coffee brewer, tags and all, and water for 12 cups in the water well. Start the automatic drip. This makes wonderful tea. We add two bags of orange-flavored tea on the side of the pot to give added flavor as the tea drips down.

> Debby and Hap Joy, The Decoy,
> Strasburg, Pennsylvania

Flavoring Tea

One way to flavor the tea is to put a drop or two of extract into it. However, this is not the tea purist's method of doing things. Personally, I feel there are so many good blends of flavored teas out there to enjoy that you can get flavor from the tea itself.

You can actually have a blend of tea made up to offer the best complement to your tap water. Send a sample of your water to Fortnum & Mason Ltd. in Piccadilly, England. They will put together a blend that goes with the makeup of your water. Your library will have information about the company and how to send the water sample.

> Patricia Morris, Marlborough Inn,
> Woods Hole, Massachusetts

Make certain that none of the herbs and flowers you plan to use in making tea have been sprayed with insecticides. Collect red clover blossoms. Wash them thoroughly and place them in a pot with water. Add ripped mint leaves (ripping allows release of mint flavor), and bring the water to a boil. Add other packaged tea blends (such as black teas) and let the tea steep for twenty minutes. Strain and serve. Add lemon or orange zest, cinnamon stick or cloves. This also makes an excellent iced tea.

> Maureen and John Magee, Rabbit
> Hill Inn, Lower Waterford,
> Vermont

Milk for Tea

Milk, not cream, is what is added to tea. Cream is too heavy, and many tea drinkers wouldn't put either one in their cup.

I did an experiment with a group of women at a church social gathering that suggests tea made by pouring the milk into the cup first, followed by the tea, tastes better. We blindfolded the ladies and asked them to taste the tea this way and also to taste the tea that had the milk added last. One hundred percent of them preferred the taste with the tea added to the milk!

> Patricia Morris, Marlborough Inn,
> Woods Hole, Massachusetts

Iced Tea

Once tea is refrigerated it usually becomes cloudy. Remove the haze by running it through the microwave until clear. Add ice.

> Edna Colwell, manager, Clayton
> Country Inn, Clayton, Oklahoma

In summer, we serve iced tea in our kitchen from an antique ceramic crock. They seem to go together in an old-fashioned way.

> Bev Davis and Rick Litchfield,
> Captain Lord Mansion,
> Kennebunkport, Maine

We make iced tea by the gallon, using loose tea covered with boiling water. Straining the tea leaves is quick and easy when you use a drip filter attachment and filter—the ones made for coffee makers.

Annie and Al Unrein, Glacier Bay
Country Inn, Gustavus, Alaska

To add delicious flavors to cold tea, add flavored gelatins to regular iced tea. Pour in slowly to taste.

Elaine Schnitzer, Summerport B&B,
Schroon Lake, New York

 ## Serving Tea

Hosting a tea is a very social occasion where you can introduce a number of guests in your home in a nonthreatening manner. Tea is a cultural way of having a cocktail party. People have something to do with their hands, sipping from teacups and munching on finger sandwiches and assorted sweets. A tea offers your guests an uplifting time due to the caffeine and sugar served.

At Britt House, we offer a strong English tea from 4:00 to 6:00 P.M. Bed-and-breakfast started in Great Britain, and tea was important to the people there. This is one of the reasons we decided to incorporate the tradition at the inn.

Our setup for tea includes a large, oak, mission-style table dressed with a lace cloth or a crisply ironed linen cloth, topped by a big bouquet of fresh flowers. To add interest to the table, we vary the size and shapes of the foods. For example, we might have a bundt cake with fluffy icing for texture, served on a pedestal for height. To vary the flavors, we serve something not so sweet, such as Irish soda bread and scones. There is usually a fresh pie mixed among all of this, and the sandwiches sometimes include cucumber and egg salad, plus eggplant dip for the health-conscious.

Carmel and Basil Luck, our English friends, taught us how to make the tea we use at Britt House. We use a strong Irish black tea (Ceylon and Golden Assam). The English drink their tea stronger than we do. So we modified the amounts they gave us, but our tea does have a "presence."

> Daun Martin, Britt House, San Diego, California

We use candlelight for our afternoon tea table.

> Maureen and John Magee, Rabbit Hill Inn, Lower Waterford, Vermont

Use only china teapots when serving tea. The thicker the pottery, the less heat you get in the cup.

> Jenny and Ken Hodkinson, Gingerbread House, West Harwich, Massachusetts

We have a teapot collection and enjoy serving tea in the pots with a tea cozy over them to keep them hot.

> Annie and Al Unrein, Glacier Bay Country Inn, Gustavus, Alaska

Author's Tip: Tea cozies can be appropriate, but be careful when making fresh tea that you don't leave the leaves in the pot too long with a cozy on top. The tea can become bitter.

An interesting assortment of teas fill a large basket on the dining room table. Our guests root through the basket in search of a tea they've never tried before.

> Bette and Ivan Nance, Annie Horan's, Grass Valley, California

We serve individual bouquets of herbs with our herb teas in the afternoon. The herb teas allow guests to experiment with flavors. We then send them home with small packages of herbs.

> Kate Kerivan, Bungay Jar, Easton, New Hampshire

Color is added to a plate of lemon slices at teatime by adding a few native blueberries in season.

> Harriette and David L. Lusty,
> Dockside Guest Quarters, York,
> Maine

Our tea is served informally in the main-floor parlor. It includes finger foods, shortbread confections, cookies, fork foods, cakes, pies, and tarts. The service is arranged on a teacart, using silver compotes for visual appeal. In summer, we serve iced tea. Lemon mint leaves from the garden are garnish.

> Mary Louise and Conley Weaver,
> Red Castle Inn, Nevada City,
> California

Charlie found an antique teacup in the foyer one day. It has created The Governor's Unsolved Teacup Mystery and is sometimes a conversation piece at 3:00 P.M. tea. Teatime here is a moment when guests can relax by the fire and enjoy each other. Muffins are a favorite accompaniment to our traditional beverage.

> Deedy and Charlie Marble,
> Governor's Inn, Ludlow, Vermont

During wintertime we serve tea in the common area. In addition to beverages, we provide foot warmers. They are antique, British porcelain warmers that are filled with hot water. We bring them out on a tray, and each guest takes one if they desire. They remove their shoes and place their feet on top of the warmer. It's an old tradition we enjoy rekindling here.

> Greg Brown and Bertie Koelewyn,
> Jefferson Inn, Jefferson, New
> Hampshire

Tea in the winter includes the provision of hot soup. The soup is heated in a cast-iron pot on top of a wood-burning stove and is served right from the pot. Bowls, spoons, and ladles are kept on a table. The hot soup is very popular with skiers who need something to hold them until dinner.

> Carriere-Zito Family, Mill Brook
> B&B, Brownsville, Vermont

For a pretty tea plate, dig up a violet from the yard and put it in a little crock on the plate with the tea treats. The plants survive nicely in the house for several days and can then be replanted in the garden.

Dorry Norris, Sage Cottage,
Trumansburg, New York

Teapots are in every guest room. Four o'clock tea is available, complete with a tea cozy. Delicate teacups are a must. They seem to make the tea tastier. A tea set in your guest room makes a friend or relative feel immediately welcome and warm.

Ujjala Schwartz, Ujjala's B&B, New
Paltz, New York

At four o'clock on the last Sunday of every month, we hold high tea, highlighted by chamber music.

Emily Hunter, Briar Rose, Boulder,
Colorado

Afternoon tea at The Gingerbread Mansion is served in one of the four parlors between 4:00 and 6:00 P.M. Items are attractively displayed on three glass-covered trays and placed on an elegantly carved sideboard. The trays protect the sideboard from hot beverages, any spilled cream, and/or sticky cake.

One tray holds the old-fashioned electric coffeepot and the pot of tea. Each sits on a wicker trivet. Included on a second tray is a small bowl for spoons that have been used.

Cups and saucers are all different, so guests may choose one that suits their whim.

Wendy Hatfield and Ken Torbert,
Gingerbread Mansion, Ferndale,
California

 # Theme Teas

Have a picnic tea. Hot water carries well in a thermos. Pack your china teacups, napkins, silverware, tea, sweets, and sandwiches. What a romantic way to spend a quiet afternoon.

For another special tea, bring out all your old family pictures and set them on the tea table. It sets the mood for relaxing and opens the way to the past for your tea guests.

Children can also enjoy a tea. Since they love to dress up, have them arrive in their parents' old clothes or provide them upon arrival with vintage hats, gloves, jewelry, and scarves.

A Mad Hatter Tea is fun for the young at heart of any age. We put out dolls from the story along with the book itself. Tea foods become quite special. Among our treats are whimsical butter shapes we make from molds such as one that represents the Cheshire Cat. We also make meringue mushrooms (see tea recipes). Remember to tell your guests to guard their thoughts when eating them, or they may grow larger or smaller. For this tea, you can also serve a cake cut into 1½-by-2½-inch pieces; pipe onto the top of each piece the words "Eat Me," as per the story.

Serve cherry or strawberry tarts. Add a few birthday candles and wish everyone an "unbirthday." Remind your guests that they have 364 unbirthdays.

When planning a Mad Hatter Tea, let your imagination run wild. Reread the wonderful story to get your own ideas.

Mary and Ray Nichols, Hannah
Marie Country Inn, Spencer, Iowa

Author's Tip: If you're looking for an interesting way to shower a bride, a tea is a perfect type of party, and a nice way to introduce a young bride to the tradition of taking tea.

Author's Tip: And why not a tea tasting, the same way people hold wine tastings? Ask each of your guests to bring two varieties of loose or bagged tea and a teapot. Serve tea in demitasse cups and spoons so that your guests taste only a small amount at one time. Provide each guest with paper and pen so they can make personal comments about each tea they taste. Later they will know which ones they want to go out and buy for their own supply. Be sure to have a large bowl on the table so that guests can pour any remaining tea from their cup as they go on to the next flavor. Also have each guest bring a tea tip such as this one: To rid your kettle of those ugly white deposits of calcium or lime, pour in about one-quarter cup of vinegar and one quart of water. Bring to a boil and allow to boil for ten minutes. Empty the pot. Wash and rinse thoroughly.

We have a tea for my daughter and her friends. We set a child-size table and chairs with a fine linen cloth. A cocoa set and teapots that have been in our family are placed on the table along with demitasse spoons. Sandwiches are served, but the children cut their own with a cookie cutter of their choice. They reach into an old tin for the one-inch-high tin cutters in many various shapes. Something sweet is also served. Sometimes they have tea, but most often, apple juice is poured out of the teakettle. Usually, they select something to read from a stack of old books, and they also choose which stuffed friends will take tea with them. Our nursery tea usually includes children four to ten years old.

> Sally and Ken McWilliams, Main
> Street B&B, Madison, Indiana

My favorite tea is served to a Brownie troop and their moms. This high tea would make an occasion full of fun as well as being a learning experience for any grouping of youngsters.

Containers of coffee as well as regular, decaffeinated, and flavored teas are placed where everyone can help themselves. As they are seated on the lawn under a cooling tree or around a warm fire in winter, several small sandwiches and sweets are served. (See recipes in this chapter.) The ingredients are named and described to all.

As seems appropriate, we tell them about the origins of the tea custom, events like the Boston Tea Party, and then discuss where other high teas are held today in their area. We then take a tour of Spring Bank. Each girl signs the guest book and takes home lavender soap as a souvenir from the inn.

> Beverly and Ray Compton, Spring
> Bank Inn, Fredericksburg,
> Maryland

Chocolate pastry teas were popular during the Victorian era. To encourage the theme here, look through chocolate cookbooks and chocolate magazines for recipes. Try to introduce the flavor of chocolate in recipes where your guests wouldn't ordinarily expect it. Try adding chocolate to butter, for example.

Early Wednesday evenings, we serve high tea, the supper tea of the northern countrysides of England and Scotland. This most substantial of the tea meals has food that is both satisfying and alluring: savory pasties (filled with beef, potatoes, carrots, and onions), Scotch eggs, cakes, and an apple-and-cheese flan (see tea recipes) that is a hallmark British dessert. This is not a dainty affair. It's a cheerful, noisy gathering of guests after a day's work.

Mary and Ray Nichols, Hannah
Marie Country Inn, Spencer, Iowa

Author's Tip: Some other ideas are:
Oriental tea with a variety of teas and *dim sum.*
Hold a poetry reading during a tea.
A garden tea is nice in warm weather.
Hold a mother-daughter tea with friends and neighbors.

Author's Tip: Sometimes, the theme is there without trying to create it. For exampkle, at Sweetwater Farm in Glen Mills, Pennsylvania, tea is appropriately served from the farmhouse kitchen. "We use all home-baked goods served on country ware," says innkeeper Linda Kaat. She is referring to the highly collectible, yellow ware and antique blue-and-white dishes native to the inn's area.

A nice idea for a shower gift, anniversary, birthday, or you name it, is a tea basket. Into a basket, tuck recipes for muffins or scones, a tin of tea biscuits, a few blends of tea, a tea strainer, perhaps a cup and saucer, and it's ready for a favorite friend. Actually, you can fill the basket with anything you wish, according to your budget.

Mary and Ray Nichols, Hannah
Marie Country Inn, Spencer, Iowa

 Beverages

ICED VICTORIAN TEA

1 cup water
2 tablespoons sugar
3 whole cloves

1   cinnamon stick
2   tea bags
2   cups apricot nectar
2   tablespoons frozen orange juice concentrate
    Club soda
    Light rum
    Orange-flavored liqueur, such as Grand
        Marnier
    Orange slices and ripe strawberries

Combine water, sugar, cloves, cinnamon, and tea bags in a sauce-pan. Simmer for 5 minutes, then allow to stand for 15 minutes. Strain into a glass container. Add apricot nectar and orange juice concentrate. Stir. Allow to cool and then refrigerate. When ready to serve, pour over ice in a brandy snifter and add club soda to each glass. Add 1 ounce of light rum and a splash of Grand Marnier to each. Garnish with a fresh orange slice and a plump, ripe strawberry, stem and all. Also wonderful without the rum and Grand Marnier. Yield: about 1 quart or 8 servings.

The Governor's Inn Cookbook, Ludlow, Vermont

GREEN ICED TEA

A handful of bee balm and sweet cicely steeped in 6 cups of boiling water for 8 minutes makes a beautiful green blend for iced tea. The taste is a combination of mint and licorice. A bee balm leaf in each glass with a violet or even a dandelion blossom make a drink fit for the fanciest spring tea. Yield: 6 servings.

Sage Cottage, Trumansburg, New York

ROSEMARY TEA

When winter comes, my favorite is rosemary tea. Since rosemary has to spend the winter indoors in our climate, I just pick a sprig or two and add about 2 cups boiling water, cover, steep for 5 minutes, and then sit back and enjoy the fragrance of a sunny summer's day. Yield: 2 cups.

Sage Cottage, Trumansburg, New York

CHURCHTOWN'S MINT TEA

About 5–6 shoots each of peppermint and spearmint, fresh from the garden, are placed in a tall metal pot (such as one for cooking spaghetti). Add boiling water to cover. Let steep for a couple of hours. Makes a delightful aroma throughout the house. Yield: 24 servings.

Churchtown Inn, Churchtown, Pennsylvania

SUN TEA

Fill a gallon jar with water. Add 8 regular-flavored tea bags and 2 of a flavored tea such as black currant. Let sit in the sun for 3–4 hours. The black currant gives the tea a great flavor. Yield: about 24 servings.

Little River Inn, Aldie, Virginia

FRESHLY SQUEEZED LEMONADE

This is a refreshing drink to serve during teatime on hot days.

    2   cups sugar
    1   cup water
        Rind of 1 lemon
        Pinch of salt
 8–10   lemons
    1   gallon water
        Lemon slices

On stove top mix sugar, 1 cup water, lemon rind, and salt. Heat to dissolve sugar. Do not boil. This is your syrup. Let it cool to room temperature.

Squeeze lemons to give you 2 cups of lemon juice. Mix your syrup, lemon juice, and 1 gallon of water. Chill and garnish with lemon slices. Yield: about 24 servings.

Little River Inn, Aldie, Virginia

CHOCOLATE LEMONADE

Use a 12-ounce can of lemonade concentrate. Mix with water according to directions, and add about ¼ cup of chocolate syrup or chocolate to taste. Our guests love this beverage. Yield: about ½ gallon.

Hannah Marie Country Inn,
Spencer, Iowa

VIENNESE MOCHA

Just in case a tea guest prefers coffee.

    ¼   cup half-and-half
    ¾   cup milk
    2   tablespoons sugar
    2   teaspoons Dutch-process cocoa
    ¾   cup freshly brewed strong coffee
    ¼   cup whipped cream
        Cinnamon

In small saucepan over medium heat, stir together half-and-half, milk, sugar, and cocoa until blended. Bring mixture to a boil, then add coffee. Pour mocha into mugs or cups and top with whipped cream and sprinkled cinnamon. Yield: 2 servings.

Grant Corner Inn Breakfast and
Brunch Cookbook, Santa Fe, New
Mexico

Scones, Tea Cakes, Breads, and Muffins

TEA SCONES

The word scone is actually from the Dutch *schoonbrot,* meaning beautiful bread.

2	cups sifted flour
2	tablespoons sugar
3	teaspoons baking powder
½	teaspoon salt
⅓	cup butter
1	egg, beaten
¾	cup milk (approximately)

Preheat oven to 425 degrees. Sift together flour, sugar, baking powder, and salt. Chop in the butter with a pastry blender until the flour-coated particles of butter are the size of coarse cornmeal. Add the egg and most of the milk, reserving some milk. Stir quickly and lightly, only until no flour shows. Add more milk if needed to make a soft dough.

Turn the dough out on a floured surface and knead gently, about 15 times. Cut the dough in half. Shape each half into a ball, press each half down into a round about ½-inch thick, and cut it into 8 wedges like a pie. Place the wedges on a greased cookie sheet, without allowing the sides to touch. Glaze, if desired, with lightly beaten egg. Bake until deep-golden brown, about 12 minutes. (Uncooked scones may be frozen on the cookie sheet and dropped in a plastic bag for baking later.) Serve hot with whipped cream or butter, marmalade, and a good blend of tea. Yield: 8 servings.

Mayhurst B&B, Orange, Virginia

PINEAPPLE SPICE SCONES

This scone recipe is used for teatime for Brownie troops at Spring Bank Inn. It is a particularly appealing scone for all ages, but the addition of the pineapple makes it most appropriate for introducing young people to the traditional teatime treat.

3	cups flour
⅓	cup sugar
2½	teaspoons baking powder
½	teaspoon salt
¾	cup margarine or butter
1	8–ounce can crushed pineapple (juice pack)
	Light cream or milk
3	tablespoons chopped macadamia nuts or almonds
1	tablespoon sugar
½	teaspoon cinnamon

Preheat oven to 425 degrees. In a mixing bowl, stir together flour, sugar, baking powder, and salt. Cut in margarine until mixture resembles coarse crumbs. Make a well in center. Stir in undrained pineapple until dry ingredients are just moistened (dough will be sticky). On lightly floured surface, knead gently 10 to 12 times; roll dough to ¼-inch thickness. Cut with floured 2½-inch biscuit cutter. Place dough circles on ungreased baking sheet. Brush tops with cream or milk. For topping, combine nuts, 1 tablespoon sugar, and cinnamon. Sprinkle about 1 teaspoon of mixture over the top of each scone. Bake about 15 minutes. Serve warm. Yield: 21.

Spring Bank Inn, Fredericksburg, Maryland

CLOTTED CREAM

Add 1½ tablespoons of buttermilk to 1 cup of heavy cream. Let it sit out, covered, for 12 hours. Then store in the refrigerator.

The Decoy, Strasburg, Pennsylvania

Clotted cream is traditionally served with scones in England, and at our inn, we also serve the real thing. Our guests always want to know what clotted cream is. The cream we use is imported. It is produced by the Jersey cow, which, in England, eats lush green grass. When the cow produces its milk, cream rises and clots at the top. Unlike whipped cream, clotted cream is slightly sour rather than sugary.

> Jenny and Ken Hodkinson,
> Gingerbread House, West Harwich,
> Massachusetts

FRENCH TEA CAKES

2   eggs
1   cup sugar
1   cup sifted cake flour
¾   cup melted and cooled butter
1   tablespoon rum
1   teaspoon vanilla
1   teaspoon lemon rind

Preheat oven to 450 degrees. Heat the eggs and sugar in a double boiler until lukewarm, stirring constantly. Remove from heat and beat until thick but light and creamy. When cool, gradually add the flour. Add the melted and cooled butter, rum, vanilla, and lemon rind. Pour into greased madeleine pans or small muffin tins. Bake for 15 minutes. Yield: 16 cakes.

> *The Summer Cottage Inn Cookbook,*
> Cape May, New Jersey

STRAWBERRY TEA CAKES

1¾   cups flour
1   teaspoon baking soda
¼   teaspoon salt
1   cup sugar
½   cup unsweetened, flaked or shredded
      coconut
2   eggs

½   cup oil
1½   cups strawberries, hulled and halved
           lengthwise

Preheat oven to 350 degrees. Stir together flour, soda, salt, and sugar. Stir in coconut. In separate bowl, combine eggs and oil. Add berries and stir gently. Gently add flour mixture to berry mixture and stir to blend. Pour into greased muffin cups, filling each cup half full. Bake for 20–30 minutes. You may top with whipped cream. Yield: 18 cakes.

Britt House Cookbook, San Diego,
California

COCONUT TEA CAKES

3½   cups flour
2   cups sugar
1½   tablespoons baking powder
3   cups sweetened flaked or shredded coconut
3   sticks butter, melted
2   cups milk, room temperature
2   tablespoons cream of coconut
5   eggs, room temperature
1   cup egg whites (about 5)

Preheat oven to 375 degrees. Into medium bowl, sift flour, sugar, and baking powder. Mix in coconut and set aside. In another bowl, whisk together butter, milk, cream of coconut, and whole eggs. Set aside. In a small bowl, beat egg whites until stiff but not dry. Pour butter mixture into flour mixture. Stir well to blend. Fold in beaten egg whites. Fill paper-lined muffin cups two-thirds full. Bake for 15–20 minutes, or until golden brown. Yield: 24 muffins.

*Grant Corner Inn Breakfast and
Brunch Cookbook*, Santa Fe, New
Mexico

LEMON CASHEW BREAD

1½ cups flour
¾ cup sugar
2 tablespoons grated lemon rind
1 teaspoon baking powder
½ teaspoon salt
½ cup unsalted cashews, toasted and chopped
¼ cup milk
¼ cup fresh lemon juice
6 tablespoons vegetable oil
2 eggs

GLAZE:
½ cup sugar
2 tablespoons lemon juice

Preheat oven to 350 degrees. Grease an 8½-by-4-inch loaf pan. In medium-size mixing bowl, combine ingredients in order given (except glaze ingredients). Pour into prepared pan and bake for 1 hour. Cool 15 minutes. Remove from pan. Poke holes in top of loaf with a toothpick. Mix sugar and lemon juice. Brush over top and sides of loaf, with special attention to the top. Let stand until glaze hardens before slicing. Yield: 1 loaf.

Grant Corner Inn Breakfast and Brunch Cookbook, Santa Fe, New Mexico

TROPICAL TEA BREAD

⅔ cup butter
1⅓ cups honey
4 eggs
4 tablespoons milk
1 teaspoon vanilla
2 tablespoons vegetable oil
4 cups sifted flour
1 teaspoon salt

1¾   teaspoons baking powder
1   teaspoon baking soda
2   cups toasted coconut
2¼   cups mashed bananas
4   teaspoons grated lemon rind
2   teaspoons fresh lemon juice

Preheat oven to 350 degrees. Grease and flour two 9-by-5-inch loaf pans. Cream butter until fluffy; add honey in thin stream. Beat in eggs; stir in milk, vanilla, and oil. Sift dry ingredients into a medium-size bowl. Stir in toasted coconut and set aside. In small bowl, blend bananas, lemon rind, and lemon juice. Add dry ingredients to creamed mixture alternately with banana mixture, blending only until moistened. Spoon into pans. Bake for 55 minutes. Cool in pans 5 minutes. Remove and cool thoroughly before slicing. Yield: 2 loaves.

Grant Corner Inn Breakfast and Brunch Cookbook, Santa Fe, New Mexico

PUMPKIN-RAISIN BUNDT BREAD

3   eggs
1½   cups sugar
1½   cups pumpkin puree
1   cup plus 2 tablespoons vegetable oil
2   teaspoons vanilla
2¼   cups flour
1½   teaspoons baking soda
1½   teaspoons baking powder
1½   teaspoons salt
2   teaspoons pumpkin pie spice
½   cup coarsely chopped pecans
1   cup raisins

Preheat oven to 350 degrees. In medium-size mixing bowl, beat eggs and sugar until well blended. Add pumpkin, oil, and vanilla, mixing well. Set aside. Sift flour, soda, baking powder, salt, and pie spice. Add to pumpkin mixture and beat. Add pecans and raisins, stirring to blend. Pour into nonstick bundt pan. Bake for 1 hour, until a toothpick inserted at center comes out clean. Yield: 12 servings.

Grant Corner Inn Breakfast and Brunch Cookbook, Santa Fe, New Mexico

LEMON YOGURT BREAD

3	cups flour
1	teaspoon salt
1	teaspoon baking soda
½	teaspoon baking powder
1	cup sesame or poppy seeds
3	eggs
1	cup oil
1	cup sugar
2	cups lemon yogurt
2	tablespoons fresh-squeezed lemon juice

Preheat oven to 325 degrees. Sift together flour, salt, baking soda, and baking powder. Stir in seeds. In a large bowl, beat eggs. Add oil and sugar. Cream well. Mix in yogurt and lemon juice until combined. Spoon into 2 greased loaf pans or 1 large bundt pan. Bake for 1 hour.

Wedgwood Inn, New Hope, Pennsylvania

WHOLE WHEAT WILD MAINE BLUEBERRY BREAD

¾	cup butter
1½	cups sugar
3	eggs
1½	teaspoons vanilla
2	cups unbleached white flour
1	cup whole wheat flour
1½	teaspoons baking soda
1½	teaspoons baking powder
¼	teaspoon salt

1½   cups sour cream
1   15–ounce can wild Maine blueberries,
     drained

Preheat oven to 350 degrees. Grease two 8½-by-4½-by-2¾-inch pans. Combine butter, sugar, eggs, and vanilla. Beat at medium speed for 2 minutes. Combine the flours, baking soda, baking powder, and salt. Add the flour mixture to the butter and sugar mixture, alternately with the sour cream. Stir in the blueberries. Bake 55–60 minutes or until tester comes out clean. Cool before taking out of the pan. Yield: 2 loaves.

Silver Maple Lodge, Fairlee,
Vermont

STRAWBERRY BREAD

3   cups flour
2   cups sugar
1   teaspoon baking soda
1   teaspoon salt
1   teaspoon cinnamon
4   eggs, beaten
1¼   cups vegetable oil
2   10–ounce packages frozen strawberries,
     thawed and chopped

Preheat oven to 350 degrees. In a large mixing bowl, combine. flour, sugar, baking soda, salt, and cinnamon. Make a well in the center of the mixture. Combine remaining ingredients and add to dry ingredients, stirring until well mixed. Spoon mixture into 2 greased and floured 9-by-5-by-3-inch loaf pans. Bake for 1 hour. Cool 10 minutes and then remove from pan.

Brass Bed, Cape May, New Jersey

RAISIN HARVEST COFFEE CAKE

1½   cups sifted flour
3¾   teaspoons baking powder

¼   teaspoon salt
¾   cup sugar
¾   cup butter
2   cups peeled and finely chopped cooking
        apples
1½ cups dark seedless raisins
2   large eggs, well-beaten
1   tablespoon milk
    Sugar for topping

Preheat oven to 350 degrees. Into a large bowl, resift flour with baking powder, salt, and sugar. Add butter and mix until mixture resembles fine bread crumbs. Stir in apples, raisins, eggs, and milk. Batter will be stiff. Spread in well-greased 9-inch square pan and sprinkle generously with sugar. Bake for 55–60 minutes. Allow to cool slightly before cutting. Serve warm. This may be made ahead and frozen. Yield: 4–6 servings.

Red Willow Farm, Kennett Square, Pennsylvania

GINGER MUFFINS

¾   cup butter
½   cup sugar
2   eggs
⅛   teaspoon cinnamon
1   teaspoon ginger
½   teaspoon allspice
½   cup buttermilk
1   teaspoon baking soda
½   cup dark molasses
½   cup chopped nuts
½   cup raisins
2   cups flour

Preheat oven to 400 degrees. Mix ingredients in order given. Grease 12 to 16 muffin cups or use cupcake liners. Fill each cup ¾ full. Bake for 10 minutes. Yield: 12–16 muffins.

Butternut Inn, Chaffee, New York

CRANBURY CORNER MUFFINS

2   cups flour
2   teaspoons baking powder
½   tablespoon salt
½   cup butter
1   cup sugar
2   large eggs
1   teaspoon vanilla extract
1   teaspoon butter-vanilla extract
2   large tablespoons sour cream (or 3 large
       tablespoons cream cheese)
3   ounces canned whole cranberries
½   cup milk
½   cup walnuts, chopped (optional)

TOPPING:
1   tablespoon sugar
¼   teaspoon nutmeg
¼   teaspoon cinnamon

Preheat oven to 375 degrees. Grease 12 to 16 muffin cups and the areas between the cups. Sift together flour, baking powder, and salt. In a mixing bowl, cream butter and sugar until fluffy. Beat in eggs, vanillas, and sour cream. Stir butter and sugar mixture into flour mixture. Fold in cranberries. Add walnuts. Spoon batter into muffin cups, filling to the top.

Mix together topping ingredients. Sprinkle a little topping over each muffin. Bake 25 minutes until golden. Cool 10–15 minutes before removing. Yield: 12–16 moist cakelike muffins.

Audrie's Cranbury Corner, Rapid
City, South Dakota

THE ORANGE MUFFINS

1   whole orange
⅓   cup orange juice
¾   stick butter
1   egg
½   cup raisins

1½   cups sifted flour
¾   cup sugar
1   teaspoon baking powder
1   teaspoon baking soda
1   teaspoon salt

Preheat oven to 400 degrees. Grate the rind from the orange. Discard the pith. Quarter and seed the orange. In a blender, mix the rind, quarters, orange juice, butter, and egg. Add raisins. Blend for 5 seconds. Transfer to a large bowl. Sift the flour, sugar, baking powder, baking soda, and salt. Stir flour mixture into orange mixture until combined. Divide batter into 16 buttered and floured muffin cups or 8 large ones. Bake for 15–20 minutes. Yield: 8–16 muffins.

Maidstone Arms, East Hampton,
New York

DUTCH APPLE MUFFINS

1   egg
¾   cup milk
½   cup vegetable oil
1   medium apple, peeled and chopped
2   cups flour
⅓   cup firmly packed brown sugar
3   teaspoons baking powder
1   teaspoon salt
½   teaspoon cinnamon

TOPPING:
¼   cup packed brown sugar
¼   cup chopped nuts
½   teaspoon cinnamon

Preheat oven to 400 degrees. Grease 8 large muffin cups. Beat egg in medium bowl; stir in milk, oil, and apple. Stir in remaining muffin ingredients all at once, stirring just until moistened. Fill muffin cups and sprinkle with the topping. Bake about 25 minutes. Yield: 8 large muffins.

Main Street B&B, Madison, Indiana

PEACH COBBLER MUFFINS

1   egg
½   cup sour cream
½   cup milk
1   teaspoon vanilla
4   tablespoons vegetable oil
3   large peaches, peeled and diced
2   cups flour
½   cup sugar
1   tablespoon baking powder
¼   teaspoon baking soda
¼   teaspoon salt

TOPPING:
¼   cup flour
¼   cup sugar
¼   teaspoon ground cinnamon
2   tablespoons butter

Preheat oven to 400 degrees. Grease 8 large muffin cups. In a medium-size bowl, combine egg, sour cream, milk, vanilla, and oil. Stir in the peaches. In a large bowl, combine flour, sugar, baking powder, baking soda, and salt. Pour in the peach mixture and stir until just moistened. Fill muffin cups. Prepare topping, using a pastry blender. Sprinkle the batter with topping. Bake 30–35 minutes. Yield: 8 large muffins.

Main Street B&B, Madison, Indiana

The trick to making most muffins is in the wrist. Once the wet ingredients hit the dry ingredients, you have only a few minutes to get those muffins into the oven to ensure they will rise high. If you spend too much time, the gases will be released, and you'll have only little mounds instead of nice and hearty, eye-opening breads.

Susan Knowles Chetwynd,
Chetwynd House, Kennebunkport,
Maine

Be careful when blending muffin batter. You don't want it to be smooth. Leaving lumps yields a high-rising, light muffin.

Beverly and Ray Compton, Spring
Bank Inn, Frederick, Maryland

Sprinkling some cinnamon sugar on top of muffins will not only add flavor, but also will make them crispier on top.

Sallie and Welling Clark, Holden
House 1902, Colorado Springs,
Colorado

The seasons can help you decide what type of bread to bake for your guests. Whatever fruit is in season can be baked into a bread when it is plentiful, at its best, and least expensive.

Roberta Pieczenik, Captain Dexter
House, Vineyard Haven,
Massachusetts

Spray muffin tins with vegetable-oil spray to eliminate the need for those messy paper muffin cups.

Carol and Jim Beazley, Beazley
House, Napa, California

Use a quality ice-cream scoop (one with a good spring) to put muffin batter into pans. It makes filling the pan quick and easy, and the muffins cook uniformly. Our scoop is one quarter of a cup, but you should adjust according to your pans.

Diane and Al Johnson, Nauset
House, East Orleans, Massachusetts

To soften hard raisins, put them into a plastic bag and then place bag in warm water.

Shirley and Stephen Ramsey,
Mayhurst B&B, Orange, Virginia

To measure honey, molasses, or corn syrup, grease a liquid measuring cup before adding the syrup. All of the liquid will come out of the cup.

Daun Martin, Britt House, San
Diego, California

Rinse a pan with cold water before scalding milk to prevent sticking.

Ruthmary Jordan, Pride House,
Jefferson, Texas

 Pies, Cakes, and Sweets

SOUR CREAM (OR YOGURT) RAISIN PIE

	Pastry dough for a 9-inch pie
2	eggs
1	cup sugar
1	cup sour cream plus 1 tablespoon lemon juice (or 1 cup lemon yogurt)
1	cup raisins
	Pinch salt
¼	teaspoon nutmeg

Beat eggs. Add sugar and beat until light. Fold sour cream and lemon (or yogurt) into the egg mixture. Add the raisins, salt, and nutmeg, and mix thoroughly. Line a pie pan with pastry dough and pour in mixture. Cover with a top crust and bake in moderate 350-degree oven for 30 minutes. Yield: 8–10 servings.

Britt House Cookbook, San Diego,
California

BRITT HOUSE FAVORITE TRIFLE

A trifle is really the British way of using bits and pieces of desserts and ending up with a most impressive teatime delicacy.

Leftover cake (orange, banana, white
pound, walnut, yellow, but not
chocolate)
Custard
Raspberry jam
Bananas, strawberries, pears, and/or
peaches

Sherry or orange-flavored liqueur such as
Grand Marnier
Mint leaves

Cut cake into slabs 1-inch thick. Place in loaf pan. Top with a layer of custard, a layer of jam, a layer of fruit, a layer of whipped cream, and a drizzle of liqueur. Then start the process over until the pan is full, ending with whipped cream. Chill thoroughly. Garnish with fruit and mint leaves. Yield: about 8 servings.

Britt House Cookbook, San Diego, California

SQUIRE TARBOX INN POUND CAKE

1	cup (½ pound) soft, lactic-acid cheese (goat or cream cheese)
1½	cups (3 sticks) softened butter
2	cups sugar
⅛	teaspoon salt
1½	teaspoons lemon or vanilla extract
6	eggs, room temperature
3	cups unsifted flour

Preheat oven to 325 degrees. Blend cheese and butter in an electric mixer. With the speed on high, beat in the sugar, salt, and extract until light. Add eggs one at a time and beat until the batter is very light and fluffy. With the mixer on low speed, add flour and blend only until mixed. Turn into a buttered and floured 10-inch tube pan and bake 1 hour and 15 minutes. Cool for 5 minutes. Invert on a rack to cool thoroughly. Yield: 16 servings.

Squire Tarbox Inn, Wiscasset, Maine

ANISE CAKES

2	tablespoons brown sugar
¾	cup flour
¼	teaspoon baking powder

¼   cup margarine
1   large egg
½   teaspoon crushed anise seeds
1   cup rolled oats

Preheat oven to 375 degrees. Combine sugar, flour, baking powder, and margarine in a bowl. Mix together until well combined and light. Add the egg and anise seeds and beat lightly. Stir in oats. Drop by tiny spoonfuls onto a lightly greased cookie sheet. Bake 8 minutes or until lightly browned. Yield: 3 dozen.

Sage Cottage, Trumansburg,
New York

CRANBERRY CHEESECAKE BARS

This is a family recipe that we serve at teatime. It is especially festive during the Christmas season.

CRUST:
2½   cups flour
1   cup butter, softened
⅔   cup sugar
2   eggs, beaten
½   cup chopped pecans

Preheat oven to 350 degrees. In a large bowl, combine all ingredients except nuts. Mix at low speed until crumbly. Add pecans. Press into a 9-by-13-inch pan. Bake for 8–10 minutes.

TOPPING:
8   ounces cream cheese, softened
¼   cup powdered sugar
1   teaspoon vanilla
1   egg
1   16–ounce can whole-berry cranberry sauce
¼   teaspoon nutmeg

Combine cheese, powdered sugar, vanilla, and egg. Beat until smooth. Pour cream cheese mixture over baked crust. Add nutmeg to cranberry sauce. Blend well. Spoon cranberry sauce in 3 lengthwise rows over the cream cheese mixture. Pull a knife through the mixture to swirl. Bake in the 350-degree oven for 30–40 minutes or until set. Cool completely. Cut into bars. Yield: about 24 servings.

Summer Cottage Inn, Cape May,
New Jersey

SPICED JAM BARS

½   cup sugar
½   cup margarine, softened
1   teaspoon vanilla
1   egg
1   cup flour
½   cup chopped walnuts
½   cup quick-cooking oats
½   teaspoon baking powder
½   teaspoon cinnamon
¼   teaspoon salt
¼   teaspoon ground cloves
½   cup strawberry jam

Preheat oven to 350 degrees. Cream sugar, margarine, vanilla, and egg. Stir in remaining ingredients except jam until well mixed. Spread half the mixture into a greased 8-inch-square baking pan. Spread jam evenly over the top of the dough, then drop teaspoonfuls of remaining dough over the jam. Bake for 25–30 minutes, until lightly browned. Cool. Cut into bars. Yield: 2 dozen.

The Summer Cottage Inn Cookbook,
Cape May, New Jersey

WALNUT PIE

3   well-beaten eggs
1   cup sugar

1   cup crushed graham crackers
½   cup chopped walnuts

Preheat oven to 350 degrees. Add dry ingredients to eggs and turn into a well-greased 8-inch or 9-inch glass pie plate. Bake for 20–25 minutes. Serve at room temperature or cold, with or without whipped cream or ice cream. Yield: 8 servings.

Red Castle Inn, Nevada City,
California

BLACKBERRY COBBLER

PASTRY:
2   cups sifted, unbleached flour
¼   teaspoon salt
½   teaspoon baking soda
2   teaspoons baking powder
6   tablespoons butter
½   cup sugar
⅔   cup sour milk or buttermilk
    Cream

FILLING:
5   cups blackberries
¾   cup sugar
2   teaspoons cornstarch
4   tablespoons butter, in small pieces

NUTMEG SAUCE:
⅔   cup sugar
¼   teaspoon grated nutmeg
2   teaspoons cornstarch
    Pinch of salt
1   cup boiling water
3   tablespoons orange juice or peach brandy

Make the pastry. Sift the flour, salt, soda, and baking powder into a mixing bowl. Cut butter into the flour mixture with two knives or pastry blender. Add sugar. Blend mixture until it is coarse. Sprinkle in the milk, and mix with a spatula or wooden spoon. Shape dough into a ball, and place it on a lightly floured surface. Knead for a minute or two, giving quick punches into the dough. Cut ball in half. Roll out one half to ½-to¼-inch thickness and lay it in an 8-by-8-by-2-inch baking pan. Cover with wax paper and let it cool in the refrigerator. Refrigerate the other half of dough, too.

When ready to make cobbler, remove dough from the refrigerator. Preheat oven to 450 degrees. Make filling: Sprinkle a small amount of the sugar over the pastry. Fill it with berries. Sprinkle remaining sugar, the cornstarch, and butter over the berries. Roll out second half of dough and place on top of berries. Make steam holes in top. Brush top with the cream and sprinkle a little sugar on top. Place the pan in the preheated oven. Once you shut the oven door, turn temperature to 425 degrees and bake 45 minutes. Remove from oven and let cool on rack a bit before serving. Serve with thick and creamy nutmeg sauce.

To make sauce: Place sugar, nutmeg, cornstarch, and salt in a one-quart saucepan. Stir well. Pour in the boiling water, stirring as you pour. Set over medium heat to boil gently for 10 minutes. Set aside until ready to serve. Reheat without boiling, and add orange juice or brandy. Yield: about 8–10 servings.

> Sleepy Hollow Farm, Gordonsville, Virginia

CHEESY APPLE FLAN

CRUST:

10	ounces finely chopped walnuts
2	sticks unsalted butter, softened
⅓	cup sugar
3	cups all-purpose flour
1	egg, beaten
1	teaspoon almond extract

Grease a 9-inch springform tart pan. Mix together all the ingredients until well-blended. Press into the tart pan. Chill 30 minutes in the refrigerator before adding the filling.

FILLING:
3	teaspoons white sugar
3	teaspoons brown sugar
1	egg
¼	cup flour
¼	cup whipping cream
2	tablespoons rum
¾	cup shredded Swiss cheese
4	medium-tart apples, peeled and sliced
¾	teaspoon cinnamon
⅓	cup brown sugar

Preheat oven to 400 degrees. Beat the 6 teaspoons of sugars and egg until thick. Add flour and mix. Add whipping cream and rum. Stir until mixed. Pour mixture into unbaked nut crust. Sprinkle the shredded Swiss cheese evenly over the egg-sugar mixture. Place the apple slices in a circular pattern on top of the Swiss cheese. With a flat hand, press the apple slices gently down into the cheese and egg mixture. Sprinkle the cinnamon and ⅓ cup brown sugar on top. Bake for 40 minutes. Yield: about 8 servings.

Hannah Marie Country Inn,
Spencer, Iowa

ALMOND SNOWBALLS

We like to serve these cookies during the Christmas season.

1	cup butter
1	cup powdered sugar, plus more for rolling cookies
1	tablespoon vanilla
1	tablespoon amaretto liqueur
2	cups all-purpose flour
1	cup finely chopped almonds (best done in food processor to coarse-powder consistency)

Cream together butter and 1 cup sugar. Add vanilla and liqueur. Beat until well blended. Gradually add flour, then almonds. Chill dough for 1 hour.

Preheat oven to 325 degrees. Break off pieces of dough with a melon-ball maker and place on a cookie sheet. Bake for 13–15 minutes. While still hot, roll in powdered sugar. (These cookies do not freeze well but will last several weeks in an airtight container.) Yield: about 3–4 dozen cookies.

Alexander's Inn, Cape May, New Jersey

ENGLISH LEMON CURD

Use this as a filling for small pastry-tart shells for teatime or as a spread for muffins and sweet breads.

4 eggs, beaten
2½ tablespoons lemon rind
8 tablespoons lemon juice
1 cup sugar
1 cup butter or margarine
⅛ teaspoon salt

Combine all ingredients in top of double boiler. Cook over boiling water until thickened, about 20 minutes. Place in clean jars. Seal and store in refrigerator. Yield: 1½ pints.

Balcony Downs, Glasgow, Virginia

CAPPUCCINO CHEESECAKE

CHOCOLATE CRUST:
1 cup flour
1 tablespoon sugar
3 tablespoons cocoa
1 egg yolk
3 tablespoons ice water
¾ stick unsalted butter, chilled and cut into 6 pieces

Preheat oven to 400 degrees. Put all ingredients in work bowl of food processor. Process until the mass forms a ball of dough. Line a flan pan (removable ring) with the dough. Bake for 10 minutes. Set aside.

FILLING:

8	ounces cream cheese, softened
1	teaspoon cinnamon
1	cup sugar
3	eggs
¼	cup sour cream
½	cup extra-strong espresso

Blend all the ingredients in food processor. Pour into crust. Bake in the 400-degree oven for 30–40 minutes. Yield: 8–10 servings.

Bramble Inn, Brewster,
Massachusetts

 Sandwiches and Other Nonsweets

CUCUMBER SANDWICHES

Hothouse cucumbers, while more expensive, have fewer seeds and thus are more desirable.

	Crustless bread, thinly sliced and cut into 3-inch squares
	Cream cheese
1	cucumber, peeled and thinly sliced into rounds

Cut bread ⅛-inch thick, if possible. Spread with cream cheese. Top with a thin slice of cucumber.

Britt House, San Diego, California

SQUIRE TARBOX NUT LOAF

6	tablespoons butter
3	cups chopped celery

3 cups chopped onions
1 cup cooked rice
1 cup ground almonds
2 cups chopped walnuts
2 cups toasted cashews
¼ cup rolled oats
½ cup sesame seeds
¼ cup sunflower seeds
2 pounds soft goat cheese (or cottage cheese)
2 teaspoons salt
2 teaspoons pepper
1 teaspoon blended herbs (basil, oregano)
6 beaten eggs

Preheat oven to 400 degrees. Melt butter in a large skillet and sauté celery and onions until tender. Combine them in a large bowl with the rice, almonds, walnuts, cashews, rolled oats, sesame seeds, sunflower seeds, soft cheese, salt, pepper, and herbs. Blend in the beaten eggs and pour the batter into three 9-by-5-by-3-inch butter loaf pans. Bake for 1 hour or until quite dark on top. Serve warm. Yield: 3 loaves.

> Squire Tarbox Inn, Wiscasset,
> Maine

SPRING BISCUIT TREATS

1 cup flour
3 tablespoons margarine
1½ teaspoons baking powder
¼ teaspoon grated lemon peel or 1 tablespoon
  minced lemon balm
3 ounces skim milk
 Violets
1 egg white, broken up with a fork

Preheat oven to 425 degrees. Combine flour, margarine, baking powder, and lemon peel or lemon balm in a small bowl. Cut margarine into flour with a pastry cutter or two knives until the shortening is the size of peas. Stir milk in lightly. Turn out onto lightly floured board or pastry cloth and pat gently into a 3-inch square. Fold in half and repeat twice more (for a light, flakier biscuit). Cut with small flower-shaped cutters. Place biscuits close together on baking sheet. Dip violet blossoms in egg white and place one on each biscuit. Bake for 10–12 minutes. Yield: 12 biscuits.

Sage Cottage, Trumansburg, New York

SPRING BANK SANDWICH

Brownie troops over for high tea sample this tasty and protein-rich sandwich: Mix together equal amounts of peanut butter, milk powder, orange marmalade, wheat germ, and raisins. Spread on toast quarters.

Spring Bank Inn, Fredericksburg, Maryland

HANNAH MARIE'S DEVILS ON HORSEBACK

What a curious name! Our supper tea (high tea) guests love them.

¼   cup raisins soaked overnight in 1 teaspoon
        dark rum and water just to cover
¼   cup cream cheese
16   large prunes
1   cup dry red wine
8   bacon slices

Preheat oven to 375 degrees. Drain raisins and discard rum and water. Puree raisins and cream cheese in a small blender or mix with a fork, mashing the raisins. Simmer the prunes in wine about 10 minutes. Cool. Fill the prunes with the raisin and cream cheese mixture (½ to 1 teaspoonful, depending on the size of the prunes). Don't overstuff, as cream cheese mixture will run out the sides. Wrap half of a slice of bacon around each stuffed prune and secure with a toothpick. Stand on one of the open ends in a baking pan with sides. Bake until the bacon is brown and crisp, about 12 minutes. Drain on paper towels. Serve warm. Yield: 16 "little devils."

Hannah Marie Country Inn,
Spencer, Iowa

BEEF PASTIES

Our pasties take many forms and are served during high tea. Use your favorite pie-pastry recipe for the crust. Cut circles of the pastry to the size you'd like your pasties to be. We cut ours in 6-inch circles, the size for fruit pies.

2	pounds beef round steak
2	tablespoons oil
1	large onion, chopped
1	cup carrots, peeled and thinly sliced
2	cups peeled, cooked, and diced potatoes (½-inch squares)
3	cups beef broth
½	teaspoon salt
½	teaspoon pepper
2	tablespoons cornstarch
⅔	cup red wine

Trim the fat from the steak and cut the meat into ½-inch pieces. Brown meat in oil in a large skillet. Remove meat and set aside. Add the onion, carrots, and potatoes to the pan, and cook until onions are limp. Add the meat broth, salt, and pepper. Bring to a boil, cover, and simmer for 1 hour until the meat is tender. Add the cornstarch mixed with the wine.

Preheat oven to 400 degrees. Place equal amounts of filling on each pastry round. Using a dampened finger quickly smooth the edges of the pastry, folding half the pastry over the filling. Use a fork to seal the edges and crimp the pastry. Make holes in the pastry with the fork to release steam. Bake about 30 minutes, or until lightly browned. Yield: 24 or more servings.

Hannah Marie Country Inn,
Spencer, Iowa

MERINGUE MUSHROOMS

We serve these at our Mad Hatter Tea, as in the mushroom episode from *Alice in Wonderland*. We dress as King and Queen of Hearts and pass around the mushrooms, daring all to take a bite. They're easy to make and are a good way to use up your egg whites.

2	egg whites from large eggs
½	cup sugar
¼	teaspoon vanilla

Preheat oven to 200 degrees. Oil the surface of a cookie sheet or baking pan lightly with oil. Dust with flour.

Beat egg whites until stiff peaks are formed. Add ¼ cup sugar and vanilla. Continue beating until the egg whites are glossy. Using a spatula, fold the remaining ¼ cup sugar into the egg whites. Prepare a pastry bag, using a plain tip to form the mushrooms. Select the tip size according to how small or large you want to make the mushrooms. Pipe the meringue mixture onto prepared baking pan in the shape of a mushroom. Bake for 2 hours. When cool, put them on a doily-lined plate.

Hannah Marie Country Inn,
Spencer, Iowa

Cookie cutters make great designer shapes for sandwiches.

Nasturtium leaves make lovely tea sandwiches. Just add mayonnaise.

Maureen and John Magee, Rabbit
Hill Inn, Lower Waterford,
Vermont

Author's Tips: Make a checkerboard of sandwiches by using alternating squares of white and brown bread. Serve with a "game" in progress—top a few of the slices with halved cherry tomatoes as the checkers.

Trim the crust off breads for tea after filling the sandwich. It's easier that way.

Use only thin breads filled with thinly sliced or finely minced fillings.

Spread each sandwich with unsalted butter before filling. The butter acts as a protector, preventing the bread from soaking up moisture from the filling.

If filling with cucumber, use cucumber varieties that have fewer seeds. Peel and slice cucumbers. Place on a dish and lightly salt the slices. Place a weighted dish over the cucumbers and let sit for a while. This will help drain moisture from them.

To enhance your presentation, have three or four different types of sandwiches, but place each type on a different plate.

Have some of the sandwiches on each plate or platter facing upward so that the type of filling shows.

To keep sandwiches fresh, cover them with dried lettuce leaves and then a dampened cloth until you are ready to serve.

Hosting a Holiday, a Party, or a Theme Dinner

Festive Furbelows and Other Goodies for a Gala

Usually, most of us like to embrace the holidays with family and friends. But sometimes we are far from home. The innkeepers are aware of the traveler's need for the kind of welcoming atmosphere that eclipses the longing for home and family during the holidays. At some of the inns, everything done is targeted to the season—from breakfast to evening snacks and decorating.

Some inns, such as the Red Brook Inn in Old Mystic, Connecticut, bring guests to holidays past with their early American dinners. The innkeepers dress fashionably according to the era and serve meals reminiscent of the times.

We can imitate some of the inns' holiday celebrations by incorporating the innkeepers' festivities into our own family gatherings. This is bound to make the holidays a little different each year.

The innkeepers have also outlined some special events they have held at their inn. Let these ideas coax your own creativity. Consider that a theme will make planning your entire party or special dinner a lot easier. For example, have you ever become so confused by so many possible recipes that you do not know which dishes to make? A theme will narrow the choices and help you focus the meal plan.

Tips for All Holidays

If you're having overnight guests for the holidays, remember to decorate their sleeping rooms festively. Let your cheer spread throughout.

> Eva Mae and Frank Musgrave,
> Edge of Thyme, Candor, New York

I use felt as a colored liner under lace tablecloths. It's inexpensive and so interchangeable for holiday entertaining. I keep a selection of colors such as green for Saint Patrick's Day and pink for Valentine's.

> Robin Brooks, Robins Nest, San
> Andreas, California

Many of our holidays are highlighted by a Victorian tradition. We place small flags on toothpicks on our muffins and fill tall vases with assorted sizes of flags whenever flowers are in short supply. The Victorian period was a very patriotic time, and the American flag was used extensively in decorating. If your home is Victorian, this practice would be particularly appropriate.

> Mary Louise and Conley Weaver,
> Red Castle Inn, Nevada City,
> California

Author's Tip: Small grapevine wreaths make splendid napkin holders. Dress them according to the season. A simple bow tied through the wreath will do nicely.

Your usual decorator pillows can be changed easily to coincide with a holiday. Take two napkins (or fabric you've hemmed in the size of a napkin) and place one on either side of the pillow. Take coordinating ribbon and gather the extra fabric at each of the corners. You have a new pillow in an instant. We do this at least during the Christmas season with our checked dinner napkins. The effect is versatility and a decorator's look for your holiday preparations.

> Sally and Ken McWilliams, Main
> Street B&B, Madison, Indiana

Gift-Wrapping Ideas

If you're invited to dinner and intend to bring a bottle of wine for the host, make the bottle a more attractive gift by adding a few fresh or silk flowers. Tie the flowers to the bottle with a piece of decorative twine or a ribbon.

> Merrily and Max Comins, Kedron Valley Inn, South Woodstock, Vermont

The holidays are times when home-baked goods are often given as gifts. Should you run out of gift tins, an inexpensive way to achieve the same results is to cover a coffee can in pretty holiday wrapping.

> Joyce and Fred Evans, Triple T Ranch, Stanley, North Dakota

Author's Tip: Gifts for all holidays and birthdays can be wrapped with colorful fabric that can be reused by the recipient. Leftover wallpaper can also make a memorable gift wrap.

Wrap a single-man's gift in the paper of your choice. Add a bow and attach a small black book (date book) to the bow.

> Jeanne Marie Tomlinson, Glendale Farms, Ithaca, New York

 ## Valentine's Day

Cupid reigns among our sugar cookies that are tied in plastic wrap with a red ribbon and placed on each guest pillow.

It's also nice to bring the holiday to your guests at the breakfast table. Our place settings are accented with large, homemade heart cookies bathed in pink frosting and topped with the word "Love" in white frosting.

> Betty Lee Maxcy, Covered Bridge Inn, Ephrata, Pennsylvania

The names of our entrees change with the holiday. A sample for Valentine's Day: Cooing Duck, Heart Beet Soup, Passion Fruit Sorbet, Shrimps in Love, Nesting Greens, Sweet Ecstasy, Forever-after Coffee. Give your entrees seasonal names and announce them to your own dinner guests at home.

Fran and Charlie Guy, Mercersburg
Inn, Mercersburg, Pennsylvania

An easy touch for your guest's breakfast: We top eggs with red hearts that are made out of pimientos with a small cookie cutter.

Eva Mae and Frank Musgrave,
Edge of Thyme, Candor, New York

 Saint Patrick's Day

We serve green eggs and ham on Saint Patrick's Day. To a mixture of beaten eggs and half and half, add fresh parsley, scallions, steamed broccoli or asparagus, cubed cream cheese, and then julienne ham. Pour into skillet. Turn once. We garnish with avocado slices. So the eggs are not actually green, but the additional ingredients are, and they give the eggs a green theme.

Chris and Jill Raggio, Ilverthorpe
Cottage, Narragansett, Rhode
Island

On Saint Patrick's Day the local herb society meets at our inn. We serve green wine and green-herb hors d'oeuvres. We exchange herb recipes and green plants.

Jackie and Lee Morrison, Laurel
Hill Plantation, McClellanville,
South Carolina

 Easter

Adults love to color Easter eggs. The leftover colors from our own Easter eggs are supplied to our guests after breakfast. They enjoy coloring their own and get to take the eggs home. If you have company coming the day before Easter, wait for them to work with you in coloring the eggs. It's one way of celebrating the holiday together.

Fran and Frank Sullivan, Wild Rose
of York, York, Maine

Mahogany eggs—dyed with onion skins and the outline of herbs—and marbleized eggs fill a twig basket at Easter and decorate the breakfast table. These eggs hail back to the early days of this country. Settlers used native plants—walnut hulls, pokeberries, goldenrod, cabbages, and onions to create lovely colored eggs. A bit earlier in the season, the eggs are placed among freshly dug violets, sweet woodruff, and moss in a huge flat basket as the centerpiece for a buffet—the perfect harbinger of spring.

Here's how to make the eggs in your own kitchen:

You will need uncooked white eggs, a metal or enamel pan, nylon stockings, string, brown onion skins, turmeric, red cabbage leaves, vinegar, alum, young ivy leaves, and tiny sprigs of thyme, rosemary, and parsley or dried pressed flowers.

To decorate: Work with one color at a time. Start with the onion skins for mahogany eggs, as they are the easiest.

• Dip ½ cup of brown onion skins into 2 cups of boiling water. Remove the skins and wrap around an egg. One layer will do. The wet skins will mold nicely to the egg.

• Tie a string around the ankle of the stocking. Slip the wrapped egg into the stocking as far as the knot. Tie another knot at the opposite end of the egg.

Skip an inch and tie another knot, repeating with as many eggs as can fit in the pan.

• Boil leftover skins for 10 minutes. Remove. Add eggs. Simmer for 10 minutes.

• Carefully untie strings and unwrap eggs. They should be a lovely dark, yellow-brown, with a marbleized design. You can reuse these same skins for the next batch, although the color won't be as bright.

• Let the eggs dry thoroughly. It was the custom in the Maryland colony to oil the eggs for a richer color. When they are completely dry, you can also use a little paste wax for a glowing shine. The eggs will dry up inside their shells and can be kept from year to year in a box.

For your next batch, try something a little more challenging—a design on the egg:
Press a tiny herb sprig or a dried flower onto the egg before wrapping it with the onion skin. When it is unwrapped, it will have a tiny green print of the herb. Repeat as often as you like or until the color and skins wear out.

Directions for various colors:
Blue: Substitute red cabbage for the onion skins. Use 1 cup of chopped red cabbage leaves plus two or three of the softer leaves for wrapping. You need two cups of water and 1 tablespoon of vinegar. Boil all together for 10 minutes, removing the whole leaves as soon as they're soft. Wrap eggs with leaves as you did with the onion skins, or place the eggs, unwrapped, into the dye.

Yellow: Boil 1 teaspoon turmeric, 2 cups of water, 1 tablespoon of vinegar, and 2 pinches of alum together for 10 minutes. Apply herbs to eggs. Tie the eggs in the stockings and simmer in dye 10 minutes.

Green: Green eggs emerge from ½ cup young ivy leaves, 2 cups water, 1 tablespoon vinegar, and 2 pinches of alum. Follow the remaining procedure stated for the yellow eggs.

Dorry Norris, Sage Cottage,
Trumansburg, New York

For Easter, paper cupcake holders are filled with Easter grass and jelly beans and placed at each table setting.

Joanne and George Hardy, Hill
Farm Inn, Arlington, Vermont

One year, an Easter table centerpiece consisted of Easter ornaments hung from a chandelier over the dining table at different heights and tied with pink ribbon. The table underneath had green grass and candles in the shape of eggs, plus wooden tulips and a lovely fresh flower arrangement.

Jan and Gene Kuehn, Victorian
B&B, Avoca, Iowa

 # Memorial Day

You can serve this on the Fourth of July as well as Memorial Day: It's a mock American flag made with food. Spread bread dough on a rectangular pan. Bake until done. On top, create the flag with blueberries in the corner for stars, strawberries for the red stripes, and bananas for the white stripes. An alternative is to decorate a yellow cake baked in a shallow rectangular pan with the fruit. You can add a colorful selection of juices to serve with the cake in the red, white, and blue theme: tomato, grapefruit, and cran-blueberry.

> Chris and Jill Raggio, Ilverthorpe
> Cottage, Narragansett, Rhode
> Island

 # Independence Day

Breakfast on the Fourth of July is celebrated with French toast garnished with strawberries and blueberries and served to guests with a flaming sparkler.

> Paul and Ellen Morissette,
> Kenniston Hill Inn, Boothbay,
> Maine

 # Halloween

When pumpkins are growing on the vine, you can use a pin to scratch your name (we scratch the name of the inn) or a welcoming greeting on the surface. Your special welcome will grow larger as the pumpkin grows bigger.

> Meri and Mike Hern, Hilltop Inn,
> Sugar Hill, New Hampshire

Deviled eggs are always popular, and I love to dress them for the particular occasion. At Halloween, I make devilish eggs. Use your deviled-egg recipe and add slivers of green onions for the horns, ripe olives for the nose and eyes, parsley or poppy seeds for the beard or whiskers, and a pimiento for the tongue. (At Easter, decorate the deviled eggs as a bunny with slices of cooked egg white for ears, small strawberries for pink eyes, and a black olive for the nose.)

Robin Brooks, Robins Nest, San
Andreas, California

A wreath made of the mugwort herb guards the front door at Halloween to keep away the evil spirits. Here's how to make one. Apply the same techniques to almost any wreath you make.

Buy a wire ring at a crafts-supply store. They come in many sizes. For a large wreath, gather lots of the plant or whatever material you are going to use as the basis of your wreath. (I use mugwort because of its herbal significance.) Divide the herb into branches, three or four inches long, then divide them into small bundles. Put one bunch on the outside of the frame in a spiral fashion, another in the middle, and one on the inside. Then, using a light wire, continue this spiral pattern around the ring, pulling the wire tightly after applying each bundle.

Wreaths six inches in diameter or smaller can be made by just wrapping a stem or two in a circle and securing the end with light wire or heavy thread. Tiny dried flowers may be secured on any wreath with glue and very fine ribbon.

Dorry Norris, Sage Cottage,
Trumansburg, New York

 ## Thanksgiving

For this holiday, we pull cornstalks from the fields and create massive bundles attached to lightposts and columns on the porch. We tie the bunches with colorful orange and yellow ribbons. The look is country and festive. You can buy cornstalks in the fall at many farmstands.

Joan and Sal Chandon, Doubleday
Inn, Gettysburg, Pennsylvania

From Thanksgiving through Christmas, we serve meals as close to the manner in which they would have been prepared and cooked in an eighteenth-century American household. Some guests help prepare the meals. We show them how to churn butter and let them use antique kitchen tools, such as an old chopper and wooden bowl to prepare the vegetables. They also learn to knead bread. Buckets with hot water serve as our dish-washing vessels. Mary Louise cooks in front of the hearth in the keeping room. Ron cooks in the old-style reflector oven. With a full house, we use all of the other common room fireplaces, and guests help watch what's cooking in the kettles.

We wear period attire, using clothing that was designed from authentic historical patterns. While we're all working and talking, we explain older traditions and often have guest speakers or a Vermont fiddler.

Many of the bowls we use are hollowed fresh squashes or pumpkins. These make seasonal serving dishes. Even the small ones can hold condiments or dips.

> Mary Louise and Ron Thorburn,
> Inn at Weathersfield, Weathersfield,
> Vermont

Thanksgiving is a natural holiday for cooking over the open hearth. Cook turkey and roast duck over the fire. Then fill your home with more victuals and scents of the season by making this cran-orange sauce: In a medium-size crane pot, cook fresh cranberries and peeled orange sections, and add sugar to taste. Boil gently, allowing the wonderful scent to fill the air. Once the berry skins have split, making a popping sound, swing the crane away from the flames and let the sauce simmer for another twenty minutes at lowest heat position. Remove the pot from the crane and cover, keeping the cran-orange sauce warm by the hearth. Serve it later with your meal. (See more on hearth cookery in the fireplace chapter.)

End your Thanksgiving meal with a toast to the upcoming season. Play carols and read a story aloud. O'Henry's "Gift of the Magi" is a wonderful choice.

> Maureen and John Magee, Rabbit
> Hill Inn, Lower Waterford,
> Vermont

 Christmas

Decorations

When decorating for the holidays, it's nice to give the decor a theme. Music is an especially important ingredient at Rabbit Hill during the holidays. We decorate our parlor with music as the theme. On the mantel are brass horn candle holders, wooden replicas of a harp and violin, and an antique music stand.

Our manger was handcrafted in Italy. On the sides of the manger, we have a jack-in-the-box featuring a pop-up Scrooge and scenes from Dickens's *A Christmas Carol.* We place music boxes in adjoining rooms. In the dining room, we play tapes of music-box melodies. Guests, arriving to the sound of all these boxes playing, are enthralled.

> Maureen and John Magee, Rabbit
> Hill Inn, Lower Waterford,
> Vermont

My philosophy is: If it doesn't move, decorate it. Combine live greens, carnations, or other fresh flowers with tiny toys and accent with silver or gold for table arrangements.

> Claire Cane, Melfair Farm, Kittery,
> Maine

We had a candlelight holiday tour at the inn. We tried to create the feeling of Christmas at home during the 1850s. Here's how we did it: A large tree had candles and holders and German ornaments. In the center of one of the rooms, we placed a large silver wassail bowl beneath a gas chandelier. Greenery and fruit surrounded the bowl. The candelabra was festooned with velvet ribbons complementary to the colors of the room. Pink tissue-paper roses acted as a garland, framing mirrors along with dried baby's breath, greenery, and gold beads.

> Betty Lee Maxcy, Covered Bridge
> Inn, Ephrata, Pennsylvania

Guests are greeted by an old-fashioned sleigh out front, chock-full of gift-wrapped packages.

> Karen and Ken West, Benner
> House, Weston, Missouri

Antique Santas are grouped together on the mantel in the main gathering room. Each Santa represents a different period and country.

> Bev Davis and Rick Litchfield,
> Captain Lord Mansion,
> Kennebunkport, Maine

Strings of popcorn and cranberries are woven into our staircase railing.

> Bonnie and Bill Webb, Inn on
> Golden Pond, Holderness, New
> Hampshire

When the holidays are over, don't throw away the popcorn-and-cranberry garland. Put it outside for the birds to eat.

> Sandy and Dave Granger, 1830 Inn
> on the Green, Weston, Vermont

Our inn was part of a house tour one Christmas. To add to the holiday flavor, we dusted part of the table with flour and placed a rolling pin nearby, along with a few cooked gingerbread men on top of the flour. We wanted to give the illusion of just-baked cookies in the kitchen. This is a nice decorating idea for a holiday party in your own home.

> Sally and Ken McWilliams, Main
> Street B&B, Madison, Indiana

We wrap our old, white, colonial home in a huge red ribbon and hang a garland with satiny red bows from the overhang, the entire length of the inn. The Doubleday looks like an enormous Christmas package dropped onto the Gettysburg Battlefield.

Our hostess, Olga Krossick, made pinecone decorations that won a local prize. To make her decoration: Form a nest at the top of a pinecone, using dried moss and glue to fasten. Add some baby's breath and place a colorful, small, artificial bird in the center. Finish it off with a red bow and hang.

> Joan and Sal Chandon, Doubleday Inn, Gettysburg, Pennsylvania

Kissing balls deck our home. To make your own seasonal Cupid of sorts, take a potato and stick boxwood stems into it from every direction. Attach a strong ribbon and hang it in a doorway.

> Michele and Edward Schiesser, La Vista Plantation, Fredericksburg, Virginia

At Christmastime, we go all out. Every year, Jim catches a heavy dose of spirit and makes painted plywood Santas from images of old Saint Nick.

> Mimi and Jim Agard, Brafferton Inn, Gettysburg, Pennsylvania

Christmas Trees

Every room of your home can have a Christmas tree. A friend taught us how to make small, fresh trees. Cut a block of oasis to fit into a deep dish, standing upright. Wet the oasis. Stick fresh-cut evergreen branches into the oasis. You can decorate the trees with colored baby's breath, ribbons, toys, and even a string of tiny twinkling lights.

> Linda and Rob Castagna, Chestnut Hill on the Delaware, Milford, Pennsylvania

Since our house is Victorian, we decorate our Christmas tree in the same mode. A Victorian Christmas tree includes deckings of period china, dolls, crystal, lace, and gold roses.

> Emily Hunter, Briar Rose, Denver, Colorado

Our tree is decked with our collection of antique ornaments for a vintage look.

Mimi and Jim Agard, Brafferton
Inn, Gettysburg, Pennsylvania

Old cut-crystal bangles are used as icicles on our Christmas tree.

Bev Davis and Rick Litchfield,
Captain Lord Mansion,
Kennebunkport, Maine

Satin bows are key accents in creating a Victorian Christmas tree. Next, select a fabric complementary to your design scheme and stitch fabric hearts. Stuff them with batting and attach ribbon loops so that they can be hung from branches. Keep the size and weight of the hearts to a minimum. Lightweight, inexpensive strands of pearls make wonderful garlands for roping around the tree along with tiny white lights.

After presents have been opened, warm the empty space around the tree with an arrangement of antique toys. You need only a few. A worn teddy bear on a child's rocker and a drum beside it are warm and fitting.

Maureen and John Magee, Rabbit
Hill Inn, Lower Waterford,
Vermont

Different-sized empty boxes are wrapped in seasonal papers and placed under the tree. It makes the tree look complete.

Mimi and Jim Agard, Brafferton
Inn, Gettysburg, Pennsylvania

During Christmas, a tree is covered with animal cookie cutters tied with red ribbons.

Dorry Norris, Sage Cottage,
Trumansburg, New York

When we decided to have a second tree—a large, 12-foot one—we didn't have the time to run out and buy new ornaments for it. Besides, such a tree would cost a fortune in store-bought baubles. Instead, we took nuts and pinecones and sprayed them with gold paint, added ribbons, baby's breath, and tiny lights, and we had a tree that took our guests' breath away. Use imagination when decorating your own tree. Make it as personalized as you can.

Sally and Ken McWilliams, Main
Street B&B, Madison, Indiana

Old or new lace draped around the tree like a garland will give your tree an old-fashioned look.

Diane and Larry Muentz,
Alexander's Inn, Cape May, New
Jersey

Table Adornments

For our annual Christmas dinner, we serve an elaborate, eight-course affair in the Victorian manner. The centerpiece is usually made up of single, old wooden balusters, topped by square blocks of oasis into which redwood cuttings, winter pears, apples on spikes, and gilded pinecones are massed. Brass candlesticks of varying heights flank the base of the centerpiece.

Mary Louise and Conley Weaver,
Red Castle Inn, Nevada City,
California

Buy the brightest apples you can. Core them and dip them into a crystal-clear floor wax. When they have dried, put a white candle in the cored area for truly authentic candle holders.

Joan and Sal Chandon, Doubleday
Inn, Gettysburg, Pennsylvania

Author's Tips: You can also make natural candle holders from bagels. Just slip some tinfoil on the bottom of the candle and insert it in the bagel hole. Decorate the bagel with a hint of evergreen and a marble-sized Christmas ball.

Take an empty can (coffee can preferably) and glue the candy canes around the outside. The curved part should face out. Secure them with a festive ribbon tied around the canes. Place holiday greenery or other flora inside. This also makes a nice container for cookies and candy.

Pineapples also make wonderful seasonal centerpieces. Wrap an evergreen bough around the bottom, and place colorful

Christmas balls every 3 inches or so on top of the bough. Place a satin ribbon between each ball.

A holiday centerpiece can be made from a small, white-birch log. Drill holes in it for candles, and decorate it with various yuletide greens and trimmings.

Sharon and Scott Wright, Silver
Maple Lodge, Fairlee, Vermont

Pinecones can be placed on your holiday table. Spray the tips with a hint of gold paint. Just before your company arrives, spray the cones with an evergreen-scented aerosol fragrance. Place them around the table.

Sally and Ken McWilliams, Main
Street B&B, Madison, Indiana

Christmas breakfast tables are set with 5-by-9-inch stockings made from a quilted fabric. We fill them with candy, fruit, and nuts.

Joanne and George Hardy, Hill
Farm Inn, Arlington, Vermont

Scraps of felt and lace can be used to make holiday napkin holders. At Christmas, for example, they are red-felt mittens with a white-velvet ribbon cuff, topped by a green-felt holly leaf and a couple of red sequins for berries. When your napkin is rolled and slipped in, it looks like a sleeve going into the mitten. To make one, trace a mitten pattern onto felt. Sew together two pieces, leaving an opening where a hand would slip in, to be used for the napkin.

Robin Brooks, Robins Nest, San
Andreas, California

Christmas Sweets

Each year, a different centerpiece of edible architecture greets guests and can be anything from a cracker cottage to a confectionery castle. You don't have to be a baker to start this tradition in your own home. If making a gingerbread house seems intimidating, relax and enjoy this similar but easier method of constructing a sweet building:

Anyone can mix up some royal icing (three egg whites to a pound of powdered sugar). This magic mortar dries to a sweet cement that will stick anything to anything. Your foundation can be square or round (for turrets) oatmeal boxes, cookie tins, or cardboard tubes. One year, a row of jelly-bean town houses was constructed out of wine boxes from our vineyard. The royal icing covers your foundation. Add your own food accents.

Beth and Franz Schober, Hopkins
Inn, New Preston, Connecticut

Winter holidays can be enhanced with frosted fruit as decorations. Here's a recipe for making your fruit glisten:

1 egg white
2 tablespoons water
1 cup sugar

In a small bowl, beat the egg white and water lightly. Dip assorted fruits in the mixture. Drain the excess back in the bowl. Roll each piece in sugar until covered. Let them dry thoroughly on waxed paper.

Tommie and Andy Duncan, Arcady
Down East, Blue Hill, Maine

Entertaining

For a holiday party or dinner, place a basket of ornaments on a table in the entryway. As each guest arrives, have them choose an ornament and place it on your tree.

Kate Kerivan, Bungay Jar, Easton,
New Hampshire

At Christmastime, each guest staying with us gets a Christmas ornament that looks like our inn and has our name and the year printed on it. If you have a holiday party at your house, you could do something like that.

Corky and Steve Garboski, Province
Inn, Strafford, New Hampshire

Spring House Christmas parties have featured opera singers presenting a recital, the lighting of plum pudding, and the cutting of a Yule log.

Ray Constance Hearne, Spring
House, Airville, Pennsylvania

We like to mark Christmas with a musical celebration of the holiday season. Antique music-box melodies play throughout the inn and Christmas carols are sung as a special feature. You can do the same in your own home. Holding a Christmas caroling session will brighten your Christmas Eve or Christmas day with the family. Christmas caroling is a very Victorian tradition.

We like to explain the history of caroling to our guests. The custom of going from house to house caroling comes from the old English yuletide practice of wassailing. Wassail, derived from old- and middle-English *wese hael,* meaning "be well," was a toast of celebration. The wassail bowl was a part of every celebration and held a special ale. It was very often carried door to door by merrymakers, who drank to the health of those who gave them a friendly welcome.

Many of our oldest carols date from the fifteenth century, when the use of carols was held in the highest esteem. The Puritans, thinking the Christmas songs and customs were frivolous, suppressed the tradition in the seventeenth century. Carols were kept alive, popularly preserved in folk songs, and were passed down through the years by families.

By the middle of the nineteenth century, the time-honored customs of caroling were rarely observed. Scholars and clergy, who had been preparing the way for revival, began publishing more and more carols until musicians at last became interested. In 1871, the Reverend H. R. Bramley and Dr. John Stainer published *Christmas Carols Old and New,* a collection of forty-two carols. It is to these men that we owe the renewed interest in carols.

The rediscovery of old carols, along with the composing of new ones, led to a nineteenth-century revival in which the Victorians gave caroling a new lease on life. Within a few years, this revival was well under way on both sides of the Atlantic, and community carol-singing was organized. By 1915 in New York City, candles were associated with caroling; a lighted taper in your window on Christmas Eve guaranteed singing at your door. Bands of minstrels along with groups of carolers gathered to raise their voices in celebration, filling the streets with the sounds of Christmas.

Nancy Rishforth, Summer Cottage Inn, Cape May, New Jersey

Combine cinnamon sticks with whole cloves, bay leaves, whole nutmeg, lemon and orange peels, and some water to cover. Place on low heat at the back of your stove. Let simmer. As the water evaporates, add more. At the end of the day, store the remains in a tightly covered jar and refrigerate. The mixture can be reheated and freshened with additional ingredients as needed. How about a pot of this banked in your fireplace coals or simmering from the crane?

Maureen and John Magee, Rabbit Hill, Lower Waterford, Vermont

 New Year's Eve

Entertainment for your New Year's Eve celebration can include something we do. Over our bar, we fill a big net with black and white balloons. Then we pull the balloons down from the ceiling at midnight with a cheer.

Rita and Allan Kalsmith, Black Lantern, Montgomery Village, Vermont

On New Year's Eve you can decorate a room inexpensively. We festoon our dining room with curly ribbon, and we fill the entire ceiling with helium balloons that have long strands of ribbon attached. Buy the ribbon in commercial-size rolls to save money.

Inside each wine glass, we place a horn with long streamers. This makes for a colorful table before the clock strikes twelve.

Barbara and Barry Lubao, Ellis River House, Jackson, New Hampshire

Our Glue Gun Game is a different kind of activity for New Year's Eve. Guests at the inn take turns gluing odd pieces of mat board, wood, glass, and many other scraps of material to make a sculpture. Each guest makes his or her own piece of art. Everyone has a lot of laughs.

Lyle and Barbara Wolf, Greenhurst Inn, Bethel, Vermont

Author's Tip: A cake complementary to the closing seconds of a New Year's Eve party is one decorated on top as though it were a clock. Use plastic numbers and hour hands, or make your own by piping black icing through a cake-decorating tip.

 # Special-Occasion Parties

During an Iowa caucus, we had thirteen candidates. For a political party, we put up thirteen red, white, and blue balloons and cascaded them from a chandelier in various lengths. On the table, we placed a donkey vase and an elephant vase, filled them with rice, and placed about three small flags in each, along with curled red, white, and blue ribbons. It made a lovely table-setting.

Jan and Gene Kuehn, Victorian B&B, Avoca, Iowa

The bottom line in entertaining is Keep It Simple with Style and prepare in advance. For a political fund-raising luncheon, I had the bakery slice 5-foot-long loaves of French bread lengthwise. On nice and new 1-by-12-inch boards, we made the bread into giant open-faced submarine sandwiches, which we decorated with ripe olives, cherry tomatoes, sardines, pickles, and other condiments. We used an electric knife to cut the sandwiches into 4-inch sections and topped each one with a small American flag. They were a smash. We raised funds and later converted the boards into shelves.

Robin Brooks, Robins Nest, San Andreas, California

We have some friends who are artists. To promote their work and our business, we have an art show at the inn a few times a year. We hire musicians such as a pianist or a string quartet, who work at a discount because they get referrals. Our inn gets great exposure as we help out our friends. You can have an artist's showing at your house. Consult with an artist as to how he or she needs to display the paintings. Usually the paintings are for sale.

Susan Hannah, Winters Creek
Ranch, Carson City, Nevada

Have a summer-in-February party. Decorate with tropical posters and paper palm trees. Serve tropical fruits and other summer foods. Give everyone a lei, and turn up the heat so they can wear shorts!

Kathy Drew, Out-the-Inn-Door,
Freeport, Maine

Author's Tip: A useful centerpiece for a seasonal summer dinner is made by starting with a large bowl or basket filled with homegrown or fresh garden salad greens and vegetables. Use a small, colorful spade and rake as salad servers. Put a small, decorative watering can filled with an herb dressing nearby, and let your guests water their own garden-on-the-plate.

Hot Springs has another season for decorating—horse-racing time. During the season, we put racing napkins in jockey colors and an old cast-iron doorstop on the table. We use a bunch of shamrock plants as a centerpiece for good luck.

Mary and Gary Riley, Williams
House, Hot Springs, Arkansas

You can do a Beggar's Banquet anytime of year. Once a year, we have a banquet in the tradition of the medieval times in England, when the rich opened their houses to the poor for meals. We serve Elizabethan dinners, which include wild game, fresh fruits, squashes, potatoes, and dill breads. We play Elizabethan-style music from recordings recommended by historical societies.

Kris McIlvenna, Greenbriar B&B,
Coeur d'Alene, Idaho

In May, we have an Elizabethan feast. We hold a special dinner for friends who dress up in period costume; women wear pearls in their hair, and men wear short, balloon-type pants. Mead is a specialty and is served in pewter goblets. Dessert includes rose-petal ice cream. Just add crushed rose petals to your usual, basic ice-cream recipe.

Megan Timothy, La Maida House,
North Hollywood, California

Author's Tip: I sometimes use restaurant menus to coincide with my dinner-table theme. For example, I once had a bon-voyage dinner party for my in-laws bound for vacation in France. The centerpiece was a menu from a French restaurant. I inserted a list of the evening's dishes, giving them Parisian titles. The menu sparked jovial conversation. My father-in-law started it off with, "Does this restaurant take a credit card?"

I have a collection of menus to complement many themes for the table, having collected them when I used to review restaurants for a newspaper column. Now, I have to depend on the generosity of the restaurant to give me one or else pay a few dollars for one.

(Incidentally, some menus look great in a custom-made picture frame, hanging in the kitchen.)

A special party at our inn is a Japanese dinner. Guests take off their shoes and are given a kimono to wear over their clothing. They sit at low tables on large floor-pillows around a low grill. (Of course, we don't burn charcoal in it, as the fumes would be toxic inside.) The food is arranged on a tray, and the guests do their own cooking at the table, which is topped by an oriental umbrella.

Jeanne Biner and Vivien Willard,
Cricket on the Hearth, Coeur
d'Alene, Idaho

To decorate for a dinner with a Victorian theme, make some fancy napkin rings. Use wired ribbon to form the ring. Secure with a glue gun. Cut a small piece of lace from a damaged doily or another find. Starch the lace, and glue it to what will be the top side of the ribbon napkin ring. Then glue dried flower buds at the center of the lace. Add a short thin ribbon. (Note: These rings also make lovely curtain tiebacks.)

Make a complementary nosegay centerpiece. Select a paper or lace doily of desired diameter. Pierce the center and draw wired dried flowers through it. Wind white florist tape around the wires, and curl the tape prettily at the ends. Next, pucker the doily from its center by gathering it underneath, and glue in place with a glue gun to shape it around the flowers. Glue dried leaves around the flowers to make a pretty arrangement. Add a crystal bead to resemble a dewdrop and thin ribbon streamers. Place at the center of the table or on the side, or make nosegays to decorate each place setting.

> Maureen and John Magee, Rabbit
> Hill Inn, Lower Waterford,
> Vermont

Author's Tip: Rabbit Hill's Victorian napkin rings and nosegays also work nicely for formal teatime decorations.

We had a surprise birthday party for our forty-year-old friend Elliott McDowell, who was born February 29 (leap year), thus making this actually only his tenth birthday. You can use these ideas to mix with almost any birthday party.

We covered tables with white butchers' paper. Guests were given crayons to write their greetings on the paper. A table centerpiece consisted of an array of confetti, candy, rubber snakes, marbles, baseball cards, a gumball machine, and a baseball mitt. On one of the other tables, we placed a new pair of high-top sneakers with a balloon bouquet tied to the laces. The ceiling was covered by helium balloons in pinks, purples, blues, and silver.

Party helpers had ponytails with large pink bows and wore short skirts and hot-pink T-shirts with "Elliott's Big 10" printed in turquoise.

Food included miniature hot dogs and hamburgers. Finger sandwiches were cut in shapes of airplanes, stars, hearts, and rabbits, and filled with peanut butter and homemade apricot jam, crab, chicken, and cream cheese and red-pepper jelly. The cake was chocolate-orange, decorated with brightly colored papier-mâché finger puppets.

Games were musical chairs to 1950s music and Pin-the-Tail-on-the-Coyote (Santa Fe–style).

The party concluded with the release of the balloons into the sky with champagne toasts to Elliott. Afterwards, one of the T-shirts was used to cover the photo album commemorating Elliott's party.

> Louise, Pat, and Bumpy Walter,
> Grant Corner Inn, Santa Fe, New
> Mexico

We have a Back-to-the-1960s Party every year here. The event features prizes for the best sixties outfit, a hula-hoop contest, and a sixties trivia quiz.

A make-your-own pizza is a highlight of the sixties party, but you can adapt it to any gathering. We provide guests with boxed pizza dough and sauce with a variety of toppings, allowing them to be as creative as they wish. What comes out of the oven is often surprising and, at times, even artful.

> Denise Anderson and David
> Karpinski, Quill and Quilt, Cannon
> Falls, Minnesota

A few loaded instant-photo cameras can turn any party into a hilarious event. Here's one for Halloween, or omit the costumes and do it for any other occasion: Supply each guest with a camera (or ask them to bring one if they can). Depending on how many guests you have, divide them into small groups or couples. Send them out with the instant camera and a list of places where they must have their picture taken. All members of the group must be in the picture, so they will have to solicit strangers to take their snapshot.

A little advance preparation is necessary, since you need to scout out locations in your neighborhood that can be covered in the time allowed. You also need to add some bonus points to the scoring to break ties. For example, at one of our recent parties, we gave the groups ninety minutes to get their photos taken in a bowling alley, in a fire station, on a city bus, in a police car, in a grocery store checkout line, under a movie marquee, and in a cemetery. All the groups got all the photos in the time allowed. Bonus points for such items as the number of fire trucks in the fire-station picture, the number of additional people wearing bowling shirts in the bowling-alley shot, the number of heads of lettuce in the grocery-store picture, and so on, were the deciding factors for the winners.

Denise Anderson and David
Karpinski, Quill and Quilt, Cannon
Falls, Minnesota

We have a hat collection at the inn. In addition to using the hats for display, we play a game with them for special dinner guests. For each guest coming to dinner, we choose a hat that matches his or her personality. We place it on the seat of the chair or at the place setting. The guests have to guess which is their designated seat, based on the hat.

Jim and Mimi Agard, Brafferton
Inn, Gettysburg, Pennsylvania

Author's Tip: Have a Western Party. Set the table with bandannas as your napkins. You can use place mats or make a tablecloth out of burlap. Napkin rings can be round, slotted, wooden clothespins upon which you write your guest's name. Another napkin ring idea that also doubles as a place card is using a small cowboy hat from a doll. Write the guest's name on a piece of paper attached to the hat with a straight pin. The elastic hatband wraps nicely around the napkin. For a centerpiece, use something western, such as a small rocking horse or an agate coffeepot filled with fresh baby's breath. You can also place two candlesticks with a string between them. Using tiny clothespins and doll clothes, hang a pair of overalls and a checkered shirt on the line to dry! Pewter plates are a nice complement, if you have them.

Tell guests it's a jeans party, so they will wear denim. Serve a barbecue dish as the main entree, perhaps with wagon-wheel pasta and pesto sauce as one of the side dishes. Green and yellow squash slices, sautéed in butter and sprinkled lightly with salt and pepper, also go well. A loaf or two of braided bread to resemble the rope of rough riders will look attractive on the table and complement the theme.

Restoration and Home Improvements

Saving Old Homes and Remodeling Newer Ones

"You know, in a house like this, you're never really the owner, but rather a temporary caretaker for generations to come."

These words, delivered by an observant friend, are emblazoned in Jim Agard's memory. He understands well that the home he and his wife, Mimi, purchased in Gettysburg, Pennsylvania, is their possession for the present but their responsibility to the future. The Brafferton Inn, as it was named by the Agards, is a monument of sorts. Although they own it, they feel an obligation to keep their house intact for those who come after them.

"We've tried to take care to enrich the home, magnify its sense of time, history, good humor, and taste, and instill a family presence throughout. That's a good thing to keep in mind when doing any restoration or renovation to an old house," says Jim, passing along his own platitude and unofficial doctrine of adapting an old house to a new age.

That is part of what innkeeping is all about—men and women saving an old home but making it usable for today's lifestyle. Many innkeepers possess the penchant to own an old home but neither the time nor the rare skills and know-how to restore the house by themselves. They often seek professional help. You may hear them tell war stories of the once deplorable condition of their now exemplary home. The point here is that they believed in their vision enough to take the risk and turn the most devastated structure into their dream house. Then they painstakingly studied and researched, looked for the best carpenters and craftsmen, and turned their souring vestiges of bygone eras into repackaged Victorian confections or barnyard beauties.

The emphasis in this chapter is on restorations, as most innkeepers who supplied information for this book own old homes/inns. There is also some advice here for those who live in newer houses that need a little renovation.

You will find solutions to general house problems. Take, for example, the way Joan and Sal Chandon of The Doubleday Inn in Gettysburg, Pennsylvania, handled this one. "One of our stairwells has a very low, curved ceiling. The average-height person would hit his head if not warned in advance. We painted the stairs green and the ceiling and walls white. We stenciled a trailing vine in white paint on the stairs and then stenciled it in green on the ceiling. The result is that on their way upstairs, people tend to look down at the ivy crawling up the stairs and thus avoid hitting their heads. On the way down, they tend to look up at the ivy on the ceiling and again keep from hitting their heads."

Another problem was cleverly resolved by Bonnie and Bill Webb at The Inn on Golden Pond in Holderness, New Hampshire. Bonnie reports, "We had a chimney that was no longer being used. Since it was in the center of the house, we used it as a conduit for plumbing and electricity when we added a new room on the third floor."

The range of old-house restoration and problem solving that goes on at inns is extensive. But inns that have been newly constructed as reproductions are also opening. Donna and Charles Tanney's inn is one example. They built their eighteenth-century saltbox—Gates Hill Homestead in Brookfield, New York—all by hand, right from bulldozing a spot for the foundation. Donna built the stone hearth with her gloved hands. She explains a challenge that required a mustering of fortitude and an I-can-do-it attitude:

"The challenge in building the hearth was to balance on a ladder, top end propped against the structure on which I was working, with the bottom of the ladder resting on a plank stretched between the beams, as there were no floors yet. Charlie set the flue's clay tiles, so I had a form of sorts. I kept my work going straight by means of 2-foot and 4-foot levels. When it was all over, there was a thrilling moment of realization. It came out exactly as I had sketched it."

The Tanneys did it all, including decorating with stenciling and refinished furniture, and they even made their own chandeliers! They are fine examples of how to face any building, renovation, or restoration challenge.

In Strasburg, Pennsylvania, Debby and Hap Joy found a charming Amish house they decided would make a fine inn. The only trouble was that the house had no electricity and no central heat. Should they buy the place and face a massive project? Debby, now proud owner of The Decoy, remembers: "Our renovations were major ones, and the expenses were great. We took out the four closets in the upstairs rooms and added four bathrooms. Thus far we have maintained the home's simplicity, and the work was all worth it."

When restoring an old home, innkeepers face many challenges. Perhaps their greatest challenge is a balancing act—modernizing the building while maintaining its history and integrity. Based on the research for this book, I would have to say that the most common change made by the innkeepers to historical homes is changing unneeded closets into bathrooms. This is the way extra bathrooms can be had without jeopardizing the home's historical status. However, there are some inns that simply cannot add baths without taking away from the home's significance. This is one of the reasons there are so many shared baths at inns. But this seems to work out. Many guests do not mind sharing a bath. Inn-goers of old Europe and early America always jointly used the bath—or the outdoor privy.

Today's old-house restorer must also face modern regulatory codes regarding matters such as smoke detectors and fire escapes. Rehabilitating an old home is not an easy task. However, looking beyond the gloomy tunnel of what must be done, innkeepers see the rewards of reviving the past and running an inn as they had always hoped. They offer a mosaic of tips for setting the cornerstone of either a good inn or private home. Either way—as innkeeper or homemaker—they are cultivating the nectar of historic preservation. That truly does make them caretakers of a sort, now doesn't it?

 ## Shopping for an Old Home

Bless their hearts, but don't pay too much attention to a parent's objection when he or she sees that you're buying an old home badly in need of repair. They may not have the vision or ambition you have to take on the challenge. Your parents don't reap the rewards from such a project as you do, so naturally they see it differently.

To determine actual expenses for utilities, ask to see one year's billings.

> Beverly and Ray Compton, Spring
> Bank Inn, Frederick, Maryland

Figure from the start that you're in for a lot of work. However, also consider that if you don't get it all done today, it will still be there the next day. Otherwise, you'll get overwhelmed and discouraged. Take it one step at a time, and take a breather in between.

The thing to avoid is a house that has to be completely gutted, unless you get the deal of the century on it. It is getting harder, not easier, to find capable and qualified workers for restoration. So you want to find a house with as many of its original features as possible.

The secret to a great buy is this real estate maxim: location, location, location—but with a slightly different twist. Look for a marginal area of historic homes into which people are beginning to move. The interest in historic homes is growing. So as long as you're not in an absolute slum, you probably won't lose on your investment.

A house that needs cosmetic work, rather than structural renovation, is best. The impact from cosmetic changes is more dramatic and thus gives you more immediate appreciation than structural work. Of course, if you plan to live in the house the rest of your life, then that appreciation doesn't matter. But if you plan to sell and move on, it certainly does.

> Ripley Hotch and Owen Sullivan,
> Boydville The Inn at Martinsburg,
> Martinsburg, West Virginia

We bought our guest cottage knowing it needed a lot of work. The foundation had to be redone. Oh, boy! We had a certain number of dollars planned for the restoration, but the foundation work alone took everything we had. When you shop for an old home, shy away from one that needs a new foundation.

When you get an estimate on the restoration from a professional, add as much as 25 to 50 percent more for those hidden things that crop up.

> Sunny and Joy Drewel, Zachariah
> Foss Guest House, Washington,
> Missouri

A strong roof system is the best assurance of a structure's longevity.

To test the soundness of the mortar on a brick or stone house, scratch the mortar joints with a cut nail to see if the joints are soft and sanded out. These houses can almost always be saved (stabilized) by scratching away 2 or 3 inches of mortar between the bricks or stones, and replacing it with new mortar. First, scratch the outside, and then do the same thing from the inside.

To appraise the soundness of a frame building, first view the structure from a distance and look for sagging and settling. If the lines of the building are still square and crisp, it's almost always OK. It's a very rare frame house that cannot be restored. I've never seen one.

> Allan Smith, Historic Smithton Inn,
> Ephrata, Pennsylvania

Love the house before you buy one that needs restoration. The work is hard, grueling, and seemingly never ending. Some things in an old home you cannot change. You may have to get used to tilting floors and crooked corners.

> Jackie and Lee Morrison, Laurel
> Hill Plantation, McClellanville,
> South Carolina

Sometimes, there are situations in an old house that you can do little to change. For example, be aware that in a house built before 1830, there are no interior cavities in the walls. This means you can't run the electrical system inside the walls, as it is normally done today. Electric wires and wire boxes will be exposed when you electrify the house. The wire is encased in a molding that will always be visible to you. This may not bother some people, but it

can be a disappointment to others. It is something to consider if
you buy a house from this period.

Miya and Les Patrick, Charles
Hinckley House, Barnstable,
Massachusetts

If you're buying a home with the idea of turning it into a bed-
and-breakfast or country inn someday, here are some of the
things you need to ask and have answered before buying:
- Is the immediate neighborhood a pleasant setting for a
B&B? Will the neighbors openly accept a B&B?
- Is the building unusual in appearance or architecture, so that
people will give it more than a passing look?
- Do you know or can you discover enough about the building
and its former owners to enable you to prepare a short history of
it—suitable for use as a press release, in support of a request for
restoration funding, and for a brochure to give guests?
- Is it possible to develop friendly relations with the business
community?
- Does the area offer a variety of activities for guests?
- What is the (B&B) competition in the area?
- The owner of a historic B&B needs to realize that the more
successful the business, the more personal attention it requires.
Information on methods and problems of recycling historic
buildings, as well as tax incentives, investment credits, and other
economic benefits, is available in the publications of the Preservation Press, National Trust for Historic Preservation, 1785 Massachusetts Avenue, Washington, D.C. 20036.

Helen M. White, Historic Taylors
Falls Jail, Taylors Falls, Minnesota

If you're looking to open an inn, small towns on the outer edges
of metropolitan areas are the best bet now—say, within a two-
hour commute of major cities. People are looking to get away
these days, which is why country inns within commuting distance
are so popular.

Ripley Hotch and Owen Sullivan,
Boydville The Inn at Martinsburg,
Martinsburg, West Virginia

You'll need a wheelbarrow full of $'s if you're going to restore a home.

Deedy and Charlie Marble,
Governor's Inn, Ludlow, Vermont

Have your checkbook ready and don't hesitate.

Kay Gill, Stephen Daniels House,
Salem, Massachusetts

Lots of home improvements can cost less when you plan ahead. For example, green wood may cost 25 percent less than its kiln-dried counterpart. The wood should be ready for use in one year.

Allan Smith, Historic Smithton Inn,
Ephrata, Pennsylvania

When financing a home, try to secure a mortgage and a home-improvement loan at the same time. Have the payments structured so that you pay one mortgage installment per month (or two per month to save money on interest over time), which includes the home-improvement loan. In our experience, banks seem more willing to help finance in this manner, if they know up front how much you plan to spend for remodeling.

If you are planning to open an inn, go one step further. List the number of rooms for let and the price per night for each room. Contact the local chamber of commerce and list the occupancy rate of rooms in the area per season, and then let the banker know. Figure out your projected yearly income. Prepare a second list showing your expenses, such as heat, electric, food, linen services, taxes, and so on, and deduct these from your expected income. Your final figure should be great enough to convince any banker.

Joan and Sal Chandon, Doubleday
Inn, Gettysburg, Pennsylvania

Seek companies that provide supplies free or at wholesale in exchange for publicity. We mailed a letter to 100 companies, describing the mansion and what we needed. We told the companies how our inn would be advertising for them. As a result, three companies responded with wallpaper, carpet, and paint.

Pat and Bob Handwerk, Harry
Packer Mansion, Jim Thorpe,
Pennsylvania

 ## Restoration Basics

Much of what is involved in restoration work has to do with confidence. I (Jim) remember once building an addition onto a saltbox I owned in Vermont. When considering the whole project, it seemed impossible. But once the footings were in, everything else quickly followed. Before you knew it, the addition was complete.

Mimi and I have found decorating, building, and historical magazines to be a big help. They generate ideas and alternatives, especially when you're having a problem figuring out a renovation.

I am a firm believer in graphing out every new floor plan. Every foot counts. As we buy antiques, we fit them into the floor plan for the proposed room or rooms. I photocopy the plans and keep them in my van, so if I'm out scouting for an antique, I can look at the size of a wall where this particular piece might fit. I give a copy to the plumber and electrician so they understand the entire plan.

I'm in the process of doing a major restoration to our top floor. I'm putting it on videotape and narrating it. It should be a wonderful visual document for the house and for the kids when I'm living in the great restoration in the sky.

Mimi and Jim Agard, Brafferton
Inn, Gettysburg, Pennsylvania

When doing restorations or renovations, confine them to the smallest area possible. Many go into renovations by tearing the whole house apart all at once. Do one room or area at a time and complete it. It seems to go a lot faster that way, too.

Robin and Bill Branigan, Roaring
Lion, Waldoboro, Maine

All of us have projects around the house we just can't seem to get around to. At the Quill and Quilt, we simply take a reservation for (or schedule an event in) the room involved and then begin work. The forced deadline adds to our resolve. Once, we had hung the final towel bar in an entirely new bathroom about ten minutes before guests who had been promised a private bath had arrived. You can do the same thing in your own home by beginning a project and then sending out party invitations or inviting friends over for an event that uses the room.

Denise Anderson and David Karpinski, Quill and Quilt, Cannon Falls, Minnesota

Research the style and materials you plan to use before starting renovations or restorations. There are many good reproduction sources available today. An excellent resource: *The Old-House Journal.*

Live in a house at least nine months before planning major renovations. Test all the seasons for air and light and patterns of movement in the house.

Marjorie and John Pratt, Inn on Cove Hill, Rockport, Massachusetts

Your local historical societies are a good place to begin your research. Old Sturbridge Village and Old Deerfield Village in Massachusetts are also excellent sources. As you begin the research to restore your home, a network of contacts will follow. This is how, for example, we found a blacksmith to re-create our ironwork in exact eighteenth-century replicas and a mason to do our masonry work.

If you can get a hold of old books referring to your house, read them as much as possible. They will indicate where things might be hidden. You don't want to tear into a wall and find out you have ruined a fireplace behind it, for example.

Mary Louise and Ron Thorburn, Inn at Weathersfield, Weathersfield, Vermont

Returning a house to the aura of centuries ago is an ongoing process. You need to mix the old with the new—modernize within historical confines. Seek local historians for help in restoring your old house.

Korda Family, Historic Brookside
Inn, Orwell, Vermont

If possible, when hiring help for your restoration project, find local people who are adept at old-house restoration.
Use available materials where possible rather than buying reproductions. We moved existing doors and used locks from extra doors, for example.

Tommie and Andy Duncan, Arcady
Down East, Blue Hill, Maine

Getting expert craftsmen to restore old houses is not always easy. When you hire one, the best way to learn the trade yourself and learn it quickly is to work with him. Be his helper and watch his every move. You can ask a thousand questions.

Allan Smith, Historic Smithton Inn,
Ephrata, Pennsylvania

If you're having restoration work done for you, it's best to fully understand wha' is going to be done. Then, communicate with your hired workmen every day. Be on the site as much as possible, so that your expectations are met. Get lien releases from everyone you hire.

Pat Hardy, Glenborough Inn, Santa
Barbara, California

When you plan a restoration or renovation, keep in mind not to take any shortcuts, especially with electrical equipment or insulation.

Fran and Frank Sullivan, Wild Rose
of York, York, Maine

An important rule of serious restoration: If you use the same tools and the same materials as the original homeowners, you should get the same results. Antique tools can be very serviceable. Early craftsmen used hand planes, shapers, and routers, for instance, to shape moldings, which you can do in your own workshop.

Allan Smith, Historic Smithton Inn,
Ephrata, Pennsylvania

Walls, Windows, Doors

Do your walls lean out? Many old homes have crooked walls due to age. If so, build new, straight walls inside the room. This may make the room slightly smaller, but you won't go mad trying to correct the situation.

> Elaine and Ray Grandmaison,
> Captain Stannard House,
> Westbrook, Connecticut

If an exterior wall becomes an internal wall due to an addition, expose the beams to show the eighteenth-century construction. Apply polyurethane to them, so that they can be kept clean.

> Sandra Cartwright-Brown, Conyers
> House, Sperryville, Virginia

Do not gut a room indiscriminately. You may destroy a valuable underlayer. We found 18-inch, tongue-and-groove planks in a wall under plasterboard and wallpaper. A portion was then removed and used as a very effective wainscot.

> Marjorie and John Pratt, Inn on
> Cove Hill, Rockport, Massachusetts

Vertical wood bumper guards on interior convex wall corners go a long way toward reducing maintenance. They were used all the time in homes during the Victorian period. Reproductions are easy to find, but salvaged antiques can be cheaper, particularly with a little sweat equity gained by cleaning, stripping, and painting them. Don't worry about getting the same ones for the entire house. Just try to match each room with one style.

> Charles A. Hillestad, Queen Anne
> Inn, Denver, Colorado

Author's Tip: Don't let an ugly, paneled wall stymie you. If you want to brighten the room, paint over the paneling. No sanding is necessary to make the paint adhere if you first apply an oil-base sealer. (The walls will really look horrendous at this point with the dark paneling still showing through.) Next, apply two or three coats of good-quality, light-colored interior house paint. The effect is wonderful; it looks like wainscoting. You can even stencil over the finished product. It's a great facelift for a room darkened by paneling.

If you are restoring or rehabilitating a home that is more than seventy-five years old and not insulated, it's almost always best to remove the plaster. Don't try to save plaster that is so old. It's like a child insisting on saving last winter's snowballs in the freezer.

 If you do replaster and want an early primitive look, don't call in a professional. Do it yourself, just like the early Americans. In early homes, the decorative woodwork was done after all the basic woodwork was installed. Thus, you can remove and replace the plaster without touching the woodwork.

> Allan Smith, Historic Smithton Inn,
> Ephrata, Pennsylvania

There was a plastic, accordion door on one of the closets. It was old and ugly. We replaced it with a machine-made quilt—stuffed with a sturdy mattress pad—and used the original hardware (door frame).

> Carriere-Zito Family, Mill Brook
> B&B, Brownsville, Vermont

Keep old trim from windows and doors. We have had many occasions where we needed a piece that was no longer made.

> Bonnie and Bill Webb, Inn on
> Golden Pond, Holderness, New
> Hampshire

I (Fran) am really proud of a door I designed and built for an odd-shaped doorway. I used 6-foot-long boards of 1-by-4-inch tongue-and-groove pine. I sawed them to match evenly and held them together with 1-by-2.5-foot boards in the shape of a Z. Black, wrought-iron hardware accents the rustic door.

> Fran and Frank Sullivan, Wild Rose
> of York, York, Maine

There were no windows or air vents in our spacious fourth-floor attic. Summer heat used to build up, affecting the rooms on the third floor. Passive roof vents were our solution. We had a 22-

inch air-intake vent installed in the ceiling and a motorized, temperature-controlled vent put in near the roofline in the other end of the attic. We had to go this route, as our roof is very steep. The normal soffit air intakes used in modern houses were not feasible.

If your old house has attic windows, you could consider installing metal, louvered vents with screens to alleviate the heat buildup. Otherwise, consultation with a qualified ventilation specialist may be advisable.

Mariam and Charles Bechtel,
Bechtel Mansion Inn, East Berlin,
Pennsylvania

Tools and Supplies

Our inn is a reproduction of a Victorian mansion. We found that we could make all of the old-style moldings with a bell saw planer. We recommend it for all sorts of reconstruction work.

Christi and Mark Carter, Carter
House, Eureka, California

Press screws into leftover soap before screwing them into wood. They will go in easier.

Marie and Dick Brophy, Isaiah Hall
B&B, Dennis, Massachusetts

Keep all your tools sharp, and your work will be cleaner.

Korda Family, Historic Brookside
Farms, Orwell, Vermont

It may sound crazy, but if you are not a born handyman and you are framing in a small job, try 2½-inch plasterboard screws and a power screwdriver to do the job. There is much less noise (no hammering), and if you make a mistake, you can take it apart quickly.

Cathy and Dave Eakin, Captain's
House Inn, Chatham, Massachusetts

A rule of thumb for newly stripped, unvarnished wood is to oil with furniture oil: once a day for a week; once a week for a month;

once a month for a year; every year thereafter. This helps bring up the patina.

Corky and Steve Garboski, Province
Inn, Strafford, New Hampshire

To repair wood that is decayed or rotted, use auto-body plastic. But first the wood must be completely dry, and all the soft decay must be removed.

Allan Smith, Historic Smithton Inn,
Ephrata, Pennsylvania

Ceilings

The ceilings of many old houses (pre–1940s) were painted with calcimine, a kind of whitewash. Ceiling paint applied over calcimine will perpetually peel. Check first by washing a patch with hot water and Spic and Span. If a white residue washes off, it is likely calcimine. Wash thoroughly and reapply calcimine.

Marjorie and John Pratt, Inn on
Cove Hill, Rockport, Massachusetts

Floors

Almost every guest comments on our floors. We have some floors that are very high gloss and shine like glass in the sunlight. Here's how to bring your floors back to life:

Sand them with a rented commercial sander. Follow with a vacuum. Use a tack cloth to remove anything missed by the vacuum. (The tack cloth, available at hardware stores, will remove any excess dust particles or dirt.) The cleaner the floor, the better the end result. Next, use a high-quality polyurethane and the thinner that goes with it. The first and second coats should be about 80 percent thinner and 20 percent polyurethane. The third coat should be fifty-fifty, and the next about twenty-five-seventy-five. Follow this with two coats of full strength polyurethane. The first coats really get down into the wood, and the next coats build up body. If you have heavy traffic, refinish the floors every spring and fall. One sheet of fine, 180-grit sandpaper stapled around a sponge mop makes a great sander to scratch the top coat so the new polyurethane will adhere.

> Rosemary and Ed McDowell, Tulip
> Tree Inn, Chittenden, Vermont

Sand floors only until the old finish has just been removed. Sanding until blond will remove patina and the antiquity that is so becoming to an old house.

> Marjorie and John Pratt, Inn on
> Cove Hill, Rockport, Massachusetts

Bathroom Restoration and Renovation

When redoing an old house, put in all new plumbing fixtures. Don't try to save money by reusing old ones that will break down and cost more later. Be sure to put in circulating hot-water lines for instant hot water upstairs.

> Nancy Donaldson, Old Yacht Club
> Inn, Santa Barbara, California

Old pipes are hard to hide in a bathroom. We built boxes around them, and then we wallpapered them so the boxes flowed with the rest of the room.

> Bonnie and Bill Webb, Inn on
> Golden Pond, Holderness, New
> Hampshire

When restoring or remodeling a bath, you might want to consider installing heated towel bars. Such luxuries are not uncommon in European hotels. Our towel-bar units are from England. On a chilly morning, toasty-warm towels make an exit from the shower or tub more satisfying.

> Marge and Cal Gage, Thatcher Hill
> Inn, Marlborough, New Hampshire

A renovation project at our inn involved moving the lavatory vanities out of all of our private baths and into the bedrooms to give the effect of old-fashioned washbasins. The practical reason for this change was to prevent the steam from a husband's shower from becoming a problem for the wife putting on makeup or doing her hair.

Mary Ann and Michael Pitchford,
Green Tree Inn, Elsah, Illinois

Author's Tip: Many private homeowners are doing this same thing, mainly to make a small master bathroom larger, provided there is adequate space in the bedroom.

If you move the bathroom into the room itself, it is likely not to have any walls. Here's where a dressing screen comes in handy to hide the commode, sink, and even the claw-foot tub.

Never paint latex over oil paint in a bathroom. It will only peel off in a matter of months if it is a much-used bathroom. If your surface was previously painted with an oil paint, you will need to sand the surface to ensure that the new coats of paint will adhere.

Joan and Sal Chandon, Doubleday
Inn, Gettysburg, Pennsylvania

For privacy and quiet, use foam board-insulation materials even in the bathrooms.

Fran and Frank Sullivan, Wild Rose
of York, York, Maine

We've found that putting cedar paneling on small bathroom ceilings eliminates mildew problems. Also, water-resistant dry-wall in our bathrooms, together with oil-based paints, works well. We've found that wallpaper peels away too easily.

Bev Davis and Rick Litchfield,
Captain Lord Mansion,
Kennebunkport, Maine

We added some bathrooms in the Victorian style. The outside of one of the claw-foot tubs was in bad shape, so we merely painted it the same color as the accent color above the picture molding.

Many Victorian bathrooms had wainscoting made of Lincrusta Walton—a linoleumlike product that looked like leather. To duplicate the look, we ordered white embossed wallpaper in a Victorian pattern from the *Renovator's Supply* catalog, put it on the lower half of the bathroom wall, and put on two coats of brown Kiwi shoe polish. We then varnished over the polish. It looks just like Lincrusta. But be careful. Shoe polish, like paint and yarn, comes in dye lots. Be sure you buy cans of the same dye lot.

> Planaria Price and Murray Burns,
> Eastlake Inn, Los Angeles,
> California

Guests used to comment on our food. Well, although the food here is just as notable as always, guests are commenting instead about our commodes. Since water is becoming a finite resource in these parts, we have turned to water-saving toilets. They are Swiss imports that use only one gallon—compared to five gallons—per flush. They have been used in Europe for years. Guests think they're attractive. We do too, but we ┌ ticularly like doing our part to conserve water.

> Jean and Dud Hendrick, Pilgrim's
> Inn, Deer Isle, Maine

When retrofitting rooms for baths and showers, try using large, clear blocks of glass brick for the walls, particularly for showers. That way it will not be so obvious that you have not matched the original moldings and paint. Furthermore, the openness of glass block eliminates some of the claustrophobia normally inherent in making the room smaller.

> Charles A. Hillestad, Queen Anne
> Inn, Denver, Colorado

 # Kitchen Renovation

Flatware for hardware? That's just one of the many interesting interior details at the inn. Knives, forks, and spoons are nailed to drawers instead of pulls. This clever application works equally well on an old, restored buffet or even on kitchen cabinets.

> Beth and Franz Schober, Hopkins
> Inn, New Preston, Connecticut

In a very small kitchen with limited counter space, we knocked through a wall with enough space behind it to put in cabinets. Between the upper and lower cabinets, we added two 24-inch by 4-foot cutting boards that roll out of the wall and make more than ample preparation space. When not in use, they push back into the wall and are covered by hinged cabinet doors, which give the entire wall a finished look.

> Louise, Pat, and Bumpy Walter,
> Grant Corner Inn, Santa Fe, New
> Mexico

Often, old cupboard doors won't stay closed. Place a thumbtack on the bottom of the door frame and raise or lower the tack to make a snug fit.

> Mary Louise and Conley Weaver,
> Red Castle Inn, Nevada City,
> California

Punched-tin cabinets now highlight our kitchen. We had the frames of the cabinets custom made. Then Gene designed the pattern, which he punched onto sheets of tin he had sized to fit into the frames. After Gene had punched in the design, he heated the surface. This gave it a coppery finish.

You will discover after you've completed this project that, while it looks complicated, it is a relatively simple process. Gene became interested in punched tin after seeing a demonstration at Old Sturbridge Village in Sturbridge, Massachusetts, many years ago. As an antiques dealer, Gene saw a variety of punched-tin patterns on pie safes. Punched tin is a true folk-art form. But it was most important for its utilitarian purposes. In the case of pie safes, punched tin allowed food to receive ventilation and kept flies away; in a lantern, it let light filter out.

To make your own punched-tin cabinets, you will need to find a design pattern. Look in books on antiques and punched tin and in quilting books. Also try crafts stores. Another option is to design your own pattern.

SUPPLIES:
> 28-gauge sheet steel (at sheet-metal shops)
> Paper patterns
> Rubber cement

Maple or hard pine wood for punching on
Center punches of various sizes, sharpened
Nail sets sharpened to a point
Cold chisels, various sizes, sharpened to a
    point
Hammer
T square
30-, 40-, 60-degree angles
Compass
Artist's sketch pad
No. 2 pencils

Door frames are made just like a picture frame with a recess in the back to accommodate the panel. Shear the metal to size, allowing ½ inch for fitting into the rabbet (the recess in the back of the door panel). Each panel requires a separate pattern. So when you have the pattern laid out to your satisfaction, have it photocopied until you have a copy for each panel.

Use rubber cement to affix pattern to the metal. Then nail the tin to the piece of wood through several of the holes in the pattern where there will eventually be holes in the metal anyway. Start punching.

Remove and straighten panel by flexing carefully. Heat the panel with a torch, and you will get a mixed coloration of straw, darker browns, and blues.

DO'S AND DONT'S:
• Lay out the pattern accurately and clearly for every punch point.
• Use rubber cement, an adhesive that rubs off.
• Do not use the wood backing block too many times without resurfacing, or it won't support the punching process.
• Make sure you have punched all the points before removing the pattern.
• Rub the finished panel with vegetable oil. This will enhance the look and act as a rust preservative. Do this twice a year to prevent rust.
• Lights can be mounted behind the panels to highlight the pattern.

Helen and Gene Kirby, Horatio
Johnson House, Belfast, Maine

 # House Exterior

When we bought the house, there was a deck over the front porch. A neighbor showed us a much older photo of the house when it had a porch. We decided to restore the porch, but we didn't put enough roofing compound down. When the project was finished, the roof leaked during a storm. My advice is to be generous with roofing compound when redoing any roof on an old house.

> Diana Kopulos and David Garrett,
> Annie Moore's Guest House,
> Laramie, Wyoming

Maintaining the exterior of any building situated close to salt water is a never-ending battle. We are sailors from way back and have successfully brought ashore some boat-maintenance techniques to apply to the exterior of homes. Here are a few:

Marine bedding compound is used in assembling any joints on porch railings here. This excludes water and prevents rot in the wood.

Yacht paint on porch decks and screen doors resists the attacks of sun and water much better than conventional house paints. The added life of marine paint makes up for its difference in price.

> Harriette and David L. Lusty,
> Dockside Guest Quarters, York,
> Maine

To remove mildew from the siding of an old home, make a solution of one cup bleach to one gallon of water. Brush it on and wipe the mildew away.

> Ellen and Paul Morissette,
> Kenniston Hill Inn, Boothbay,
> Maine

Our afternoon sun can be rather intense in the summer, and arriving guests walk along a 45-foot-long veranda on the west side of the inn. To offer shade and a leafy effect, we train hop vines on wires climbing up two stories to create a marvelous natural screen. Additional sun screens are provided all year by white canvas hung like a curtain and tied back with red-canvas tiebacks attached to the supporting columns along the veranda.

Mary Louise and Conley Weaver,
Red Castle Inn, Nevada City,
California

We reconstructed a wraparound porch at the inn, and although we have French doors and many windows, the porch blocked out a considerable amount of light inside the house. A guest suggested installing skylights on the porch roof. It worked, letting in nearly the same amount of light the porch had blocked out.

Lynda and Joe Petty, Park House,
Saugatuck, Michigan

Decorating and You

Innkeepers Show How Personal Style Really Works

You don't need a degree in interior design to coax your home into the retreat of your dreams. You don't even need a lot of money. All that is required is imagination and confidence, plus a passion for your tastes. In short, you need to recognize and identify your own personal style and then let it work for you. This means you don't follow fads in decorating. Nothing is in or out, and everything is chosen and placed according to the way you like it. The thousands of inns across the country have shown how individual taste is a design statement in and of itself. By taking cues from the innkeepers, you'll see how fast you'll begin to develop your own exciting ideas and make your dream home a reality.

While personal style offers the freedom of creativity, there are still some basic decorating rules you should follow. The most important one is to commit yourself to decorating your rooms fully. Put whatever you want in the room, but be sure to pull the room together and complete it. A new bedspread with your old curtains—that you don't even care for anymore—won't complete the effect. Outfit the room entirely, right down to careful decisions on accent pieces. Compare the process to buying clothes for yourself. My mother always taught me: "You'll be sorry if you buy the pants without the blouse. If you do, you may wear the pants with something less than complementary." Every time I didn't listen, I dreaded the purchase, and oh, what a waste of hard-earned baby-sitting money. Her golden rule of fashion buying applies to decorating a room. Don't make one move without the other. Placing a straw basket in the kitchen, for example, is not enough to create the country look. You've got to go all the way and make the most of the money you do invest in decorating.

When planning your room, no matter what the decor, it helps to visualize each section of the room as a separate vignette. Create scenes or pictures with furniture groups and accessories. This helps pull the room together yet give it individual points of focus and interest.

There are many decorating shortcuts that can make the process easier on the pocketbook. Try to use what you have and add to it. But if certain pieces no longer work for you, don't be afraid to sell them and put the cash toward something new or bargains found at garage sales and secondhand shops.

The architectural style of your house should not affect your decorating. For example, if you have a contemporary structure but love country, work toward ways of coaxing that look inside. Maybe you can add hewn beams and a cozy fireplace, country wallpaper and Early American colors throughout. Fill the house with antiques. You don't have to have a historic or old home to have the warm look of country.

Innkeepers are becoming known as creators of great decorating themes for individual rooms. They give a room atmosphere by establishing a central motif. This is a good way of approaching decorating that will help you if you are not as easily prone to making decorating decisions. Innkeepers give their motifs the crowning touch by naming their rooms.

In our own home, taking a cue from the innkeepers, my husband and I accented our guest room with two framed reproductions of paintings by one of our favorite American artists— Grandma Moses. My husband is an art-history buff and I am an art admirer, so the theme reflects our interests. We added cheerful country wallpaper, an old buggy bench for seating, and a large book about Grandma Moses on the nightstand, and we then christened the room by hanging a real painter's palette on the door. We call it our Grandma Moses Room and have painted that name on the palette.

Our master bedroom is done in Shaker decor, so we named this room the Shaker Sweet. My office was easy enough to name. We call it the Author's Alcove and plan to hang an open wooden book on the door with the name of the office on the front cover.

Innkeepers have many tips for making a home look as though

it was taken from a history book or a magazine cover. But at the same time, their rooms say, "Come inside and make yourself at home." This seems like the right blend for any home. Their decorating ideas and philosophies will fuel your own imagination and build your passion for your own personal style.

 ## Decorating Basics

First, regard the whole prospect with enthusiasm. While the details can seem daunting at first, it is one of the most creative things you can do in your home and one of the most satisfying.

Start your planning by considering the uses of each area you are decorating. Consider that you will need to take different approaches in your planning. Kitchen and dining rooms need to be functional yet give off an energetic decor, while bedrooms must be restful.

Don't be afraid to mix decor with caution. Be eclectic, if you wish. A good rule to follow is that when you are mixing period furnishings and those from different countries, touch on each period or country in each room so that you maintain harmony throughout.

Here are a few quick, basic rules:

Don't skimp. Cheap fabrics wear out fast.

Always line curtains, as they hang better and last longer. The lining takes the brunt of the sunlight.

Lamps are the jewels of a room. Choose them carefully, making sure that their size is appropriate.

> Penny and Michael Schmitt, Inn on
> the Common, Craftsbury Common,
> Vermont

Make a scrapbook when you do any decorating. In it, keep swatches of wallpaper, fabrics, paint chips, and other pertinent information, such as what book the wallpaper came from and the design number. This is a useful resource later when you need to identify fabric and other textures for replacement and redecorating.

Linda and Rob Castagna, Chestnut
Hill on the Delaware, Milford, New
Jersey

When decorating a room, keep in mind the goal to make it a warm environment. You do this with colors, fabrics, and accent pieces. Candles in the room, for example, create a soft and romantic feeling.

I give workshops on stress management; in them, I talk about the importance of our environment. Today, we need our own comfortable nurturing spot to retreat to. Your house or apartment needs to be your home for the mind and spirit as well as for the body. Don't let your life-style or financial situation be an issue in making a home. Remember to make it a place that suits your personality, allowing yourself to use your senses (of color, shape, texture, and aroma) as directional signals. These components will help you and your family and friends relax. Home is where the heart is, and that heart is you!

Ujjala Schwartz, Ujjala's B&B, New
Paltz, New York

Consider what's outside your window when you plan your decorating. Bring the outside in, if you like the view. For example, we have a weathered barn outside our living room. Therefore, we decided not to hang curtains and to work with the barn's shades of brown and all the greenery from the outside in decorating the inside. We selected a light beige for the walls and upholstered pieces, and a small red oriental carpet.

Karen and Manfred Wolf, White
Goose Inn, Orford, New
Hampshire

Avoid trendy colors when decorating, or you'll find yourself having to redecorate every year.

For paint colors, off-white is much more pleasing than white, especially in a four-season climate.

Marjorie and John Pratt, Inn on
Cove Hill, Rockport, Massachusetts

My (Joan's) only advice on decorating is to keep your rooms cheerful. Avoid depressing, dark colors, even if they are authentic. Generally, if your room's windows face north, decorate in light, airy colors. If they face east or west, beware of any fabrics or rugs that may fade from direct sun. But should your room's windows face south, let your imagination run wild.

> Joan and Sal Chandon, Doubleday
> Inn, Gettysburg, Pennsylvania

When decorating, don't overlook catalogs for ideas as well as for goods, including linens, curtains, and accessories. Our curtains, mostly lace, draw rave reviews from guests, who love their old world charm. Although they look like they were bought in Europe, they actually came from an American department-store catalog. With catalogs, you can shop at your leisure, and, most of the time, you can depend on the merchandise to be delivered to your door in a matter of days.

> Denise Anderson and David
> Karpinski, Quill and Quilt, Cannon
> Falls, Minnesota

We hired someone to decorate our inn. She was a free-lance decorator, rather than one with a company. We liked that, as she was not bound to push any particular products. The key to selecting a decorator is to see how well that person picks up on what you like. Also, you have to be willing to put in your own sweat equity. Visit furniture shops and shop for fabrics with the decorator.

> Marni and Bill Graham, Graham's
> B&B, Sedona, Arizona

When you like old things, you may collect a lot and want it all on display. At the same time, you don't want clutter or an impossible dusting job. The solution is to change your accent pieces every now and then. Display others and store the rest. This makes your home more interesting.

> Kris McIlvenna, Greenbriar, Coeur
> d'Alene, Idaho

Theme Decorating

Decorating can be fun when you take a situation and work to complement it. Look at a room closely, and think about what will suit it best. Each room is an individual. For example, we have a dormer in one room that resembles a sharply angled pup tent. A theme for the room suddenly emerged. The window is at the end of the room, so I designed curtains to look like the tent flap was open on both sides. I chose burlap material and a muslin lining. The window overlooks a creek, which adds to the campfire theme. I named the room the Nevada Suite. Kerosene-style, electric lanterns—similar to those used in tents—hang from a ceiling beam. Room accents include a western wallpaper border, a large cactus, and colorful, striped rugs and blanket.

Susan Hannah, Winters Creek
Ranch, Carson City, Nevada

Develop an overall motif when decorating a room, a theme that suits you as an individual. Build on your interest. Is it sailing? Have a nautical corner. Our interest is antiques appropriate to gardening and old barns. Our B&B was built from an old barn, so we collect old gardening implements. Choose things that have meaning to you, and your house will develop a sense of place, a certain effect that no decorator can achieve for you.

Kate Kerivan, Bungay Jar, Easton,
New Hampshire

Choosing a theme helps your decorating scheme. Included in our theme are hearts. We use them quite a bit but feel we have the right balance. We carry the theme right down to the heart-shaped butter mints we make and heart-shaped flower beds out front.

Adella and Bob Schulz, Sweet
Adeline's, Salida, Colorado

Before we opened the inn, we decided that each guest room would have a theme based on one of our collections. One room holds our nautical objects, including seafaring paintings as well as old lobster traps, which we use as luggage racks.

Bill comes from a musical family, so he had collected a lot of old instruments. In our Music Room, we have an old organ and an old violin that we made into a lamp.

Since train collecting and collecting old bottles are hobbies of ours, we decorated two rooms in those motifs.

Judy and Bill Wolfe, Birchwood
Inn, Temple, New Hampshire

Each of my guest rooms reflects a different kind of turn-of-the-century travel. In the Airplane Room, I used an antique propeller above the bed instead of a headboard. The bathroom-mirror frame in the Steamship Room is a brass porthole. A chair in the Buggy Room is an antique buggy seat, and old hubcaps are above the bed in the Automobile Room.

Robin Brooks, Robins Nest, San
Andreas, California

Each of our rooms is named after one of the ships built by Nathaniel Lord, the builder of the mansion. Bev did counted cross-stitch and embroidered name plaques for each room's door.

Bev Davis and Rick Litchfield,
Captain Lord's Mansion,
Kennebunkport, Maine

A room is not the only thing a homeowner can name. Give your house a name. Our house had a name before we opened the inn. We built our home, and one day, as the framing went up, we noticed that it was surrounded by cedar trees. Cedarym (using the Old English spelling) became the name of our house. Naturally, we kept the name when we opened the inn. Naming your home will only make it more special. You don't need an inn to do that. The name can be used on your stationery, your front door, or your mailbox. We know some homeowners who have tasteful hand-crafted signs placed by their walkway.

Mary Ellen and Walt Brown,
Cedarym B&B, Redmond,
Washington

I (Linda) wanted to create a warm Victorian look in our inn. Immediately, the color red for wallpaper came to mind for our drawing room. Now, choosing red is risky, you might say. I went to the wallpaper store and brought back samples. (Never select wallpaper without bringing a sample home.) It appeared that the red would work, indeed, as it picked up on the rug. Bold prints are a trademark of Victorian decor, and you can't be afraid of them. They are toned down with lots of lacy accents, printed bandboxes, and Victorian antiques.

We added Victorian finger lamps that burn oil for our dining-room tables, instead of candles. This coaxed the nineteenth-century look. Cotton-and-lace sheets also will give you a very Victorian romantic feel. The key is to not listen to anyone who tells you that you're doing the wrong thing, just because it sounds unusual. Not everyone will like what you do, but at least you'll do it your way.

> Linda and Peter LaRose, Inn at
> Thorn Hill, Jackson Village, New
> Hampshire

Keep the Decor Consistent

We try to keep everything within the time frame of 1908 or before. When you decorate your home, stick to the same decor throughout, or at least don't mix and match within the same room. Of course, there is a certain amount of mixing that can be done. An eclectic blend of modern and antique pieces can work if you can strike the right balance. However, not all mixtures work. Georgian and country get confusing, for example.

> Eva Mae and Frank Musgrave,
> Edge of Thyme, Candor, New York

Never be timid when using color, and never worry about what anyone else will think of your ideas. Be true to your tastes, and you'll find a consistency throughout your home. Follow your instincts, and you will surprise yourself at the continuity your ideas will present. The only time you fail at home decorating is when you begin to worry if others will like it!

> Marilyn Coughlin, Hutchinson
> House, Faribault, Minnesota

Be sure to retain the integrity of the architecture and decor of your home. Modern conveniences can be hidden. For example, when we needed a bit of refrigerator space in the dining room, we found a new, small refrigerator that resembles a 100-year-old safe.

Demay and Jim Pringle, Pringle
House, Oakland, Oregon

To complement the history of our inn, which was built in 1814, we keep furnishings simple and serve food appropriate to the period. Herbs hang from the kitchen ceiling and over the fireplace, which we have adorned with hearth-cooking gear.

Betty Lee Maxcy, Covered Bridge
Inn, Ephrata, Pennsylvania

 ## Painting

At the Shire Inn, we start repainting a room by consulting the shelter (decorating) magazines for the lovely photographs they provide. But we apply only those things that we think will work in our own home. A lot depends on the situation and lighting of a room, which may make it impossible to apply an idea you see in a magazine.

We begin by developing a scheme for the entire room. We ask, "Is it a dark room that needs some life, or do the windows provide southern exposure, allowing for darker colors?" Our color palette starts to form. Decisions where to paint and whether to use any wallpaper will be made. Note: Don't match wallpaper to paint. Match paint to desired paper.

Be consistent with the paint. Don't leave a touch of white on the windowsill if there is no other white in the room, for example. Work with three, possibly four, colors matched to the paper—two accent colors and one or two neutrals.

We recently finished our Orleans Room. (All guest rooms are named after counties in Vermont.) It has a 150-year-old rope bed, two large windows with southern exposure, and excellent views of the first branch of the White River. Since the room receives effulgent sun, we decided to go darker, with richer-toned colors.

Mary Lee chose a nondescript wallpaper with green, pink, and a dash of pale yellow in it. The color palette for paint was adopted—green and pink and our neutrals, ivory and yellow.

The ceiling trim and baseboard were painted green. This acted as a nice encasement, framing the paper. Since only half the room was being papered, we decided not to lean too heavily on the dark side, and we agreed a solid pink would not look well. We went with the yellow. Ceiling, doors, and window frames were painted ivory.

Now, where to use the pink? There was a spot between the window moldings and the windows themselves that needed paint. This accent color amounted to only 2½ inches of space, but it certainly made the entire room pop out at you. The point we're trying to stress is that by being consistent, we were able to create a designer look. You can too.

Mary Lee and James Papa, Shire
Inn, Chelsea, Vermont

As a reminder, old houses have lead paint, and removing it from walls and such can be very dangerous to one's health. Seek professional advice.

Barbara and Carl Beehner, Steele
Homestead Inn, Antrim, New
Hampshire

The combination of simulated whitewash on the walls and re-production colors on the woodwork is an unbeatable look. Simulated whitewash hides a wealth of evils.

Mimi and Jim Agard, Brafferton
Inn, Gettysburg, Pennsylvania

We keep a handy jam jar filled with the paint that we used on our woodwork. When we need to do touchups, we don't have to rack our brain, trying to remember which paint we used or where we put it. Also, we don't have to drag out the big paint cans for a little touchup.

Linda and Rob Castagna, Chestnut
Hill on the Delaware, Milford, New
Jersey

Keep a directory listing all the paints and colors (including the serial number) that you used in decorating. When it comes time to touch up, you can match the exact paint and wallpaper you've used in each room.

> Cathy and Dave Eakin, Captain's
> House Inn, Chatham, Massachusetts

To remove paint from old brass hardware, soak in Lysol toilet-bowl cleaner.

Crud and paint on cast-iron can be removed by taking it to a machine shop where machinists will have it bead-blasted.

> Robin Brooks, Robins Nest, San
> Andreas, California

For low paint maintenance, use a high-gloss paint on all surfaces so that dirt wipes off easily. However, if you prefer the richer tone of flat latex, here's a compromise: Use high gloss on the moldings, doors, and window frames and flat paint on the main wall surfaces and ceilings.

> Charles A. Hillestad, Queen Anne
> Inn, Denver, Colorado

 # Wallcoverings

We use wallpaper everywhere, because it gives rooms individual personalities.

A wallpaper border can be placed a little more than halfway down the wall to act as a chair rail.

When decorating a bedroom, select your bedspread first and decorate around it. If you choose curtains or wallpaper first, it can be a real problem to find an attractive bedspread.

> Bonnie and Bill Webb, Inn on
> Golden Pond, Holderness, New
> Hampshire

Consider covering with wallpaper any steam pipes running up
the walls in rooms. It's a nice effect.

Mary Lee and James Papa, Shire
Inn, Chelsea, Vermont

Author's Tip: Use a room's wallpaper or a coordinated one to make
book covers for old books whose covers are badly worn. Stacked
unevenly on a bookcase, blanket chest or dresser, they make an
interesting accent. Don't actually paste the wallpaper onto the
book. Just fold and tape it.

Decorative wallpaper borders can simulate a headboard for a
bed. Simply adhere the border to the wall, above the bed, and
between the two posts of the bed.

Kay Easton, activity director,
Middlebury Inn, Middlebury,
Vermont

To remove wallpaper, prepare a fifty-fifty solution of water and
vinegar. Apply it with a sponge. As the paper loosens, peel it off
the wall.

Sunny and Joy Drewel, Zachariah
Foss Guest House, Washington,
Missouri

We've covered some of our walls with burlap for a rustic appearance. Buy the burlap by the yard. Cut it to fit the wall, and staple
it in the corners.

Lynda and Joe Petty, Park House,
Saugatuck, Michigan

Fabric can be used in the same way wallpaper border is used. Cut
the fabric to the desired width. Use wallpaper paste to adhere the
fabric to the wall. Cover it with polyurethane. Paste a lace border
along the upper and lower edges.

Daisy Morden, Victorian House, St.
Augustine, Florida

In old houses, you often find wallpaper over very old plaster,
even on the ceilings. I call it structural wallpaper, and I usually

leave it intact. Removing it means a major patching job, and it simply doesn't seem worth the trouble.

Mimi and Jim Agard, Brafferton Inn, Gettysburg, Pennsylvania

Directly after stripping wallpaper off old, dry, and crumbling plaster walls, roll on a coat of oil-base primer paint. This stabilizes the old plaster; it binds it together, prevents further crumbling, and greatly reduces the dust and mess created by further repair work.

Harriette and David L. Lusty, Dockside Guest Quarters, York, Maine

 # Stenciling

Almost anyone can stencil. The secret is to work with a very dry brush. You get that by patting the wet brush on a paper towel or an absorbent paper plate.

Sunny and Joy Drewel, Zachariah Foss Guest House, Washington, Missouri

Author's Tip: The art of stenciling proliferated in the 1800s when decorating walls with wallpaper became desirable in Europe but too expensive to do in America. Itinerant artists, such as Moses Eaton, Jr., traveled to homes in New England, looking for work. Today, we tend to think of the art as only fitting in homes decorated in country, colonial, Federal, and such. But nowadays, stencils are also made for contemporary decor and eclectic looks.

It's important to establish your placement when stenciling a room. You don't want to end up by the window frame, for example, with half of one element of the pattern. Grid it all out with a pencil or chalk by placing dots where the pattern falls. When you place the stencil on the wall, I find masking tape works well to hold it in place. But rub the tape over your clothes so that it doesn't stick too well and peel the paint off your wall. You can start to stencil on the outside of the pattern and go lighter toward the middle for a shading effect.

Daisy Morden, Victorian House, St. Augustine, Florida

One of the ways we create an authentic look is through stenciling. I (Jim) have a special way of stenciling. Since the house is 200 years old, I don't want the stencils to look as if they were put on yesterday. I apply them very unevenly and with a very light, delicate hand. I even leave out parts. Sure enough, they look 200 years old.

Here's how: I use a standard, flat-tipped, round brush and acrylic paint. I tap out my brush, thereby removing excess paint and distributing the paint evenly on the bristles. I apply just a breath of color, missing some areas purposely—sometimes leaving out an edge, other times a tip of a leaf, and then the center part of the leaf in another section.

Sign your stenciling and date it with lettering in matching paint, either freehand or with a stencil.

Jim and Mimi Agard, Brafferton Inn, Gettysburg, Pennsylvania

Stenciling our bathroom walls became our decorating solution when, year after year, many of our old walls rejected new wallpaper. The result of stenciling a wall is immediate, the effort minimal, and it is one sure way to create a soft country look inexpensively. In addition, the variation of wall stencil patterns and modes today is endless.

Amy Donohoe, manager, Barley Sheaf Farm, Holicong, Pennsylvania

Stenciling can also be done on the outside of some bathtubs. Our claw-foot tub was in bad shape, so we painted it, and then a friend stenciled over the paint. A nonglossy protective paint sealer was sprayed over the stencilings.

Tommie and Andy Duncan, Arcady Down East, Blue Hill, Maine

Try using a smaller stencil or parts of a large one to decorate just the window and door moldings in a room. Stencil directly onto the molding, either just around the corners or the entire frame.

Cindi and Alan Ehrgott, Coloma
Country Inn, Coloma, California

If you stencil around a room, extend the design to another part of the room—in the closet, onto a piece of furniture, a lamp shade, or even a wastebasket. You'll find that once you start stenciling, you'll want to keep on going.

Diane and Al Johnson, Nauset
House, East Orleans, Massachusetts

Colorful stenciling on ordinary vinyl window shades is an inexpensive way to add a bit of color-coordinated zest to any room and make the shades more attractive.

Denise Anderson and David
Karpinski, Quill and Quilt, Cannon
Falls, Minnesota

Stenciling on Fabric

You can stencil on almost any fabric. Muslin is a popular choice, but I do most of my stenciling on solid-colored chintz. You need to use specially made paint that is for washable items. It's easier to stencil on fabric, because you don't have to get into odd positions as you do when stenciling walls. The trick is to keep the fabric taut. I lay my fabric out on a long table and work with a different brush for each color. It goes faster that way.

Gail Istler, Locust Hill, Morrow,
Ohio

A beautifully coordinated room can be created with a few yards of muslin, some stencil paint and brushes, and a little effort. For one of our rooms, we made a stencil of the flower design in the wallpaper. I (Annie) stenciled the design along the bottom edge of a muslin dust ruffle, along the edge of an opposite painted wall, on the ruffles of the curtains, and along the bottom of the window shade.

To stencil on the muslin, I put a few layers of newspaper under the fabric and hold the fabric down with masking tape. Hold the stencil in place on the fabric with masking tape. Then begin to stencil. The paint dries quickly, so you can move the stencil to the next area and just keep going.

Annie and Al Unrein, Glacier Bay
Country Inn, Gustavus, Alaska

Stenciling Floors

After the floor has been painted (see page 219 on how to paint floors), you block off the areas you want to stencil with masking tape. We did a diamond pattern in our long front hallway, making the design first with the tape. With a brush, we painted half the diamond areas in red and the other in white. When they were completely dry, we stenciled a maple leaf in the center of each diamond in a yellow-ocher color.

John made the maple-leaf stencil from a real leaf that he had pressed dry for a pattern. Before sealing the floor, we waited for six months so that it appeared worn. We then sealed it with three coats of polyurethane.

Betha and John Mueller, Wisconsin
House, Hazel Green, Wisconsin

You can also stencil a pattern directly over stained hardwood floors. Clean the floors thoroughly and stencil with bright colors so they will show over the stain. Acrylic paints are good to use, as you can wipe them off quickly if you make a mistake. When dry, apply a couple of coats of polyurethane.

To stencil stair risers, paint the risers. Let dry and then stencil. Coat with polyurethane.

Lois and Roy Jackson, Churchill
House, Brandon, Vermont

Stenciling a Rug

One bedroom has a stenciled floor. I made a matching hooked rug, picking up the pattern from the stencil. I transferred the stenciled border around the floor to a hooked-rug backing. When it was finished, I had a matching area rug. (I have also used fabrics such as burlap to stencil and then make into a rug.)

Daisy Morden, Victorian House, St. Augustine, Florida

Cutting Your Own Stencil

Not all stencils are precut. Sometimes, you have to cut out the designs as you would if you had created your own stencil. There are electric cutters you can buy for stencils. But I use a sharp cutting knife, as I like the control it gives me. I make stencils from anything. You don't have to use Mylar, the clear plastic often found in kits. More than once, I've awakened late at night, feeling the need to make up a stencil. I've scavenged for material to make the stencil. Once I used the plastic from a school notebook! Draw your pattern with a marker, and cut it out by taping it to a wooden cutting board. Run your cutter along the pattern.

Daisy Morden, Victorian House, St. Augustine, Florida

I (Jackie) design my own stencils and cut them from exposed X-ray film.

Jackie and Lee Morrison, Laurel Hill Plantation, McClellanville, South Carolina

Stencil Preservation

If you happen to discover hidden stenciling in an old house you are restoring, don't attempt to take on that portion of the restoration without some professional advice. We were fortunate to have a ninety-two-year-old woman in our neighborhood who is a stenciling authority. She restored the stenciling but left a portion as is to show what it looked like before.

Gretchen Schmidt, Dorset Inn, Dorset, Vermont

Window Treatments

I have twenty-seven windows with crisscrossed Priscilla curtains. On each window, the tieback is tacked down with nails that have wide enough heads to hold a magnet. I use decorative and whimsical magnets, such as flowers and miniature houses. This gives the curtains a special look and provides something to do with your magnet collection, in addition to scattering it about the refrigerator.

Glue lace edging to the bottom of window shades for a softer look.

> Rosemary Kip, Widow Kip's, Mt.
> Jackson, Virginia

Author's Tips: Dress up window shades with matching slipcovers or bedspread fabric, which you can have laminated to the shades.

Small grapevine wreaths make great tiebacks. So do dried flowers made into a ring.

We made some of my favorite window curtain treatments with lace ordered from the bridal-veil section of sewing shops.

> Mary and Gary Riley, Williams
> House, Hot Springs, Arkansas

My philosophy concerning window decor is this: I dressed many children, but never a window!

> Freda B. Houpt, Amos A. Parker
> House, Fitzwilliam, New Hampshire

Decorative fans—as large as the ones used as fireplace screens and done in such materials as fabric, brass, and heavy paper— make attractive decorations in front of a window. Placed on the ledge, they even provide added privacy.

> Denise Anderson and David
> Karpinski, Quill and Quilt, Cannon
> Falls, Minnesota

Rub candle wax on wooden curtain poles, and curtains will slide on easily.

Mary Louise and Conley Weaver,
Red Castle Inn, Nevada City,
California

My favorite window treatment uses old chintz draperies gathered on a wooden pole with a 3-inch header and poufed to one side. Use screw-in, bull's-eye drapery holders (round brackets) to push the fabric to the side. Let the curtains down for privacy. Another nice look is to use three bull's-eyes—one on each side and one in the middle of the window. Find the antique chintz at thrift shops or garage sales.

Sandra Cartwright-Brown, Conyers
House, Sperryville, Virginia

Wide, about 1½- to 2-inch floral ribbon makes great casual curtain tiebacks. Look for the old-fashioned variety.

Elaine Schnitzer, Summerport B&B,
Schroon Lake, New York

Sheets make easy curtain treatments. Simply run a rod through the wide hem. Hang. Draw back with a lace tie, or gather and pouf the top.

Phyllis Niemi-Peacock and Bud
Peacock, Palmer House, Falmouth,
Massachusetts

Lace tablecloths can be made into curtains.

Pat Hardy, Glenborough Inn, Santa
Barbara, California

You can cover a window with something as simple as a piece of fabric folded into a triangle and hung across the top of the window, point down. This covers half the window, and you don't even need rods. Velcro attached to the window and fabric will do.

At the inn, our window treatments are also unusual. All of the Priscilla-style curtains were made from curtain lining. This gives a soft look to all the rooms and is a very inexpensive way of creating a designer look.

> Pam Stewart, manager, Little River
> Inn, Aldie, Virginia

We use old monogrammed pillowcases as coverings for the tops of French doors and old damask tablecloths for the bottom halves. These let a wonderful old mellow light into the room. Cut and sew rod pockets to size.

> Ruthmary Jordan, Pride House,
> Jefferson, Texas

Sheets can be used as lining for drapes.

> Alice-June and Franz Benjamin,
> Chateau Victorian, Santa Cruz,
> California

 ## Decorating with Sheets

We have used quality, plain white sheets to make ruffled pillow shams. They go on all the beds that have quilts. The shams are great accompaniments to the quilts and wash up so easily. Sew up the sham with the ruffles around all of its sides.

> Pam Stewart, manager, Little River
> Inn, Aldie, Virginia

When I (Robina) was actively doing interior decoration, I did some unusual things. For many of my clients, I upholstered walls inexpensively, using starched sheets as an economical and lasting substitute for wallpaper. The sheets look like wallpaper when done, and they can be scrubbed. If too much scrubbing causes the sheets to come off the wall, simply slap on a little more starch, and it will hold them again. When you get tired of the pattern, zip the sheets off, wash, and use them for something else. Then wash down your wall and paint or paper, or even re-sheet.

Here's how to starch sheets to walls:

SUPPLIES: Flat sheets (one king-size sheet will cover approximately 8½ feet of wall; Razor-type knife; Soft sponge; Liquid starch (quality brand) in pink or blue (dries clear, except blue will make white areas appear whiter); Straight edge (I use a metal yardstick); Spatula (to push fabric firmly into corners and along top and bottom edge); Drop cloths, small wet towel, staple gun, plumb line, ladder, bucket for starch.

- Be sure walls are clean and smooth. Patch cracks. Sand. If sheet has a lot of white areas, paint walls white.
- Check sheet design for match. Measure height of wall. If extra length is required to accommodate pattern match, undo hems.
- Decide where you want to start (inconspicuous corner). Starting at the top, sponge starch onto wall in an area about halfway down and 3 to 4 feet across.
- With sheet design right side up, staple sheet onto wall near corner. (Remove staples later.) Start sponging more starch over sheet, and then staple excess width of sheet to wall so that weight does not pull sheet off wall as you work. Then sponge starch over sheet to about halfway down the wall and 3 to 4 feet across. It will be taut and smooth. Trim top edge.
- Lift sheet at bottom, and starch bottom half of wall. Then starch sheet over this. If only doing one wall, trim bottom edge and side edge in corner. If doing entire room, leave untrimmed at this stage.
- Return to top. Starch wall halfway down. Remove staples and starch sheet onto wall. Staple extra width again if necessary, and continue until entire sheet is starched to wall.
- Around windows and doors: Starch walls around windows and doors. Push sheet firmly around frame with spatula. Smooth with sponge. Trim fabric and wipe window or door frame to remove excess starch.
- Joining sheets: When first sheet is finished, continue starching wall, then begin using second sheet, overlapping to match patterns. When sheet is wet with starch, pattern underneath can be seen through top sheet, so matching is easier. Using straight edge and sharp blade, make a straight cut through both layers of sheet on the wall. Peel away extra top piece, then gently lift top edge of sheet and peel away extra piece underneath. Sponge. Cut the bottom edges together.

Notes on sheets: Sheets are different than most other fabrics. Always measure and cut with a razor knife or scissors. Don't tear straight, as you do with fabric.

After your walls are finished, any bubbles can be removed by sponging on a little more starch.

Robina and Dick Conway, Almond
View Inn, Paso Robles, California

I covered a bathroom in bed sheets—the walls and even the tub. Then I had a lining of Plexiglas installed in the tub to make it practical.

In old houses, covering with fabric camouflages a multitude of flaws where the plaster is often less than perfect. Chintz is a nice choice since it has body.

A word about decorating with sheets. I have used sheets for many unusual projects. However, if sheets are not put together properly, they will not look well. They will look like sheets. Select a full-bodied design with strong colors.

Betty York, Four Chimneys,
Nantucket, Massachusetts

Sheets and a dust ruffle make pretty slipcovers for very little money.

Phyllis Niemi-Peacock and Bud
Peacock, Palmer House, Falmouth,
Massachusetts

 # Lighting

Lighting is often overlooked when decorating. Yet it is most important from a functional and aesthetic view. In general, avoid overhead lighting. Use lots of small table lamps and lights over important pictures that can double as night-lights. Consider small lights in bookcases, cupboards, and shelves. And don't forget outdoor lighting. (Washes from below are best, not floods.)

Kate Kerivan, Bungay Jar, Easton,
New Hampshire

Candlelight, exclusively in the living room, helps set the mood of our home, like a parlor in the 1800s.

David and Marie Louise Smith,
Bodine House, Muncy,
Pennsylvania

Many a guest has gone home and immediately put this one to use: Night light in dim corners at Red Castle is provided by the lacy sparkle of miniature Christmas lights inside a willow basket filled with airy, dried baby's breath and hydrangea blooms.

Lighting a favorite ficus or indoor palm tree from below creates a shadow pattern on the ceiling and is also effective as a night-light.

Mary Louise and Conley Weaver,
Red Castle Inn, Nevada City,
California

Flour-scoop sconces reflect candlelight around the room. Hang them on the wall with the handle at the bottom. Mount a candle at the inside of the base.

How about a cheese-grater lantern? Wire a light bulb to any grater, antique or new. Hang it on a wall. Soft light peers through the tiny holes. (If the grater is too new, rough it up and then tarnish it with varnish or stain.) You can get the same effect on a table by placing the grater over a candle.

Beth and Franz Schober, Hopkins
Inn, New Preston, Connecticut

You can color-coordinate a floor lamp with your decor. Try to find an old wrought-iron floor lamp; buy a glass globe and an attachment for it. Using ordinary latex paint to match paint and other trim in the room, brush two coats onto the inside of the globe.

Marilyn Coughlin, Hutchinson
House, Faribault, Minnesota

We have old gaslight fixtures in odd spots. I have covered some of them with straw hats. One bathroom came with fluorescent light fixtures on either side of a mirror. Ugly! I covered them with French-bread baskets.

Betty York, Four Chimneys,
Nantucket, Massachusetts

 ## Decorating Hints for All Rooms

Have an unwanted big door that sticks out between rooms? We happen to have four such doors in our dining room. To break up the monotony, you can drape a colorful old shawl, Mexican blanket, or any kind of bright material over the top. It's a boredom breaker, conversation maker, and room brightener all in one.

Roberta Crane and Wayne
Braffman, Tyler Hill B&B, Tyler
Hill, Pennsylvania

Don't forget to decorate behind the door. A bow wreath is hung on the back of each guest-room door. When the door is closed, it adds a special touch.

Karen and Ken West, Benner
House, Weston, Missouri

Give a flat door interest by taking wood (even picture framing) and mitering it into squares for a paneled effect. We have done this on our parlor walls underneath the chair rail. It has an authentic look.

Jane and Ed Rossig, Strawberry
Inn, New Market, Maryland

You can add laths (flat narrow strips of wood) to the ceiling. Run them lengthwise and crosswise to make 1-foot squares. Gives an antique look.

Lynda and Joe Petty, Park House,
Saugatuck, Michigan

If you need bookcase space, try two ladders placed vertically opposite from one another with boards running across the rungs. If the ladder is wood, stain or paint it.

Kris McIlvenna, Greenbriar Inn,
Coeur d'Alene, Idaho

Leftover or new yarn, wound into a ball, makes a nice room accent when placed into a basket. Select complementary colors. Stick in a pair of large knitting needles. Don't be surprised if someday you have a guest who tries knitting.

Ursel and Frank Walker, Gate
House Inn, Jackson, California

Car-seat upholstery fabric is good for your heavily used furniture. I found a maroon fabric that gives the look of old-fashioned plush on our parlor couch. It doesn't fade or spot, wears like iron, and cost less than five dollars per yard!

Anna Horton, High Cotton Inn,
Bellville, Texas

Author's Tip: If you don't have a foyer and your front door opens into the living room, create a place to receive guests. Add a coat rack just inside the door and a mirror for checking out the *chapeau* before exiting the house. An umbrella stand also helps create the illusion. We created a separate area, resembling an old colonial tavern. We placed wainscoting (narrow-grooved paneling) three-quarters of the way up the left-hand entry wall and topped it with a wall-to-wall Shaker peg rail. Period hats hang from the rail along with a wreath. We put a tavern table in the center of the wall, with a checker game in progress and a colonial pewter mug ready for a refill.

Armoires make great accent pieces in any room. They can be left partially open to reveal nice pieces inside. We have armoires in all our rooms. We top them with baskets of dried yarrow, lavender, and roses.

Mitzi and Lew Jones, Old Pioneer
Garden, Unionville, Nevada

Our armoire is in the dining room and holds our wines. We close the doors after dinner. But while they are open, they reveal the wines. On the inside of the door we hung curtains that match the wallpaper, providing a nice balance in the room.

Jacques Allembert, Four Columns,
Newfane, Vermont

Our spiral staircase is very high and has a lovely curved wall. It looked very bare, even with the Williamsburg Chinese-print wallpaper. So I hung an embroidered kimono on the wall.

Betty York, Four Chimneys,
Nantucket, Massachusetts

Author's Tip: A decorator's touch can be accomplished by purchasing fairly wide molding (4–6 inches) and mounting it about one-third of the way down the wall from the ceiling. The wide top of the molding provides a small shelf all around the room and a border, should you decide to wallpaper.

A quilt is a nice accent in almost any room. Here's a recipe for making a quilt easily. Select three complementary fabrics that will accent a room well. Seam lengthwise, alternating the strips and using two strips of each fabric, for a total of six strips. (The length and width of each strip will be determined by the size of the bed on which the quilt will be used.) Form a fabric sandwich. The top layer is the coverlet you've just created, the middle layer is batting, and the bottom layer can be a sheet, lining fabric, or any other fabric. Hand-stitch this sandwich on all four sides. Insert a wide lace ruffle on three sides for a feminine, Victorian effect, leaving the side that extends to the head of the bed unruffled. Secure the layers in place by tying them together by hand at regular intervals with a crewel needle and crewel thread.

Maureen and John Magee, Rabbit
Hill Inn, Lower Waterford,
Vermont

Is a room so small that you want to make it appear larger? From the floor to ceiling, mount 1- to 2-inch strips of mirror in the corners, one on each side of the ninety-degree, concave angle. The eye defines size by the corners of the room. The mirror strips visually eliminate the corners altogether.

Charles A. Hillestad, Queen Anne
Inn, Denver, Colorado

Old hot-water or steam-heating radiators can be an eyesore. Here are ways to handle the problem: Build a ledgelike table around them. Put a thick slab of marble on top to make a usable surface. Or on shorter radiators, make window seats for cold days, cold people, or plants.

> Mary and Gary Riley, Williams
> House, Hot Springs, Arkansas

Kitchen Decor

Our casual breakfast room has a different kind of chair rail. Instead of the usual molding, we bought a wooden molding that resembles a rope and painted it to coordinate with the room and show the rope effect. The rope rail would also look well in a room with a nautical theme.

> Linda and Mike Levitt, Six Water
> Street B&B, Sandwich,
> Massachusetts

The kitchen ceiling is tin. To complement it, there are 100 or more tin cookie cutters hanging on the wall.

> Deanne Raymond, Greenwoods
> Gate, Norfolk, Connecticut

Bathroom Decor

Bathroom sinks that don't have a cabinet underneath can be dressed with fabric. Fasten the fabric skirt to the sink with a hot-glue gun. The fit is really tight and smooth.

> Ellen and Paul Morissette,
> Kenniston Hill Inn, Boothbay,
> Maine

Ordinary guest towels can be turned into beautiful ones with the addition of lace or a coordinating fabric sewn on to one edge.

> Daisy Morden, Victorian House, St.
> Augustine, Florida

To completely change a bathroom, put up cedar paneling on the walls. It comes in a kit.

> Pat Hardy, Glenborough Inn, Santa
> Barbara, California

In bathrooms, I often use flower bricks for toothbrush holders. They can either be antiques or modern reproductions and are usually made of porcelain or china. One of the reasons I like to use them is that they are in keeping with the period of the house—circa 1835.

> Betty York, Four Chimneys,
> Nantucket, Massachusetts

Pile unwrapped rolls of colored toilet tissue in a basket for a decorator's touch in the bathroom. This eliminates the problem of running out of toilet tissue, and when the color is coordinated with the bath, it's very attractive. A guest gave us this idea.

> Phyllis Niemi-Peacock and Bud
> Peacock, Palmer House, Falmouth,
> Massachusetts

To hide that extra roll of toilet tissue, we place it in a decorative crock. It's much more attractive this way.

> Pam Stewart, manager, Little River
> Inn, Aldie, Virginia

In each bath, we have a small, damask wall hanging that masks an extra roll of toilet tissue. Each one is hand-painted to depict wildflowers.

> Bev Davis and Rick Litchfield,
> Captain Lord Mansion,
> Kennebunkport, Maine

So that you're never out of toilet paper, make this handy holder: Cut fabric about 40 inches long and 7 inches wide. Make a small hem along the edges. Loop and sew the 7-inch edges together. Then 1½ inches down, sew again. Sew across about 8-inches from the bottom loop. Decorate with lace and bows and push a dowel through a 1½-inch casing at the top. Hang with ribbon from a decorative hook in the bathroom. Insert two rolls of toilet paper.

Ann and Clyne Long, Center
Street, Logan, Utah

Bedroom Decor

It's easy to make a canopy for a bed. You'll need plant-hanger hooks, two 6-foot-long dowels (1-inch round) that you have stained or painted, and clear fishing line. Put four hooks in the ceiling above the four posts of the bed. Hang equal lengths of fishing line from the hooks, and attach each one to an end of the dowels. Drape sheets or other decorative fabric over the framework you've created.

Pat Hardy, Glenborough Inn, Santa
Barbara, California

You can make a king-size bed canopy by sewing together two lace tablecloths.

Fran and Frank Guy, Mercersburg
Inn, Mercersburg, Pennsylvania

Use metal rods (¼-inch diameter) cut to fit on three sides and foot of the bed. Buy the barrel curtain-rod holders for ¼-inch rods, and mount them on the inside of the legs of the bed. The dust ruffle is gathered onto the rods like a curtain for the sides and foot of the bed. The dust ruffle never interferes with bed making and is easy to remove for washing.

Cathy and Dave Eakin, Captain's
House, Chatham, Massachusetts

Large lace tablecloths can work well as bed coverings.

Chris and Jill Raggio, Ilverthorpe
Cottage, Narragansett, Rhode
Island

When curtains and wallpaper are still good in a room, but the matching bedspread has worn out, cover the bedspread with a crocheted coverlet. The colors still show through this way, and you won't have to redo the entire room.

Nancy Donaldson, Old Yacht Club
Inn, Santa Barbara, California

Paper, English-reproduction face masks lean against pillows in each guest room for an interesting and humorous decoration.

Here is a bit of a trade secret at The Brafferton: One day, I (Jim) was standing in an antiques shop with my hand resting on a wonderful, primitive fireplace mantel. I loved its simplicity and wished I had a decent reason to buy it. Then it came to me. Why didn't I buy old mantels and put them in each bedroom? This would give the rooms a focal point. I would stencil the wall where the firebox would ordinarily be placed if it were a working fireplace. I figured I could also have wonderful fun creating trompe l'oeil. It worked. We now have seven mantels. Now and then you come up with a decorating solution that is perfect!

Jim and Mimi Agard, Brafferton
Inn, Gettysburg, Pennsylvania

Author's Tip: A friend of mine came up with the idea of using a colonial secretary desk to store her clothes. She selected one with glass doors on top so that her pretty sweaters would show through and add color. Other tops went in the drawers. She hasn't decided if she will use the tilt top and pigeon holes for desk supplies or as a makeup table.

Here's a tip for dressing up a simple poster bed. It was born out of the fact that very wide ribbon was unavailable in my area. I bought taffeta and simply cut 3-inch-wide and 5-foot-long pieces of fabric. I made four large, full bows with long streamers and attached one to the top of each post. This is so simple and so pretty.

Betty Doan, Vincent-Doan Home,
Mobile, Alabama

Inexpensive, plain-white silk or cotton pillows can be made into accent pieces that look as if you paid a fortune. Sew inexpensive lace doilies onto both sides of the pillows. You can also use antique lace. The result: decorator pillows for the bed.

Fran and Frank Sullivan, Wild Rose
of York, York, Maine

 ## Floor Decor

Several of our hardwood floors are painted. The result is an attractive and long-lasting look. And the floors can be cleaned easily with a damp mop and mild detergent. Floors can be painted a solid color or in a pattern, such as diamonds, to resemble a rug. To paint: Free the floor of all dirt, dust, and dampness. Choose a quality deck paint. Give the floor two coats of paint (using a roller, and a paintbrush in hard-to-reach areas), allowing the paint to dry completely between coats. Then apply at least two coats of high-gloss polyurethane, allowing time to dry between coats. We recommend twenty-four hours drying time between coats.

Shirley and Stephen Ramsey,
Mayhurst B&B, Orange, Virginia

Our 1790 farmhouse has very old pine stairs. They are quite scarred, but the wood is lovely. We didn't want to cover them completely, but they needed some protection. So we purchased carpet samples inexpensively, in all different colors, and cut mats for the top of each stair. The many colors have an attractive, kaleidoscope effect.

Joanne and George Hardy, Hill
Farm Inn, Arlington, Vermont

 ## Decorating with Collections

Decorating with your collections is a good way for your personality to come through in your home. We have sheep on our farm so it's only natural that we have a sheep collection to decorate our inn. We collect everything and anything with sheep on it, including pictures, needlework, rugs, and towels; ceramic and wooden sheep; and sheep doorstops. We also have one wall in a living room filled with a sampler collection.

Carolyn and Jeff Rawes, Ash Mill
Farm, Holicong, Pennsylvania

Collections displayed together have the most impact. Distributing one piece here and there in your home will not command the attention a well-placed collection will.

Marie and Dick Brophy, Isaiah Hall
B&B, Dennis, Massachusetts

We have an artifact board as a wall decoration. It changes all the time. Cover a pegboard with upholstery fabric, or paint it a complementary color for your room. Wire your favorite antiques and collectibles onto the board. We did one of the boards with antique cooking tools. It's a great conversation piece and a nice way to show off collectibles—especially of this kind. The board includes a tin chocolate mold, egg beaters, a chicken-egg mold, a corn grater handmade by my father in 1904 when he was nine, and a butter paddle.

Betsy Grater, Betsy's B&B,
Baltimore, Maryland

Using your collections as home decor should not be overdone. We have a few pewter pieces in the old cooking fireplace and a display of oil lamps that are put to use during power shortages.

Faith and Charles Reynolds,
Historic Merrell Tavern Inn, South
Lee, Massachusetts

Champagne corks are collectibles at our inn. They adorn the open hearth in our kitchen. They symbolize all there is to celebrate in life!

Linda Kaat, Sweetwater Farm, Glen
Mills, Pennsylvania

I have a collection of monogrammed linens, which one quickly begins to appreciate because of their fine workmanship. The largest numbers of monogrammed towels have CBL in three different styles, having belonged to the honorable Clare Boothe Luce.

Sandra Cartwright-Brown, Conyers
House, Sperryville, Virginia

 # Wall Hangings

For balance, always place wall hangings in an uneven number. If several items are to be hung on one wall, measure the space by marking it off on the floor or bed with string. Try arranging the items within this space before putting nail holes into the wall, especially in an older home where the plaster crumbles.

Barbara and Carl Beehner, Steele
Homestead, Antrim, New
Hampshire

Author's Tip: If you have something you don't want to frame but wish to put on your wall anyway, hang it with a tablespoonful or so of toothpaste at each corner and a little across the middle. If you ever take the piece down, just wipe the wall clean of the toothpaste. No one will ever know it was there.

Hanging Artwork

Paintings, drawings, and framed prints should be hung 62 inches from the floor to the center of the work. My formula: Let's say the painting is 2 feet high. Measure the distance from the hanging wire (when it is pulled tightly as if it were hanging) to the top of the painting—likely an inch or two. Place the painting on the floor, a few feet away from the wall, in the correct horizontal spacing. Go to the wall and measure up 62 inches (maximum 66 inches) from where the center of the painting will be. Place a dot. If the painting is 2 feet high, it would be correctly placed if it were positioned 12 inches above and 12 inches below the dot. Therefore measure up 12 inches. Subtract the difference between the taut hanging wire and the top of the work, and put a dot. This is where you place your hanging device. I have found that this method creates a consistent, imaginary line running through the center of every image on your wall.

Jim and Mimi Agard, Brafferton
Inn, Gettysburg, Pennsylvania

A time saver in keeping any room looking orderly: Pictures and mirrors do not require frequent straightening if they are hung by two sawtooth metal hangers attached to the upper corners of the frame. The brackets engage two appropriately positioned nails in the wall. Throw away the usual screw eyes and wire.

Harriette and David L. Lusty,
Dockside Guest Quarters, York,
Maine

We use groupings of paintings of a similar nature (a group of oriental paintings on silk in one room, a group of architectural engravings in a hall). Massed in this way, a number of smaller pieces can take on far more importance than if placed individually. Even expensive prints done this way seem more important. In grouping them, don't try to square off the outside edges. Work from the inside, arranging them around the largest piece. Center them on an imaginary "plus" sign, and let the outside of the whole grouping be uneven. Although this may seem unnatural to you as you do it, it is actually the most pleasing to the eye.

Ripley Hotch and Owen Sullivan,
Boydville The Inn at Martinsburg,
Martinsburg, West Virginia

A picture grouping can be enhanced by hanging a few stems of silk flowers of various shapes and colors, baby's breath, and delicate branches, all tied with ribbon.

Lila and Rick Peiffer, Bluebelle
House, Lake Arrowhead, California

Author's Tip: An alternative to mounting a painting on a wall: Buy a wooden artist's easel (styles and prices vary greatly), and place it in a corner of the room. Perch a favorite painting on the ledge. You can even display a large, colorful book on an easel.

Hanging Quilts

There are several ways to hang a quilt. Here are two we've used. To hang from wood: Have someone at a mill cut two pieces of wood about ½ inch thick by 2 inches wide. Sandwich the top of the quilt between the two pieces of wood. Use screws with nuts at either end of the wood. Screw them in to press the quilt between the two pieces. Add wire from the nuts to hang on the wall. You can drape the quilt over the top of the wood so that the wood doesn't show; this also will take some weight off the bottom.

To hang with clips: Use wide clips every 10 inches across the quilt. Hang the clips from cup hooks on the wall.

> Mary Louise and Ron Thorburn,
> Inn at Weathersfield, Weathersfield,
> Vermont

If you have a less valuable quilt, you can sew fabric tabs onto the top of it and hang the quilt on a round dowel. I used a bamboo pole.

> Denise Champion, Haikuleana,
> Haiku, Hawaii

Quilts on a wall have a dramatic impact. If you have a quilt that is worn and cannot be shown off full-length on a wall, mount a curtain rod on the wall and drape the quilt halfway over it. Don't be afraid to fix quilts that are badly in need of repair. We have some thirty-seven quilts at the inn. Almost all are in mint condition. Ten were handed down through my (Merrily's) family. A quilt has no value to anyone (except maybe a serious collector) if it's in very bad shape. We say, make use of the quilt. Cut it down and frame what is in good shape, or use it as a throw over a bed or upholstered piece.

> Merrily and Max Comins, Kedron
> Valley Inn, South Woodstock,
> Vermont

Another way to hang a quilt on the wall is to drape it over an antique rake that has a long wooden handle. It's a great way to

display the old rake and provide a method of hanging that won't
damage the quilt.

> Barbara Barlow, Riverwind, Deep
> River, Connecticut

Hanging Doilies

Starch and stiffen your doily, and hang it with a straight pin on
a wall alone or in a picture grouping. We have three hanging over
a bed. We have never needed to launder them, as they don't get
soiled on the wall. But if you feel the need to clean them, just take
them down, wash and starch again, and hang. This way, you can
display your doily and not have to frame it.

> Sharon and Scott Wright, Silver
> Maple Lodge, Fairlee, Vermont

Author's Tip: Should you decide you want to frame a doily, here's
what you need to do: Clean and starch the doily before pinning
it to a complementary mat board. You can make your own board
and cover it with wallpaper that matches the room, for example.
Place it in a frame. A cross-bar frame would give it an old-
fashioned look. If you don't think you can do it, or you need an
odd-size frame, bring it to a reputable frame shop.

Hanging Nostalgia

We have given one room a romantic theme by accenting it with
our parents' framed wedding certificates and engagement photos.

> Ruth and Bill Brown, Windward
> Inn, North East, Pennsylvania

In our Rose Room, we have hung several groups of old valentines. They were Jim's mom's, but one can often find such cards
at antiques shops and auctions. They have helped make this
particular room a favorite for romantic occasions, such as hon-
eymoons and anniversaries. As one guest explained when she

changed her vacation dates to coincide with the availability of the room: "The Rose Room has emotional significance. Oh, those valentines!"

Glynrose and Jim Friedlander, Isaac
Randall House, Freeport, Maine

Some greeting cards make attractive wall hangings. Select complementary frames.

Ruth and Cliff Manchester,
Bramble Inn, Brewster,
Massachusetts

From time to time, the U.S. Postal Service issues stamps that are just plain pretty. When we see a stamp design that we like, we buy a block and have it framed. Each block of stamps is a little bit of American history for the wall.

Rosemary and Ed McDowell, Tulip
Tree Inn, Chittenden, Vermont

Don't leave grandma's memorabilia in the closet. Frame it. Carl's grandfather's silk boots, which he wore at age five, are in a lovely shadowbox with a picture of him wearing them. Also framed are a tailor's brush from a great-uncle and some upholstery items used by my grandfather, plus lots more. Saving and continually treasuring family heirlooms makes the statement that we are family oriented. And to share these treasures with guests, just as you can do in your own home, suggests we treat them as guests— not just paying customers.

Barbara and Carl Beehner, Steele
Homestead, Antrim, New
Hampshire

Use the top of a small washboard (you can buy antique or reproduction washboards) for your favorite family portrait. Depending on the size of the washboard, you may want to use one large picture or several small ones. Here's how:

Measure the size of the area to be framed (the top above the cleaning ridges). Buy wood stripping. The size will depend on your washboard's dimensions. (I used ¼-inch-square stripping.) Cut the stripping to fit around the area being framed, cutting one piece to fit each side.

Get a piece of glass to fit this area and a piece of matting in your choice of color.

Place your picture(s) and the matting into the opening, and cover them with the glass. Fit the wood stripping into the frame, and nail in tiny brads to hold it all in place. You may varnish or paint the wood stripping.

Hang the washboard on the wall. Depending on where you put it (it makes a nice addition to kitchen or laundry room), you can use the bottom portion of the washboard for notes. Buy sticky notepad paper to write your reminders.

Audrey Nichols, Heritage Inn,
Salmon, Idaho

Old toys can be an important part of your decor. Use whatever toys you have and a little imagination. We placed a basket full of old toys in a room. It makes you remember your past. You can't help but take time out to relax. It's important that your decor helps you do that.

Deanne Raymond, Greenwoods
Gate, Norfolk, Connecticut

Antiques and Collectibles

How to Use and Display Treasures

When browsing among antiques, how many times have you said to yourself: "Well, I really like this piece, but what can I do with it?" You proceed to put the item down, wishing you could justify its purchase.

The same goes for those precious family trinkets you discover amid the attic's cobwebs. When you can't figure out a raison d'être, you pack them away again for another hundred years.

The solution to all this confusion over antiques is being able to develop a purpose for the relic in question. And coming to the rescue, once again, are the innkeepers. You can find a utilitarian, decorative, and/or collectible reason for purchasing nearly anything sold today at antiques shows and shops. The abundance of antiques in use at the inns is proof that old things, which have been replaced by modern technology, can still have plenty of purpose. But many inns use their antiques as they were originally intended to be used, even some of the seemingly less practical devices. Knoll Farm Country Inn in Waitsfield, Vermont, for example, uses an old butter churn to do what else—make butter and buttermilk.

There are also plenty of pieces being "recycled" for modern uses, particularly nonfurniture items. Innkeepers have used good old ingenuity to develop a purpose for even the most seemingly functionless curio. A whimsical use may even evoke laughter from some purists. But Marilyn Coughlin, owner of The Hutchinson House in Faribault, Minnesota, puts it this way: "Using ordinary objects in new and inventive ways will reveal your personality as well as your sense of fun. Display the ordinary in unorthodox ways."

How about using a nonelectric, iron-shuttered toaster as a lampshade, a wooden ironing board as a coffee table, or a wooden cigar box for your recipes? A sad iron (named sad, meaning heavy, not suggestive of the drudgery of old pressing irons) can be a doorstop, and an old British toast caddy can hold letters on their way to the mailbox. Like anything that lies dormant, prized bibelots tucked away in a box or a closet will suffer the aches and pains of growing even older without seeing the light of day. Out in the open, however, and in use, they become objets d'art.

Besides showing clever ways of using antiques, innkeepers also have important advice on buying antiques at shops and auctions, as well as tips on caring for your prized possessions.

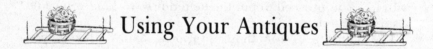

Using Your Antiques

Kitchen and Serving Items

Old pie safes, missing the front tin panels, can be found at bargain prices. Give one of these new life by installing thin, brass curtain rods behind each window or opening in the doors and gathering material on them. We have such a cabinet in our kitchen, in which we keep cookbooks.

To display decorative Victorian napkin rings, we placed them in an old pedestal candy jar and set it on the sideboard.

> Karen and Ken West, Benner
> House, Weston, Missouri

The bottoms of early sewing machines, usually made of wrought iron, have been topped with a number of surfaces and used for kitchen tables and center islands—just to mention a few clever modern-day applications.

> Iris and Bill Simantel, Hearthstone
> Inn, Eureka Springs, Arkansas

An old pair of ice tongs makes a great paper-towel holder. Open the tongs and insert the roll, then hang the tongs or stand them on the handles.

Kathy Drew, Out-the-Inn-Door,
Freeport, Maine

Those once-useful, but big, flour sifters can make attractive dishtowel hangers. Nail the sifter to the wall. Hang a dishtowel through the handle. Put dish rags in the top of the sifter. And hang potholders from the knob that turns the sifter.

Audrey Nichols, Heritage Inn,
Salmon, Idaho

An antique breadboard is a nice server for cookies and snacks.

Cathy and Dave Eakin, Captain's
House, Chatham, Massachusetts

We used an old floor joist to make the top of a kitchen counter. We cleaned and sanded it and put six coats of polyurethane on top.

The top of an early dough cabinet now hangs on a wall and holds our dishes. We found it at a farm sale.

Sunny and Joy Drewel, Zachariah
Foss Guest House, Washington,
Missouri

Old ladders can have a variety of uses. We have one leaning against a wall in our sun porch. The rungs are rounded, but we still display items such as our baskets and some dried flowers. And as long as your old ladder is freshly painted, you can even use it in the kitchen to dry homemade pasta and also to hold wet dishtowels for drying.

Sally and Ken McWilliams, Main
Street B&B, Madison, Indiana

Author's Tip: The most worn-out wooden ladder can be sanded, painted, and hung from the ceiling for a variety of uses. We have one in our kitchen. It hangs from plant hooks and four decorative chains. Here we display antique baskets, kitchen utensils, and dried herbs and flowers. You can also hang one above a kitchen island and use it as a handy rack for pots and pans. For an even more rustic look, don't even bother to paint it.

Antique block-and-tackle pulleys hang from beams in our kitchen ceiling. We hang many items from them, including pans, dried herbs from our garden, and baskets.

> Barbara and Carl Beehner, Steele
> Homestead Inn, Antrim, New
> Hampshire

We've taken an old brass mailbox (originally from an apartment building) and converted it into a spice rack.

> Debbie and Ed McCord, Shellmont
> B&B, Atlanta, Georgia

Retired brick molds make charming spice racks.

> Robin Brooks, Robins Nest, San
> Andreas, California

Author's Tip: Old brick molds are also great serving trays. Since there are a few sections in each mold, fill each one with different dips, crackers, and vegetables and even napkins.

A deed box holds candles. An early biscuit crate houses our soap powder, dish detergent, and scouring pads.

> Beverly and Ray Compton, Spring
> Bank Inn, Frederick, Maryland

Relishes, served in our dining room, come off an antique wooden sausage stuffer. We added legs.

> Judy and Bill Wolf, Birchwood Inn,
> Temple, New Hampshire

We bought the inn's turn-of-the-century coffee grinder before we bought the inn. Then we needed to buy the inn to go with it. Now it's in use as a planter at the reception desk!

> Judy and Jack McMahon, Inn at
> Starlight Lake, Starlight,
> Pennsylvania

Author's Tip: Love that ladle? Then buy it, even though its bowl is marred or scarred and can't be used for serving food. Fill the bowl with dried or silk flowers, and mount it on a wall.

Individual butter pats are served in antique blue-glass salt dishes.

> Linda and Mike Levitt, Six Water
> Street B&B, Sandwich,
> Massachusetts

A cobalt blue milk of magnesia bottle is used as a liqueur bottle on a silver tray.

> Patricia Parks, Eton House,
> Fayettville, Arkansas

Old half-pint milk bottles are used for individual servings of maple syrup.

> Bonnie and Bill Webb, Inn on
> Golden Pond, Holderness, New
> Hampshire

An old milk can is a perfect spot to display your collection of decorative and country magnets.

> Evelyn and Gilbert Davidson,
> Davidson's Country Inn, Pagosa
> Springs, Colorado

Milk-bottle carriers hold and serve jars of homemade preserves.

> Kate Kerivan, Bungay Jar, Easton,
> New Hampshire

Author's Tip: Fill milk bottles with sugar, if you want to give them color and show up the embossed lettering. This is also a nice way to store sugar.

You can make use of chipped china or crystal by turning scarred pieces into vases. Baby's breath tucked in among silk flowers looks lovely in a long-stemmed crystal goblet, for example.

> Phyllis Niemi-Peacock and Bud
> Peacock, Palmer House, Falmouth,
> Massachusetts

Author's Tip: If you choose to repair chipped crystal, file the area in a circular motion with a super-fine emery board. Clean the goblet.

Long-retired frying pans make attractive wall hangings. You can tole paint on the bottoms and add a bow at the handles.

> Audrey Nichols, Heritage Inn,
> Salmon, Idaho

You don't have to be able to use kitchen gadgets in order to enjoy them. They can be displayed in attractive groupings in the kitchen.

> Marilyn and Gene Gundersen,
> Pudding Creek Inn, Fort Bragg,
> California

The kitchen ceiling is tin. To complement it, there are 100 or more tin cookie cutters hanging on the wall.

> Deanne Raymond, Greenwoods
> Gate, Norfolk, Connecticut

We had been collecting antique knife rests and now have enough to place one at each guest's table setting. Knife rests add an elegant and lovely touch and can be found in sterling silver, pewter, or cut-crystal.

> Deedy and Charlie Marble,
> Governor's Inn, Ludlow, Vermont

We set a formal table with sterling silver and china, using our collection of antique salts. and salt spoons. Some guests have put the salt in their coffee. So now we explain.

> Barbara and Carl Beehner, Steele
> Homestead Inn, Antrim, New
> Hampshire

An arrangement of antique bottles on an interesting tray or plate can be a centerpiece for any table. Mix shapes, sizes, colors, and heights.

> Rebecca E. Shipman, Inn at
> Buckeystown, Buckeystown,
> Maryland

A popular spot is our coffee corner, where a 1915 gas stove is the butler for coffee any time of day. Coffee is made in an automatic, drip coffee maker on top of the stove. Stove drawers hold spoons. Cups can be found in the warming oven.

Mary and Bill Fisher, Schoolhouse
Inn, Melvern, Kansas

An old wood stove in the kitchen holds our microwave oven.

Tommie and Andy Duncan, Arcady
Down East, Blue Hill, Maine

One of our guest rooms has an old potbelly stove to hold gourmet coffees and teas. It's hard to find these antiques in good condition. But don't despair. Brush the stove with a drill and steel-brush attachment. Remove any chrome, and take the stove to a body shop for rechroming. Meanwhile, paint the piece with special black stove paint, the kind that's used for fireplaces.

Audry Kuhnhauser, Audrie's
Cranbury Corner, Rapid City,
South Dakota

Contact a professional sandblasting company, possibly one that engraves headstones. Disassemble all parts. Have the stove sandblasted and nickel pieces renickeled. Paint the body of the stove with black stove paint. Reassemble. Voilà, you've saved yourself about $500. If you need any parts recast, have them done at a foundry. Nickel-plating shops and foundries are listed in the Yellow Pages.

Sallie and Welling Clark, Holden
House 1902, Colorado Springs,
Colorado

Treasures for a Bathroom

Don't be afraid to buy something old that you like but don't have immediate use for. I once bought a pair of legs from an old piano. I liked them, but I had no idea when they might come in handy. We recently renovated a sink and vanity in a bathroom, putting the unit in the corner. We used one of the decorative piano legs to hold up the vanity. It looks terrific, and what a conversation piece!

Sandra Cartwright-Brown, Conyers
House, Sperryville, Virginia

In our Gordon Snidow Room, the sink is recessed into an old, Hepplewhite, round-front dresser.

Linda and Jerry Lundeen, Inn of
the Arts, Las Cruces, New Mexico

Antique cabinets can be made into sinks. Mimi came up with the idea of having pottery bowls thrown by a professional potter to be used as sinks. We had holes cut into the tops of the old cabinets by our plumber, who also did the rest of the hookups. There isn't much you can do with a bathroom. But this creates a fixture of interest.

Mimi and Jim Agard, Brafferton
Inn, Gettysburg, Pennsylvania

I've placed a wonderful, old brass bugle in a bathroom as a toilet-paper holder. Turn the bugle with the bell to the floor. Place the roll of paper over the mouthpiece.

Marilyn Coughlin, Hutchinson
House, Faribault, Minnesota

Our inn's signature—part of its Gothic Romanticism—is the un-expected use of antique objects. Audacious effects surprise guests at every turn. One of those surprises is towels offered on antique, wooden, store-mannequin arms.

Mary Louise and Conley Weaver,
Red Castle Inn, Nevada City,
California

Old crocks hold my towels (rolled up) in the bathroom, as I don't care for traditional towel racks. I've removed the blades from old planing tools and hung the planes on a wall. Guests can hang a used towel or bathrobe from the handle.

Barbara Barlow, Riverwind, Deep
River, Connecticut

We use an old clothes wringer for a towel rack.

> Elaine and Ray Grandmaison,
> Captain Stannard House,
> Westbrook, Connecticut

Author's Tip: You can also use a clothes wringer to hold bathroom tissue. Just slip the roll onto the handle.

Washboards can be used in many ways. We attached robe hooks to them and hung them in the bathrooms.

> Joanne and George Hardy, Hill
> Farm Inn, Arlington, Vermont

Author's Tip: We hung a washboard in the laundry room as appropriate decoration for a country-style home. I have also seen them turned into fronts for homemade medicine cabinets.

Quilt racks can be used as towel racks.

> Ruth and Cliff Manchester,
> Bramble Inn, Brewster,
> Massachusetts

Objects of Interest in a Bedroom

Iron Victorian tack-room brackets were placed over a bed for hanging a swag of fabric. The bracket was placed about 3 feet over the center of the bed. The fabric was draped over it and attached to the headboard with a bow, and then brought down the side of the bed.

> Lois and Paul Dansereau, Silas
> Griffith Inn, Danby, Vermont

The headboards in one of our guest bedrooms are of pressed tin, which were the grate covers of ceramic gas heaters. When the heaters were in use during the winter in the twenties, the grate covers were removed. In summer, they were put back in place, creating an ornate front.

> Linda and Jerry Lundeen, Inn of
> the Arts, Las Cruces, New Mexico

Make use of an old window frame by turning it into a headboard. We added a mirror to the back of the frame and hung it horizontally just over a bed. And we use a school desk as a bedside table.

Marilyn and Gene Gundersen,
Pudding Creek Inn, Fort Bragg,
California

Tobacco humidors have been made into nightstands.

Kate Kerivan, Bungay Jar, Easton,
New Hampshire

In one of our Victorian rooms, we have a chrome shaving stand with a mirror for the guests' convenience. We use the soap dish for a flower arrangement.

Tommie and Andy Duncan, Arcady
Down East, Blue Hill, Maine

Antiques make great luggage racks. We use a wringer washing machine for one. A suitcase can be placed on either side, where the tub used to go. And an old, wooden potty seat serves just fine for suitcases when the lid is down.

Margaret and Geoffrey
Loebenstein, Wildwood Inn, Ware,
Massachusetts

We use steamer trunks for luggage racks. They also are excellent for storing extra blankets and pillows.

In each guest room is an antique meat platter, which is used as a tray for organizing two wine glasses, napkins, small carafe for water, corkscrew, and chocolates.

Bev Davis and Rick Litchfield,
Captain Lord Mansion,
Kennebunkport, Maine

Our inn, decorated in museum-quality period pieces, is also an antiques shop. Guests may even purchase the bed they slept in.

Korda Family, Historic Brookside
Farms, Orwell, Vermont

Common-Area Treasures

A preacher's pulpit is in our guest registration area. You can use one in your home as a dictionary stand or a place for a guest book.

> Tracy and Jim Stone, Inn at
> Mitchell House, Chestertown,
> Maryland

A former church pew makes a nice bench in any room. Decorate it with an old hymnal, a pair of cotton gloves, and a basket of flowers.

An antique doll carriage is a decorative accent for a room and can hold magazines and books.

> Karen and Ken West, Benner
> House, Weston, Missouri

I use wooden drier racks for drying herbs and flowers. I've also heard of them being used to hold current newspapers and magazines.

> Barbara Barlow, Riverwind, Deep
> River, Connecticut

We made a coffee table from a hatch cover on an old freighter.

> Lois and Paul Dansereau, Silas
> Griffith Inn, Danby, Vermont

A large fireplace bellows is being used as a coffee table in one room. In another room, we're using an old sea chest for the same purpose.

> Tommie and Andy Duncan, Arcady
> Down East, Blue Hill, Maine

Flat-topped trunks have been used as coffee tables.

> Kate Kerivan, Bungay Jar, Easton,
> New Hampshire

Revive an old lampshade frame with a doily.

> Marilyn Coughlin, Hutchinson
> House, Faribault, Minnesota

I have a 1920s lamp with a slip for a lampshade. The slip is an 1830s lace garment in a pink/beige color. I cut off the top of the slip and made the bottom into a lampshade. It's perfect.

> Daisy Morden, Victorian House, St. Augustine, Florida

Old oil lamps have been electrified.

> Ruth and Cliff Manchester, Bramble Inn, Brewster, Massachusetts

Antique, French, children's torso mannequins are draped with scarves or lace collars clasped by heirloom jewelry, and then put to use as lamps.

> Mary Louise and Conley Weaver, Red Castle Inn, Nevada City, California

Old, hand, water pumps have been made into table lamps.

> Kate Kerivan, Bungay Jar, Easton, New Hampshire

Most of our lamps were made from antiques, such as molds, wine presses, and whale-oil lamps.

> Barbara and Carl Beehner, Steele Homestead Inn, Antrim, New Hampshire

Small kerosene lamps can be put to use in the twentieth century. We have one in each room in case of power failures.

> Tommie and Andy Duncan, Arcady Down East, Blue Hill, Maine

Antique fire extinguishers have been converted into hallway lamps. Outside lighting at the inn is cast by electrified, old glass lanterns.

> Jane and Frank Emanuel, Middlebury Inn, Middlebury, Vermont

Older homes relied on cross-ventilation to facilitate air movement during warmer seasons. Doorstops were used to prevent doors from slamming closed. At the inn, we use antique flatirons, brass bookends, and old jugs as doorstops, depending on the decor of the room.

> Mariam and Charles Bechtel,
> Bechtel Mansion Inn, East Berlin,
> Pennsylvania

An old lithograph stone with etchings is used as a doorstop.

> Tracy and Jim Stone, Inn at
> Mitchell House, Chestertown,
> Maryland

Antique, ceramic foot warmers make great doorstops.

> Pat Hardy, Glenborough Inn, Santa
> Barbara, California

For an interesting doorstop, take old button-top shoes and fill them with mortar.

> Audrey Nichols, Heritage Inn,
> Salmon, Idaho

Containers and Other Storage Items

A former post-office desk is in use at our inn as a wine rack. Each letter slot contains a bottle of wine.

> Ursel and Frank Walker, Gate
> House Inn, Jackson, California

A quart milk ladle, hung from an old ox yoke, holds matches for our wood stove.

> Carriere-Zito Family, Mill Brook
> B&B, Brownsville, Vermont

An old tin scoop holds our brochures.

> Betsy Grater, Betsy's B&B,
> Baltimore, Maryland

Wooden cranberry scoops can be hung on the wall as decoration. We have attached pertinent data about the inn and the area to the bowl of the scoop. You can do this for your guest room and place your own notes and greetings inside it.

> Judy and Fred Siemons, Lyme Inn,
> Lyme, New Hampshire

A former cranberry barrel, which is strong, provides an attractive container to hold wood for our parlor stove. A cranberry scoop holds magazines.

> Marie and Dick Brophy, Isaiah Hall
> B&B, Dennis, Massachusetts

We employ three antique crocks as wastebaskets for our guest rooms. Use them with plastic liners.

> Betha and John Mueller, Wisconsin
> House, Hazel Green, Wisconsin

Retired sap buckets make great wastebaskets. Covered tins hold our playing cards.

> Ruth and Cliff Manchester,
> Bramble Inn, Brewster,
> Massachusetts

Big crocks are used to hold kindling near wood-burning stoves.

> Rita and Allan Kalsmith, Black
> Lantern, Montgomery Village,
> Vermont

Author's Tip: At our house we use a replica Shaker dish rack in our foyer. It holds brochures of the area, maps, a guest book, and our outgoing mail.

Cut-glass salt cellars make great catchalls. In our rooms, we have them holding straight pins, safety pins, needles, and thread.

> Tommie and Andy Duncan, Arcady
> Down East, Blue Hill, Maine

Antique cradles are great catchalls for other antiques including teddy bears, mini-quilts, and afghans, and old lace, which can be draped over the top.

Margaret and Geoffrey
Loebenstein, Wildwood Inn, Ware,
Massachusetts

Entertainment

Stereo components have been placed inside an old press cupboard, so the stereo is handy but doesn't look out of place in a living room furnished with eighteenth-century antiques. The television is inside an old armoire; this is also a good way to handle bedroom televisions and video equipment.

One of our most popular antiques is a stereopticon. You can get inexpensive stacks of old cards of scenes and stories for your guests to enjoy.

Ripley Hotch and Owen Sullivan,
Boydville The Inn at Martinsburg,
Martinsburg, West Virginia

Old magazines are in each guest room for reading pleasure and discovery.

Judy and Bill Wolfe, Birchwood
Inn, Temple, New Hampshire

The modern look of televisions in a Victorian home like ours can be subdued by placing the television on an old sewing machine table. These can be purchased quite inexpensively. The wrought iron can be painted easily. If the wooden top is missing, it is quite simple to reattach a new top by using a piece of finished plywood.

Iris and Bill Simantel, Hearthstone
Inn, Eureka Springs, Arkansas

Vintage Clothing

I have a few old Victorian swimsuits hanging by the hot tub. Some guests want to know if they have to wear them in order to use the hot tub. Other guests just try them on for fun.

Audry Kuhnhauser, Audrie's
Cranbury Corner, Rapid City,
South Dakota

Author's Tip: Old doll clothing in a frame makes an attractive accent in an appropriate room.

Stylish old clothes can be used as decoration. An old lace nightgown on a padded hanger is draped across the foot of one of our beds.

Those delicate hankies of old can be put to good use by placing them over an old Bible or a book of verse on a bureau or small table.

Frank and Honesty Buczek,
Thompson Park House, Owego,
New York

Author's Tip: Use a printer's box not only for small collectibles but also to place inside a dresser drawer to hold jewelry. The smaller slats hold tiny baubles and treasured cuff links. Knock out a few sections, if necessary, for storing larger jewels.

We have old clothing in glass cases, including a wedding gown that was offered in the first Montgomery Ward catalog.

Marilyn and Gene Gundersen,
Pudding Creek Inn, Fort Bragg,
California

Using clothing from the Victorian era reinforces the time period we're creating. A period bridal gown and a dried bouquet hang in one of our guest rooms. Lovely, funny, old hats, including flapper clothes, are on stands and bedposts in guest rooms. They give our guests plenty of giggles when they try them on.

Little touches that make a room look used are enjoyed by guests—a piece of jewelry in an antique dish on a dresser or a pair of lace gloves on the mantel with yesterday's corsage.

> Iris and Bill Simantel, Hearthstone
> Inn, Eureka Springs, Arkansas

An antique dress hangs on an old dressmaker's form in one of the bedrooms. We've wondered if guests have ever tried it on during the course of their stay.

> Chris and Jill Raggio, Ilverthorpe
> Cottage, Narragansett, Rhode
> Island

Opened trunks make a nice display setting for Victorian clothing.

> Karen and Ken West, Benner
> House, Weston, Missouri

Author's Tip: Old steamer trunks once had the family name stenciled on the outside. Stencil your family name on your antique trunk to add authenticity, while making a conversation piece out of it.

Sewing Equipment

An old spool cabinet holds our bills and receipts in the narrow drawers.

> Beverly and Ray Compton, Spring .
> Bank Inn, Frederick, Maryland

Large spindles from old textile mills are used for candle holders. Different sizes can be grouped together. The gigantic spindles hold ice buckets.

> Hudson House, Cold Spring, New
> York

Place two, tall, wooden spools side by side in your front hallway or exit area and put outgoing mail between them.

> Jim and Mimi Agard, Brafferton
> Inn, Gettysburg, Pennsylvania

Author's Tip: The small, wooden sewing spools used for sewing machines at home can be used as holders for very thin candles. Or you can use them as decorative ornaments. You can either stencil or paint a design on them. Tie a thin, color-coordinated satin ribbon at the top of the spool's neck, and you have an attractive piece for a printer's box or an accent for a sewing room. When you paint, avoid areas on the top or bottom of the spool where the manufacturer's label, indicating its origin and age, may still be affixed.

Collectibles for Indoor Plants, Flowers, and Gardens

Antique scales make great plant hangers. We have one over a bathtub.

> Tommie and Andy Duncan, Arcady
> Down East, Blue Hill, Maine

We use old children's chairs to hold plants.

> Jan and Gene Kuehn, Victorian
> B&B, Avoca, Iowa

We hang plants in little buckets from each spoke of an old yarn winder.

> Judy and Bill Wolfe, Birchwood
> Inn, Temple, New Hampshire

Desks from old schoolhouses can double as plant stands; those with lids can be used as display cases for collectibles.
  Just because a wicker chair seat might be worn with age, doesn't mean the piece no longer can function. Use it as a plant holder.

> Pat Hardy, Glenborough Inn, Santa
> Barbara, California

Maple-sugar buckets, which have been put to rest when they can no longer be used for sugaring, are indispensable in the garden. We use them to sit on, carry tools, cover tender plants from frost, make supports to hold up shading frames or berry netting, to

stand on to reach tall trees, and to gather ashes from the fireplace
to spread on the garden.

> Carolyn and Arnold Westwood,
> Windfields Farm, Cummington,
> Massachusetts

An old stone pediment from a building column has made a great
plant stand for a Christmas cactus.

> Ripley Hotch and Owen Sullivan,
> Boydville The Inn at Martinsburg,
> Martinsburg, West Virginia

An ornate bird cage of yesteryear is great for housing a plant.
Hang the cage from the ceiling, or put it on a stand or table.

> Karen and Ken West, Benner
> House, Weston, Missouri

Horse-drawn sleighs are filled with seasonal flowers and plants
outside the inn.

> Jane and Frank Emanuel,
> Middlebury Inn, Middlebury,
> Vermont

Any antique that you admire but can't find any use for can be
converted into a vase or container of some kind. Place a glass jar
inside the container, such as in ladies' high-top button shoes, and
you have a unique flower holder.

> Mary Louis and Conley Weaver,
> Red Castle Inn, Nevada City,
> California

If you're looking for lovely antique vases, don't overlook glassware originally intended for other purposes. We've found that
topless apothecary jars make wonderful flower holders. With
their stoppers intact, these jars can be quite expensive. But if
purchased topless, they're a bargain. One of our most admired
vases is an 1895 light-blue apothecary jar that cost us only three

dollars. With the top, it would have been about twenty to twenty-five dollars.

> Denise Anderson and David
> Karpinski, Quill and Quilt, Cannon
> Falls, Minnesota

Antique family teacups serve as tiny vases for flowers. You also can use them on a vanity to hold cosmetic puffs or cotton balls.

> Bonnie and Bill Webb, Inn on
> Golden Pond, Holderness, New
> Hampshire

Antique strawberry boxes make great vases for dried arrangements. We have some complete with original advertising: "Seagraves Strawberries-Elsah: The Place to Get Quality."

> Mary Ann and Michael Pitchford,
> Green Tree Inn, Elsah, Illinois

Small, glass mason jars are vases on our breakfast table.

> Sharon and Scott Wright, Silver
> Maple Lodge, Fairlee, Vermont

Painted milk cans hold dried flowers. Antique gravy boats hold potpourri.

> Kris McIlvenna, Greenbriar, Coeur
> d'Alene, Idaho

Antique bottles can be used as flower vases.

> Marilyn and Gene Gundersen,
> Pudding Creek Inn, Fort Bragg,
> California

We disassembled an old chimney when we first arrived and have used the bricks for different projects. They make excellent borders around flower beds.

> Bonnie and Bill Webb, Inn on
> Golden Pond, Holderness, New
> Hampshire

Antique apothecary jars are great for filling with potpourri.

> Ripley Hotch and Owen Sullivan,
> Boydville The Inn at Martinsburg,
> Martinsburg, West Virginia

An antique tricycle in our front flower bed serves as a trellis for our climbing flowers.

> Barbara and Barry Lubao, Ellis
> River House, Jackson, New
> Hampshire

 # Buying and Caring for Antiques

I feel that one should buy fewer pieces if the budget is tight, but buy quality. You will accumulate enough in time.

If you buy an antique and must replace a part of it in order for it to be functional, save the original part for future resale. If a mirror needs replacing, do so. But save the old mirror and put it back into the original frame to return its value at resale.

> Alan Stott, Hannah's House, Pigeon
> Forge, Tennessee

When buying an antique quilt, consider that if it's not in mint condition, its value is probably at its peak. A rip, a fade, or a repair severely reduces the value of the coverlet.

> Mary Louise and Ron Thorburn,
> Inn at Weathersfield, Weathersfield,
> Vermont

If you want to make an antique double bed into a queen-size one, you can add an extension. Extensions can be found on display in some furniture stores or auction centers.

> Audrey Nichols, Heritage Inn,
> Salmon, Idaho

Old iron beds can be sanded and painted easily with cans of spray paint. First, cover any brass with paper and tape, if you want it to show.

Another way to extend the size of a bed to accommodate a larger mattress: We took the iron side rails of the original bed to a welder, who cut them and then added another six inches of angle iron.

> Lois and Paul Dansereau, Silas
> Griffith House, Danby, Vermont

If you see an antique headboard that you really like, but you want a queen-size bed, merely attach the headboard to the wall, then push the bed frame up against it. No one will know it's not attached to the bed.

> Sallie and Welling Clark, Holden
> House 1902, Colorado Springs,
> Colorado

After removing an old wood finish, I rub and rub the surface with a mixture of one part boiled linseed oil, one part turpentine, and one part vinegar. After rubbing, I use a very fine pumice. When the surface feels smooth and slick, I immediately take a clean cloth and wipe it down, leaving a water- and stain-resistant surface that is very durable.

> Catherine Clayton, manager,
> Balcony Downs, Glasgow, Virginia

Try cleaning and waxing with furniture polish (a quality wax, not a highly commercial brand) instead of refinishing. It preserves the wood and enhances the value, and you may discover that the piece doesn't need a refinishing job.

> Shirley and Stephen Ramsey,
> Mayhurst B&B, Orange, Virginia

If you like a certain antiques shop, it's good to go back often. The owner gets to know you and may even call you when he or she has acquired something you like. Also, knowing the shop owner will help yield better discounts.

> Beverly and Ray Compton, Spring
> Bank Inn, Frederick, Maryland

Shopping at salvage sales is a great way to bring some unusual old items into your home. We've purchased several different porch railings, for example. If you like the item, buy it. You'll find a use for it eventually.

> Sunny and Joy Drewel, Zachariah
> Foss Guest House, Washington,
> Missouri

When considering a certain antique, don't let the lack of luster stop you from purchasing the piece. Quite often, a good cleaning and polishing is enough to spruce up the piece. Remember, you want it to look like an antique, not a reproduction.

> Joan and Sal Chandon, Doubleday
> Inn, Gettysburg, Pennsylvania

Author's Tip: If there's a vintage book you want, but it is mildewed, don't shy away from buying it. You can remove a good part of the mustiness. Set the book in the sun. Fan the pages frequently. Then brush off the dried mold.

We have priced reproduction country furnishings and found that the originals in mint condition cost less.

> Jackie and Lee Morrison, Laurel
> Hill Plantation, McClellanville,
> South Carolina

Sea-grass baskets are natural to this area. Their construction is an art form passed down by coastal blacks since the early 1800s. The art is still carried on here. They can be cleaned with a mild liquid dishwashing soap and cool water. Let them dry naturally, away from heat. Stains or mildew can be removed by using a light chlorine bleach and water, then carefully drying the basket away from heat.

> Jackie and Lee Morrison, Laurel
> Hill Plantation, McClellanville,
> South Carolina

Never let antique clothes hang in a wooden closet or wardrobe. They should be kept in acid-free boxes. Handle clothing with white cotton gloves.

Jae and Tom Breitweiser, Cliff House, Madison, Indiana

To frame an antique print, use acid-free matting and backing so that you don't discolor the print.

Florence and Dick Fillet, St. Francisville Inn, St. Francisville, Louisiana

When you go to an auction or an estate sale, look carefully to see how many dealers are there, and bid with them. You can identify them before the auction begins. They look at the merchandise carefully and seem to know several people in the crowd—because they all show up at sales and auctions and bid on many items. You can again spot dealers during the auction. Since they're buying for resale, they will generally stop bidding at half the retail value of an item. If you keep an eye on these folks, and they are bidding on something you like, come in late on the bidding, and go just above the dealers. You're almost guaranteed to get a good buy at far below what you'd have to pay in a shop.

One problem with this approach is that you may be bidding against a collector, who is willing to pay more than retail value just to fill out a collection. The truth is, you're going to be burned occasionally. But it will average out. I (Ripley) once bought an entire collection of tea-leaf china (225 pieces) for $200 this way. The collection now is worth in the thousands.

Avoid auctions of merchandise brought to a motel or hotel from another town. There are likely to be plants (shills hired by the auctioneers) among the bidders at such an auction for the purpose of artificially inflating the bids. If an auctioneer is upping the bid and you can't see who is doing the bidding, stay out. (Owen once brought an entire auction to a halt by demanding loudly and publicly to see who was doing the bidding and wanting to know who she was. The woman sneaked out, and a break was called. The bidding did not resume.)

Ripley Hotch and Owen Sullivan, Boydville The Inn at Martinsburg, Martinsburg, West Virginia

One idea we can stress to beginning antiques buyers is to try to find someone with expertise in the antiques you're interested in buying. A good way to buy antiques is through a picker. A picker is someone who usually works for auctioneers or dealers. He may go door-to-door in neighborhoods, asking if people have furniture they want to sell. Once inside the house, he ferrets out items he knows he can sell. He then turns around and sells the items to antiques dealers or to you at prices much lower than those in retail antiques shops.

Mary Lee and James Papa, Shire
Inn, Chelsea, Vermont

Cut Flowers, Plants, and Gardens

Adding Colorful, Fresh Accents Inside and Out

The addition of plants inside the home year round and accents of colorful flowers outside during the growing season enhance a home's appeal inside and out, and they do much more.

Flowers, plants, and gardens are part of the amenities at inns. Filling vases and/or unusual containers, fresh-cut flowers can be found anywhere from the front porch to the common areas and even individual guest rooms.

Some innkeepers are ardent gardeners specializing in, say, herbs. Their plant-life metier becomes a part of the essence of the inn. Dorry Norris at the Sage Cottage in Trumansburg, New York, for example, is a devoted herbalist, and her guests reap the benefits of her knowledge of the field. She even offers classes on the subject to guests staying at the inn.

Usually, whatever the innkeeper grows makes its way onto the breakfast or dinner table, either as food, garnishes, or decorations. In addition to growing parsley for a garnish, for example, many of them have even learned which flowers are edible, in order to use them to garnish a meal.

Although the variety of hints offered by the innkeepers on this subject is quite diverse, they all believe that paying a little more attention to flowers and gardens reminds one to relax and forget about the troubles of the day.

 Flowers

To give your cut flowers longer life, cut the ends on an angle. Make sure no leaves are below the water level. Change water daily.

> Marie and Dick Brophy, Isaiah Hall
> B&B, Dennis, Massachusetts

Always use warm water for cut flowers. Flowers with woody stems will last longer with a crushed cigarette in the water.

> Mary Louise and Conley Weaver,
> Red Castle Inn, Nevada City,
> California

Bleach will help fresh flowers and the water in the vase look fresher. Add about one-half teaspoon per quart of water.

> Carolyn and Jeff Rawes, Ash Mill
> Farm, Holicong, Pennsylvania

7-Up soda (at room temperature), mixed with half as much cool water, will help extend the life of freshly cut flowers.

> Louise, Pat, and Bumpy Walter,
> Grant Corner Inn, Santa Fe, New
> Mexico

Flower vases dulled by brown film can sparkle again. Chop a small potato into very small pieces, and place them in the dulled vase. Add one-half cup vinegar. Shake well. Wash in soapy water and rinse.

> Britt House Staff, San Diego,
> California

Wildflowers make wonderful bouquets in the summertime. Pick them late in the day when it's cool. As soon as you pick them, soak them right up to their necks in a bucket of water. Let them stand overnight before arranging. This way, they will keep for up to a week.

Janice and Jack McWilliams, Inn at
Gristmill Square, Warm Springs,
Virginia

We plant wildflowers everywhere in the summer. They're wonderful for fresh arrangements. When the wildflowers aren't available, we use other wild plants. Blueberries and cottonwoods budding in the spring make lovely arrangements. Evergreen boughs are great in winter.

Annie and Al Unrein, Glacier Bay
Country Inn, Gustavus, Alaska

Use a meat/poultry baster to add water to vases and potted flower arrangements to prevent water damage to antique tables and other furniture.

Mary Louise and Conley Weaver,
Red Castle Inn, Nevada City,
California

Flowers create an aura of life and provide delicate, natural scents. To keep expenses down, buy daisies or mums, which come in many shades and varieties and last two weeks. You needn't have large arrangements. One or two flowers in a vase with fern and baby's breath will do.

I often use baskets to arrange flowers. Fill an old jar with water, and place it in an interesting basket. Arrange your flowers so that the jar doesn't show.

Seasonal flower arrangements are also fun. In the fall, I decorate with full branches of leaves or I place leaves around a pumpkin or gourd. In the winter, I cut evergreen branches and arrange pinecones and red sumac or rose hips around a basket.

Ujjala Schwartz, Ujjala's B&B, New
Paltz, New York

When buying flowers, ask the florist when they came in or how long they have been at the shop. If the flowers are faded, it could be a sign that they are old. Ask if that is so, as some flowers only have the appearance of being faded.

When dried flowers look old, dust them lightly and spray them with hairspray. The spray helps hold them together and slows down crumbling or falling apart.

To make flower arranging easier, make a small ball of tangled chicken wire that fits into the bottom of the container. Insert the stems of your flowers, and they will be held in place. You can also crisscross the top of your container with transparent adhesive tape, making small areas in which to insert the flowers. Make sure the tape doesn't show.

Arranging flowers isn't easy for many people. Don't try so hard to make your arrangements perfect. Arrange flowers at different heights, and stop fussing with them as soon as they look good.

> Marie and Dean Dulaney, Blossom
> Tyme B&B, Gambier, Ohio

Marguerite daisies are easy to grow. They bloom prolifically all summer and fall and last a long time when cut for arrangements.

> Marjorie and John Pratt, Inn on
> Cove Hill, Rockport, Massachusetts

Daffodils are a good investment. They require no care, and they spread every year. We have them at our driveway entrance for a great splash of color as our guests enter.

> Bonnie and Bill Webb, Inn on
> Golden Pond, Holderness, New
> Hampshire

The stems of roses will hold the weight of the rose, without bending over, if you place one tablespoon of epsom salts around the base of each rosebush and water it in. I don't know why it works, but it really does. A guest gave us this tip, and it has worked for all eighty of our rosebushes.

Baskets of red impatiens line our wraparound porch. You don't have to wait and watch too long for hummingbirds when you have impatiens. When red impatiens are this abundant, hummingbirds are attracted to them.

> Linda and Gene Merlino,
> Lamplight Inn, Lake Luzerne, New
> York

Geraniums in pots are a good summer floral investment. They are easy to move to a deck, a pool, a picnic area, or an empty garden spot. Wherever the party or occasion, they allow for instant garden or color.

Janice and Jack McWilliams, Inn at Gristmill Square, Warm Springs, Virginia

 # Indoor Plants

To tell if a plant needs to be watered, stick a finger into the dirt. If it comes out dry up to the first knuckle, the plant needs water.

Joe Rice, gardener, Vermont Inn, Killington, Vermont

If you display a plant on a scale, you can watch the weight to see when it needs to be watered.

Small chunks of leftover soap work as both a nontoxic bug killer and plant food (phosphates). If you add tobacco to the brew, you have a great mixture for eliminating aphids. Chop the soap up in a food processor, then dissolve it in water. Pour or spray the mixture onto the plants.

Robin Brooks, Robins Nest, San Andreas, California

Indoor plants love to go outside for the summer, but bring them out gradually so as not to shock them. On the first nice day, let them out for one hour, then take them back inside. Repeat for two or three more days. After this period, they are used to the change and can stay outside.

Pat and John Emerson, Emersons' Guest House, Vergennes, Vermont

The pot you use affects the wetness of the soil. Clay pots dry out faster than plastic ones. So you may need to water plants in clay pots more often.

For indoor plants, we use room-temperature water with fourteen drops of liquid fertilizer added per gallon. Omit the fertilizer from November through February.

Plants do better if you don't fuss with them too much.

> Mary and Gary Riley, Williams
> House, Hot Springs, Arkansas

Place germinating-seed containers on heating pads to expedite growth. I (Lynda) have heard you can accomplish the same thing by placing the containers on top of the refrigerator where it's warm.

> Lynda and Joe Petty, Park House,
> Saugatuck, Michigan

We grow our own lettuce for garnishes with a grow light in our basement. Make a 4-by-4-inch pot from the bottom third of a plastic one-half–gallon milk container. It will accommodate five leaf-lettuce plants. We plant two new pots every three to four weeks and always have enough leaves to use as garnishes throughout the winter.

> Robin and Bill Branigan, Roaring
> Lion, Waldoboro, Maine

Adding baby's breath to indoor green plants, such as ivy, gives the plants a pleasing, lacy touch.

> Karen and Ken West, Benner
> House, Weston, Missouri

Sugar bowls, old teapots, and teacups make novel plant holders. Place crushed charcoal at the bottom for drainage.

> Pat Hardy, Glenborough Inn, Santa
> Barbara, California

 # Gardening

If you don't have land for a garden, and besides, you aren't the type who likes to mow the grass and till the soil, a rooftop garden is the answer. We built a redwood deck on one of our roofs with a covering and a totally enclosed solarium. The solarium has a fireplace, so we can sit and have breakfast out here even in cold weather. We have hanging plants all over the outdoor section and plants in large standing pots.

> Genny Jenkins, Healdsburg Inn,
> Healdsburg, California

Don't let the lack of planting areas stop you from planting a garden. Use clay pots and large barrels filled with a mixture of potting soil and topsoil, and watch your garden grow above ground!

> Judy and Jack McMahon, Inn at
> Starlight Lake, Starlight,
> Pennsylvania

Author's Tip: Fill an old wooden wheelbarrow with colorful flowers in the summer. Display the cart on your front lawn. In the winter, the wheelbarrow can hold potted plants indoors.

Planting small trees in whiskey barrels on wheels makes it easy to move the trees around to difficult parts of the garden.

> Alice-June and Franz Benjamin,
> Chateau Victorian, Santa Cruz,
> California

Purchase colorful plants in bloom. Petunias and snapdragons in 4-inch pots work well. Mass them together in a shallow container or basket. Disguise the top of the plastic pots with sphagnum moss. A tight circle of 4-inch pots works well around the base of deciduous trees. After the blooms are spent, the plants can be set out permanently in the garden.

> Mary Louise and Conley Weaver,
> Red Castle Inn, Nevada City,
> California

Because our time is precious, gardening must be fairly maintenance-free. One of our techniques: bark mulch in beds looks nice, keeps down weeds, and holds moisture.

> Ruth and Cliff Manchester,
> Bramble Inn, Brewster,
> Massachusetts

To discourage weeds from growing, position about 2 inches of heavy bark mulch around your beds. It helps a great deal.

Mary Ellen and Walt Brown,
Cedarym B&B, Redmond,
Washington

Compost is easy to get started and really gives you a better soil. To start a compost heap, find an inconspicuous area of the garden, but one that is easy to get to. You may want to delineate the section with a small fence. Start the pile with cuttings from the garden. Add food and bones. When the pile gets big enough, put a plastic tarp over the top. This will keep any weed seeds from spreading. After one year, the compost will be ready to spread in your garden.

Beverly Roger Allison, Sleepy
Hollow Farm, Gordonsville,
Virginia

Mothballs keep snakes and other critters out of the garden. Be sure to put down plenty of mothballs; you need a lot for them to work.

Mary and Gary Riley, Williams
House, Hot Springs, Arkansas

Mothballs, sprinkled on dirt, will keep cats from using your big plants for litter boxes.

Robin Brooks, The Robins Nest,
San Andreas, California

We have changed our gardening to include more flowering shrubs, which curb fungus and insect problems.

Faith and Charles Reynolds,
Historic Merrell Tavern Inn, South
Lee, Massachusetts

Anyone can have a small pond in a garden. Dig a deep hole the depth and size you want. Buy a heavy-duty plastic liner at any hardware store. This forms your pool for holding the water. The dirt from the hole can be used as an embankment around the pond. It doubles as a dam. Clean out the pond once a week. Keep it stocked with goldfish (to alleviate mosquitoes), snails, and aquatic plants.

Megan Timothy, La Maida House,
North Hollywood, California

Enhance garden space with a hot tub. Use an ozonator as well as chlorine. You guarantee sanitation and avoid odor and red eyes.

Margot and Tom Doohan,
O'Duach'ain Inn, Bigfork, Montana

If you have deer eating up your garden, chase them away with soap. A few bars of deodorant soap strung up into trees or tied to plants in the garden will keep them away harmlessly. I don't know what the reason is behind this, but it has worked beautifully for our garden.

Dee and Bob Bundy, Bundy's B&B,
Gretna, Nebraska

Use railway ties and washed gravel to make walkways through flowers and vegetable gardens.

Audrey Nichols, Heritage Inn,
Salmon, Idaho

The key to raising bulbs successfully is good drainage. Prepare the soil well, so water does not sit around the bulbs, causing them to rot. Planting bulbs in raised beds is a good idea if you don't have good drainage.

Mary Ellen and Walt Brown,
Cedarym B&B, Redmond,
Washington

Don't skimp when buying good bulbs. Buy high-quality bulbs from a reputable supplier. Remember you're making a long-term investment.

Plan your garden well. The tallest growing bulbs should be in the back, bordered by shorter ones in the front. Early-blooming bulbs are fun to plant where they will be easily seen from your windows or be adjacent to frequently traveled walkways, so you can enjoy a sensation of spring when little else is blooming.

Remember that bulbs have different growing and flowering periods. Plant accordingly, so that your garden will bloom throughout the full growing season.

Bulbs can be used to bring early color to a perennial garden when planted in clumps of five or six throughout the garden.

Early or mid-season daffodils add a nice touch to a field or around the edge of a pond, if planted in clumps 5 to 10 feet apart or at random, to look as though they grew on their own.

> Merrily and Max Comins, Kedron
> Valley Inn, South Woodstock,
> Vermont

Author's Tip: To make gardening easier, take a tool caddy along with you. Create clever caddies according to your needs. One idea is to take an old golf bag and fill it with rakes, hoes, and shovels. Use the smaller pouches for tinier tools.

It's much easier to organize your garden if you plant in raised beds. At the Quill and Quilt, we used 1-by-16-inch boards with common corner braces to create 4-by-8-foot beds. We planted an assortment of the fruits and vegetables that we serve to our guests, as well as the flowers we cut and place in the rooms. We find our guests walking among and admiring the beds. We make sure all the plants are labeled. Beds organized this way also add encouragement to the gardener, since it is easier to see progress in the contained area.

We then build our menus around whatever is ready for harvesting. We also offer guests the chance to pick their own fruits, vegetables, and flowers. Or, if they are willing, we offer them the chance to try their hand at weeding! Try to imagine your friends' reaction if you had a dinner party with a pick-your-own salad for starters!

If you're an organic gardener, leftover bones burned in your fireplace will add bonemeal to the wood ashes and make an excellent nutrient to mix with your garden soil.

Putting together a perennial garden can be a costly venture. However, a little creativity can produce a great deal of cost-saving. Simply place an ad in your local newspaper (during spring or fall), requesting slips, divisions, or cuttings from other local gardeners, with special emphasis on heirloom varieties. Garden-

ers love to share their success and are usually more than happy
to help out.

Denise Anderson and David
Karpinski, Quill and Quilt, Cannon
Falls, Minnesota

To attract butterflies, plant flowers such as zinnias and marigolds.
There are also numerous varieties of butterfly bushes and flowers, which were grown during the Victorian era, that are planted
specifically to attract the insect.

Mariam and Charles Bechtel,
Bechtel Mansion, East Berlin,
Pennsylvania

Recognize the limitations of your garden. Forget about trying
plants that won't make it in your surroundings.

My house is surrounded by trees and is too dark for plants
needing sun. I have lush-looking plants anyway. My secret is
filling antique containers and lined baskets with clippings from
overgrown plants and even certain weeds that won't grow on my
property. The effect is an instant plant that costs nothing and that
you can change when you want. Use oasis to hold the clippings in
place in the pot.

Kay Gill, Stephen Daniels House,
Salem, Massachusetts

When we purchased our inn in 1982, there was everything to do.
The grounds, we decided, would have to wait until later. However, friends cut (actually hacked) down the bamboo and 6-foot
weeds on the property. We kept the back area mowed until 1986.
Beneath a great deal of weeds and brush, we could see the
gardens that we knew had once flourished on the property. Plants
and bulbs were more than 100 years old, and we wanted to bring
them back to flowering. So we hired weeders. Unfortunately, we
would discover later that the cash we spent hiring people to keep
the gardens weeded was not financially smart.

You see, the inexperienced people we hired had no interest or
skill for the task at hand. We should have hired a gardener in the
first place. In 1986, we hired a landscape architect to do a plan
for the entire grounds area. She recommended a gardener-
couple. They completely dismantled the rock garden and sur-

rounding area gardens, carefully and temporarily stored all of the old plants in our barn, and reconstructed the entire area, using the original plants. Some of the antique plantings are no longer available in nurseries; we gladly send roots home with all interested guests.

It took about thirty-five days to complete the back area of the inn. The total result is so rewarding. We just wish we had back the $900 we spent trying to do it with casual, inexperienced labor. I guess our bottom-line advice is: If you have gardens you want restored, seek professional help.

> Deedy and Charlie Marble,
> Governor's Inn, Ludlow, Vermont

I'm a landscape architect, so one of our attractions is our garden. Plan yours to include an evening-fragrance garden, especially if you live in an area conducive to strolling or have a patio. Use mostly white flowers. They are luminescent during the nighttime. Nicotiana is a favorite. It's white and fragrant, and its blooms open at night.

> Kate Kerivan, Bungay Jar, Easton,
> New Hampshire

Herbs

Herbs don't grow well indoors in winter in the Northeast. However, many of the tender perennials do survive the winter in the house. Rosemary, bay, scented geraniums, and ginger manage with a lot of TLC.

> Dorry Norris, Sage Cottage,
> Trumansburg, New York

Dr. Bonner's Peppermint Soap and some water will get rid of pests on indoor-growing herbs.

> Kate Kerivan, Bungay Jar, Easton,
> New Hampshire

Mint can be quite prolific in the garden. You can contain its growth by sinking a round drainage pipe into the ground and placing the mint into it. You can buy such a pipe in a hardware store.

The hotter and drier the soil, the more pungent the herbs. Although they will not look as nice as herbs growing in moist soil, they will be perfectly pungent.

Lynda and Joe Petty, Park House,
Saugatuck, Michigan

The best time to pick herbs is in the early morning, when they are fresh and have not withered from exposure to the sun.

Christi and Mark Carter, Carter
House, Eureka, California

When you first plant your herbs, don't cut them back too much in the first year. You are providing growth for the rest of their life.

Stuart W. Smith, Churchtown Inn,
Churchtown, Pennsylvania

Fireside Tips

Build a Better Fire, Have a Better Time

The winter warmth of a cozy country inn always conjures up the following scene in my imagination:

The light of the full moon cast a glow over the stormy night. As the wind whirled across the prairie, swirls of snow seemed to compass a path back to the inn for the young couple. As the shivering twosome neared the stately Victorian, partially hidden by drifts of snow, its gingerbread woodwork resembled the top of a chocolate cake, highlighted with powdered sugar sprinkled through a doily. Flickering gaslights helped the anxious man and woman find the doorway. The large turreted building creaked and moaned in the night wind as the couple huddled on the porch, scraping their icy boots on the old iron mud catcher.

They were about to knock on the door when the innkeeper, her furrowed brow unwrinkling slightly at the welcome sight, opened the door widely. She whisked the chilled couple inside and ushered them into the keeping room to be warmed by the hot fire in the big fireplace.

"Sorry we worried you," they said. "We were having such a wonderful time on the toboggan run and then the horse-drawn sleigh, that we hadn't noticed how bad the storm was getting. We lost our way back to the inn."

As the innkeeper served her special spirited brew—her inn's trademark—and her homemade confections, the couple had the comforting sensation of being pampered by a loving parent.

This portrait of a "dark and stormy night" is fictitious, but the symbolism is quite real. Many an innkeeper has kept the embers burning, waiting for guests he or she was worried about. Fireplaces at inns not only warm scenarios such as this, but also are perfect mood setters.

Not all of us have fireplaces, but if you want one in your home, you can get one easier than you think by having one built in. We did that in one of the homes we once owned.

We chose a prefabricated unit, which basically means it has no poured concrete foundation or brick chimney. This type of setup is the perfect solution for many smaller homes, as it can be installed almost anywhere. Now, don't get the wrong picture; it is not a freestanding unit, but it is fully installed with its own flue and metal chimney (which you don't see except on the roof) and ceramic firebox. We selected a finely crafted wooden colonial mantel and old bricks for facing and for the hearth. The finished effect was dazzling. We changed the entire personality of the house. Real estate agents say a fireplace is one of the best investments you can make in your house.

Another consideration is the installation of a wood stove. These units, when installed properly and in the right spot in your home, can heat your entire house. They, too, are warm and cozy, and one can enjoy almost the same amenities offered by built-in fireplaces.

 ## Starting a Fire

My (Ripley's) grandfather taught me how to start a fire and keep it going properly, and his method always works (provided you have good wood that's reasonably dry). Basically, it's this: Always keep the pieces of large wood in a pyramid shape—this creates the necessary draft around the logs (for example, if using six pieces, place three on bottom, two next, one on top). The top piece will always burn the fastest and should be moved down when you put on a new piece.

Ripley Hotch and Owen Sullivan,
Boydville The Inn at Martinsburg,
Martinsburg, West Virginia

Fire starters can be useful and decorative. Gather pinecones small enough to fit into muffin tins. Dip the pinecones in a kettle of hot paraffin. Let them cool. Fill each muffin cup with two teaspoons of sawdust and hot paraffin. You can add different colors of food coloring. Place a pinecone in each muffin cup. When cool, remove the pinecones and place them in a wicker basket, set next to the fireplace.

Audrey Nichols, Heritage Inn,
Salmon, Idaho

We have several fireplaces and have found that bringing the wood in the night before helps it to dry and also warm up. This helps the fire to start more quickly and burn better. In very cold weather, we usually have a fire at breakfast.

Faith and Charles Reynolds,
Historic Merrell Tavern, South Lee,
Massachusetts

Pinecones wrapped in newspapers will start your logs burning right away.

Susan Hannah, Winters Creek Inn,
Carson City, Nevada

With seven fireplaces—five working ones—we found Cape Cod lighters to be a saving grace. Cape Cod is not a brand name, but a style of lighter that can be purchased in a fireplace-supply shop. No newspaper is necessary. Kindling helps, but it isn't required. These lighters are filled with kerosene and have a porous ball that sits in the fluid. When ready, just light the ball and set it under the wood. Easy! And the ash is so clean, we only sweep our fireboxes once or twice a season.

Tracy and Jim Stone, Inn at
Mitchell House, Chestertown,
Maryland

We have five fireplaces, and when we first took over the inn we took lessons on fire starting from innkeeper De Davis. He was a veritable lexicon on operating and maintaining a fireplace. One of the things he did was to break white-birch bark into fine strips with which he underlaid each fire. It's a beautiful effect but a lot of work, and it may not be easy to find the white-birch bark.

We usually use newspapers to start a fire. However, we don't just crumble sheets and throw them in. No, my little secret is that I (James) tear the paper into long strips, but I do not completely rip some through to the bottom. I leave about ½ inch. This way, although the paper is in strips, it is still bound together. We don't have pieces falling around in every direction. Just lay the paper in the fireplace. Next, I take kindling and make a tick-tack-toe board over the paper. I then place a log or two on top. It is so important to build a good coal system under your fire. So make sure the fire is tended every ten minutes or so during the first half hour.

> Mary Lee and James Papa, Shire
> Inn, Chelsea, Vermont

If you don't have kindling wood, use newspaper knots to start the fire. Roll two to three full sheets of newspaper lengthwise and then into a single knot. This is an old Scandinavian trick that really works.

> Kathy Drew, Out-the-Inn-Door,
> Freeport, Maine

The tendency is to clean out the fireplace every time you use it. However, it is better not to clear out the ashes, as a bed of coals helps produce more heat for the next fire you build. Leaving the coals will warm the room more.

> Elizabeth Gundry Hooper, Corner
> Cupboard Inn, Rehoboth, Delaware

Author's Tip: When acquiring wood for the fireplace or wood-burning stove, the aroma of the burning logs is nicest from woods of fruit and nut trees, such as apple, cherry, beech, hickory, and pecan. You do pay a price for this nostalgic effect. Fruit wood is more expensive and harder to find.

Keeping the Fire Going Safely

When the fire starts to wane, puff it up again with a bellows. The forced air gets the flames active again.

> Jeanne Marie Tomlinson, Glendale
> Farms B&B, Ithaca, New York

We often pitch candle stubs into the fire. They provide the loveliest colors among the flames.

> Chris and Jill Raggio, Ilverthorpe
> Cottage, Narragansett, Rhode
> Island

If smoke backs up into the room, soak a wet towel in vinegar. Wring it out. Swirl it around the room. It really works to clean out the air.

> Marie and Dick Brophy, Isaiah Hall
> B&B, Dennis, Massachusetts

Keep a throw rug in front of your hearth so that popping embers don't singe you, the rug, or the floor.

> Emily Hunter, Briar Rose, Boulder,
> Colorado

Fireplace Decor

A 3- to 5-inch ruffle around fireplace mantels can help in creating that warm, country feeling.

> Demay and Jim Pringle, Pringle
> House, Oakland, Oregon

Author's Tip: During the summer, a gaping hearth with no fire going is not always a pretty sight. There are many ways to brighten this area. Placing large baskets of flowers in front is just one way. Another way to cheer the fireplace in summer is to install a decorative fireboard, a piece of wood that can be painted on or stenciled and placed over the entire open area of the firebox.

If you want a temporary closing for your fireplace during the warm months, here's how to make a freestanding fireboard as I (Jim) did for our fireplaces: Build a frame out of 1 × 3s to fit the size of your fireplace opening. Attach Masonite to fit the frame with finishing nails on white glue. Prime, paint, and decorate. Build two to three floor brackets to hold the fireboard in place.

To permanently close off the fireplace: Make a frame with scrap lumber—1 × 1 or 2 × 2. Cut a piece of ¼-inch Masonite to fit the opening. Hold the Masonite in position with white glue. Hold temporarily with tape until glue dries (overnight). Remove tape. The gap between the fireplace and the Masonite may be unacceptable. Fill it with caulk, and paint along this portion, as well as the Masonite. To paint Masonite, use a latex or oil primer before painting with your color. You can actually make the fireboard look like the inside of the fireplace. Using Spackle, make faux bricks. Paint them red, with gray paint between "bricks" to simulate mortar. The other option is to stencil it or paint on a landscape or flower arrangement.

> Jim and Mimi Agard, Brafferton
> Inn, Gettysburg, Pennsylvania

You can use hinged wooden doors to close off a fireplace for the season. Purchased shutters that fit the opening will do nicely.

> Stuart W. Smith, Churchtown Inn,
> Churchtown, Pennsylvania

We keep an antique copper boiler on the hearth to hold logs and fireplace tools. It looks pretty and is useful.

> Mary Lee and James Papa, Shire
> Inn, Chelsea, Vermont

 # Fireside Entertainment

Ghost Stories

Some inns claim to have kindred spirits living in their homes. The innkeepers are usually very cautious about making such claims, and some shy away from such conversations with guests. But when a guest or staff member runs into such an apparition, the house buzzes with speculation. The stories of such sightings are often retold when guests gather in front of a fire. Here are a few that you might retell at your own fireplace gatherings.

One of our first apparitions was seen by one of our waiters. He saw a man sitting alone and asked if he wanted a glass of sherry. The man declined. The waiter said it was an apparition sitting on the couch. I (Mary Louise) ran out in time to catch the man leaving the hall, dressed in knickers and a vest. If you see a ghost in your home, your local historical society will lead you to people who will help you trace who it is.

One of our guests not too long ago spotted a new apparition. She described a young girl, whom she had seen. Another guest at a different time described the same girl standing by a fireplace. We traced the girl and found she was an ancestor of one of the original home owners.

> Mary Louise and Ron Thorburn,
> Inn at Weathersfield, Weathersfield,
> Vermont

I was never one to believe in ghosts. But something gave me food for thought.

When we first moved into the house, I (Ruth) was cheerfully unpacking boxes with my daughter. We heard a noise in the back room downstairs and called down to see who was in the house. No one replied, but the noises continued. I went downstairs and locked the front door. We continued to open boxes, and I let the matter pass.

One of our first guests walked into that same room. He took four steps in and quickly took one giant leap backward. 'I cannot stay in that room,' he said rather calmly and matter-of-factly. 'There is a presence in there.' So we put the man into another room, and he was satisfied. Other guests have also reported noises and sightings, having no prior knowledge of any other guest's finding. Since then we have identified the presence.

> Ruth Keyes, Red Brick Inn, Old
> Mystic, Connecticut

Originally we just used the inn periodically. We knew there was a ghost. But since the house was hardly in use for twenty-five years, the specter stayed on. When we moved in permanently, the ghost eventually moved out, realizing we were staying.

If you have resident spooks in your home, don't tell your friends or overnight guests, unless they say something strange happened. Some people think such a phenomenon is great;

others don't. If you feel there is a presence in the house, research it to put your mind at ease.

Hettie and Joe Hawvermale,
Folkestone B&B, Berkeley Springs,
West Virginia

Activities

In December, we supply all the materials for guests to get started on a pomander to take home. It is a special treat to hang in your closet or to use as decoration in a large wooden bowl. Pomanders will fill the air with a fragrance reminiscent of another time. To make pomanders, use

6	oranges (lemon, lime, or apple may also be used; skins should not be too thick)
8	ounces whole cloves
2	ounces ground cinnamon
2	ounces ground cloves
1	ounce ground nutmeg
1	ounce ground allspice
½	ounce ground ginger
2	ounces powdered orrisroot

Push cloves into fruit in close rows. Cover entire fruit. Mix spices in a bowl. Roll fruit in this mixture and leave, uncovered, for several weeks. Turn pomanders in this mixture daily.

After several weeks, remove and add a ribbon so that the pomanders can be hung. Wait several months before storing the pomanders in an airtight container. They should last you several years.

Patricia W. and Donald R. Cornish,
Palmer Inn, Noank, Connecticut

Crumpets toasted on the fire are delicious. Set out a tray of crumpets for your guests. Give everyone a long toasting fork.

Hold the crumpet over the fire until it browns. Spread with butter and enjoy.

> Jenny and Ken Hodkinson,
> Gingerbread House, West Harwich,
> Massachusetts

A puzzle in progress gives guests something to do in the winter or while they're waiting to go to dinner.

> Robin Brooks, Robins Nest, San
> Andreas, California

The fireplace is our favorite spot for playing the old-time parlor game of charades. Once you get started, your guests will really enjoy themselves. Sometimes the old corny games are the best.

> Joan and Sal Chandon, Doubleday
> Inn, Gettysburg, Pennsylvania

When romance is kindling at our inn, Jerry may be asked to perform a wedding ceremony. Not only an architect and inn-keeper, he is also a lay minister who conducts nondenominational services.

> Linda and Jerry Lundeen, Inn of
> the Arts, Las Cruces, New Mexico

Hearth Cookery

Cooking in your home fireplace adds rich flavors to your food. Kettles are used to cook the food, and they are placed over hot coals, not directly on the flames. Flavor comes from the hard-woods that you need to burn. Softwoods will yield only ash, not fiery coals. Piles of coals are shoveled onto the hearth, where you place the cooking pots.

If you are attempting this at home for a large group, you really need a spacious hearth that is away from wall-to-wall carpeting. You can cook in almost any fireplace, but your space will be limited in more modern fireplaces. You need a good draft, too, or you'll smoke the house.

> Ruth Keyes and Vern Sasek, Red
> Brook Inn, Old Mystic, Connecticut

Cooking in the fireplace becomes less threatening as soon as one realizes that there are the same adjustments of low, medium, and high as on an electric or gas stove. On the hearth, a pot or fry pan placed on a trivet, off the coals, is on low. Banked directly in the coals, it would be at the highest temperature. The position of a fireplace crane and the use of S hooks regulate heat. The crane swings, so you can regulate its position from directly over the flames (high temperature) to a forward position (low temperature). S hooks allow you to raise or lower the cooking pot, further regulating the heat exposure. Understanding this allows for great control.

Installation of a fireplace crane for simple cookery adds a flair to any dinner party or family meal. Try simplifying fireplace cooking by first partially cooking the meal with regular appliances and finishing the presentation in the fireplace, from which you serve the meal. Never take shortcut safety measures. Have on hand a fire extinguisher, a bucket of sand, and a bucket of water. The cook should wear layered clothing of natural fabrics.

Protect the forward portion of the hearth from cooking stains with several applications of butcher's wax or floor wax. Soups, stews, and chili are wonderful foods to simmer from the crane. Many cookies and appetizers that can be oven-baked can be done in an iron griddle placed on the hearth.

Maureen and John Magee, Rabbit
Hill Inn, Lower Waterford,
Vermont

Snacks

A popcorn popper and a jar of unpopped corn on the mantel in winter is a surefire friend maker for do-it-yourself guests to enjoy by the fire.

Corky and Steve Garboski, Province
Inn, Stafford, New Hampshire

To prepare chestnuts for cooking in the fireplace, soak them in hot water for at least half the day. Place them in a specially made chestnut roaster (resembles a popcorn popper), and cook until they start to split open. Note: The soaking usually causes the nuts to split as they cook.

Ruth Keyes and Vern Sasek, Red
Brook Inn, Old Mystic, Connecticut

Household Hints

Everyday Wisdom for Any Family Circle

At the larger inns, hired help often clean up after the guests have gone. Even the smaller inns have someone who assists the innkeeper with household chores. Otherwise, the most important tasks—spending time with guests and serving mouthwatering breakfasts, lunches, or dinners—could not be done with the detail and attention that make an inn so special.

With today's wives and husbands both working, it is not unusual for them to have help as the innkeepers do. One innkeeper offers a suggestion on how to hire and find help and what you can expect.

Even with help, unless you have constant, around-the-clock maid service, there are household responsibilities you cannot escape and unpredictable mishaps that do occur. The innkeepers offer a large bag of tricks here on how to make your housekeeping chores easier. They remind us that, although they clean with guests in mind, we too can think about cleaning in the same way. Eva Mae Musgrave of The Edge of Thyme in Candor, New York, adds, "Don't forget to clean even the little things, such as light switches, glass globes on lamps, light bulbs, and the tops of tile walls in bathrooms—the kinds of things it's easy to forget, but that a visitor will notice."

The innkeepers' methods are tried-and-true and often come from secrets passed down through family generations. In fact, Mary Louise and Ron Thorburn of The Inn at Weathersfield in Weathersfield, Vermont, say they often look to old cookbooks first for a solution to a household problem. "There you find ways and means of taking care of nearly any problem the old-fashioned way—thriftily and without chemicals," explains Mary Louise.

Ruthmary Jordan of Pride House in Jefferson, Texas, finds original solutions to domestic problems by harkening back to her roots. Ruthmary notes, "Growing up on a remote plantation in the boonies of Louisiana, we were forced to make do on many occasions. This paved the way for how we often resolve problems today—we rummage through our old, bound trunks and boxes to find articles or remedies that fit our needs. This brings about unusual and certainly one-of-a-kind results that are full of character."

 # Making Housekeeping Easier

Should you decide to get help for household chores in your own home, the way we hire help at the inn applies here:
- Most important, look for someone who is honest and has a pleasant personality.
- Remember that you should treat your help well, but you are the boss.
- Sometimes it is better to hire someone who has little or no experience but is willing to learn, than someone who knows it all and may not conform to your needs.

Andrea Dale, Northfield Country
House, Northfield, Massachusetts

Keep a cleaning bucket filled with items that you use for cleaning the entire house, such as sponges, brushes, soaps, cups, wastebasket liners, and assorted cleaners. Tote the bucket to each room. This makes cleaning a lot faster and more efficient.

Diane and Al Johnson, Nauset
House, East Orleans, Massachusetts

I go around cleaning the inn so meticulously that people have joked I should wear one of those carpenter's belts around my waist and insert cleaning utensils into the leather brackets. Actually, this is a good idea. It keeps both hands free, and wherever you go to clean, your tools are right there, even in knotty corners and high spots.

> Sally and Ken McWilliams, Main
> Street B&B, Madison, Indiana

As a woman, I have my own toolbox—not only with hammer, nails, and screwdrivers, but also with glue, curtain brackets, picture hangers, and a wide assortment of other related materials.

> Susan Hannah, Winters Creek Inn,
> Carson City, Nevada

Author's Tip: Be imaginative and make your own household toolbox. One idea is to take a workman's lunch box, spray-paint it a color you like, and fill it with items that suit your needs.

With three flights of stairs, we leave a handy tray on each floor to collect items that need to be taken elsewhere in the inn.

> Kris McIlvenna, Greenbriar Inn,
> Coeur d'Alene, Idaho

 # Cleaning

Cleaning Solutions

Vinegar mixed with water becomes an all-purpose cleaner.

> Marie and Dick Brophy, Isaiah Hall
> B&B, Dennis, Massachusetts

Here's a recipe for an all-purpose cleaner: one-quarter cup sudsy ammonia, one cup isopropyl rubbing alcohol (70 percent), one-half teaspoon liquid dishwashing detergent, and enough water to make a half gallon.

> Beverly and Ray Compton, Spring
> Bank Inn, Frederick, Maryland

Nail-polish remover works magically and quickly to clean the shiny, chrome-colored part of a toaster or small broiler oven. Place a small amount of remover on a cotton ball and gently rub.

Corky and Steve Garboski, Province
Inn, Strafford, New Hampshire

Rubbing alcohol can be used when all else fails.

Cathy and Dave Eakin, Captain's
House, Chatham, Massachusetts

Cleaning Tools

Just a reminder that old toothbrushes are great cleaning tools for getting into small places, including under the hinge on the shower door!

Robina and Dick Conway, Almond
View Inn, Paso Robles, California

Cobwebs can be quickly snatched with our country cobweb-grabber that we sell at the inn. We take a calico-decorated work glove, stuff it with paper or other material, and mount it on a long dowel for a handle. This is decorative as well as useful, especially for cobwebs in high places. You can then wash the glove.

Evelyn and Gilbert Davidson,
Davidson's Country Inn, Pagosa
Springs, Colorado

Our 100-year-old ceiling beams and wide-board pine walls need little care except for dusting, which can be done easily with spray polish on a dust mop for easy reaching.

Kate Kerivan, Bungay Jar, Easton,
New Hampshire

Make a tool for dusting high corners by covering a dust mop with pantyhose. Dispose of the hose once you have dusted. You can also use it for dusting baseboards and floor moldings.

Eva Mae and Frank Musgrave,
Edge of Thyme, Candor, New York

Lamb's wool dusters shorten dusting time and do a better job than most other dusting tools. They are particularly good for chair rungs.

Faith and Charles Reynolds,
Historic Merrell Tavern Inn, South
Lee, Massachusetts

We have added Victorian-style brass "dust corners" to stair treads. They look nice and keep dust out of the corners. You can purchase them through advertisements in Victorian magazines.

Karen and Ken West, Benner
House, Weston, Missouri

Super-absorbent, prefolded diapers make great household rags.

Pat Hardy, Glenborough Inn, Santa
Barbara, California

Window Cleaning

Use a single-edge razor blade to clean windows. Simply scrape the window. No more liquid cleansers or paper towels. No more streaking. It really works well!

Jody and Raymond Maas, Pelham
Inn, Philadelphia, Pennsylvania

Use newspapers to shine windows after washing them.

Audrey Nichols, Heritage Inn,
Salmon, Idaho

Save the white vinegar you used to clean the coffee maker. It can be used later to wash windows.

Shirley and Stephen Ramsey,
Mayhurst B&B, Orange, Virginia

A squirt of lemon-scented liquid soap in window-washing water cuts tobacco film like magic.

Robin Brooks, Robins Nest, San
Andreas, California

Cleaning Specific Items

Bronze, brass, and copper can be cleaned by making a paste of salt, vinegar, and flour. After scrubbing, wash, rinse, and wipe dry.

> Beverly and Ray Compton, Spring
> Bank Inn, Frederick, Maryland

To clean copper, rub it with a mixture of lemon and salt.

> Britt House Staff, San Diego,
> California

Author's Tip: To clean silver, coat the item with toothpaste, then run it under warm water, working the toothpaste into a foam. Rinse off. For stubborn stains, use a worn, soft toothbrush. This is pleasant to work with.

Clean wood cutting boards with warm water and bleach. Then rinse well.

> Marie and Dick Brophy, Isaiah Hall
> B&B, Dennis, Massachusetts

If you have left a glass coffeepot on the burner with little or no liquid inside, you can remove the burn rings on the inside in the following way. Place small ice cubes in the pot with a few teaspoons of salt and a little water. Swirl this mixture around for a minute or two. Dump out and rinse. This is much cheaper than commercial solutions.

> Rosemary and Ed McDowell, Tulip
> Tree Inn, Chittenden, Vermont

For wood with an otherwise satisfactory finish but a gummy dirt buildup (the kind you can scrape with a fingernail), try a mechanic's waterless hand cleaner. Apply with fine steel wool and wipe with a soft cloth. It will liquefy the gummy grime and leave a soft shine. This is especially good for stair railings and dining-room chairs.

> Anna Horton, High Cotton,
> Bellville, Texas

Clean the toaster daily. Not only can it cause the smoke alarm to sound, but burnt crumbs interfere with the toaster's own thermostat.

> Cathy and Dave Eakin, Captain's
> House, Chatham, Massachusetts

Clean stained glassware with a denture tablet added to a container of water.

Occasionally pour a quarter cup of dishwashing detergent, specifically for cutting grease, down the kitchen drain when you're sure you won't be using the drain again until morning. It keeps your drain clear.

To prepare your oven for tomorrow's cleaning, leave a cup of ammonia in the oven overnight with the door closed, so that the fumes soften the grease. This works particularly well with a gas oven.

> Beverly and Ray Compton, Spring
> Bank Inn, Frederick, Maryland

After cleaning the oven, rinse it with a mixture of vinegar and water to finalize the cleansing.

> Marie and Dick Brophy, Isaiah Hall
> B&B, Dennis, Massachusetts

Bathroom Cleaning Advice

A little bleach inside the commode prevents ring-around-the-potty when it's not used for several days.

> Robin Brooks, Robins Nest, San
> Andreas, California

Paper towels in a holder in the bathroom are useful for wipe-ups (including hair).

> Carolyn and Arnold Westwood,
> Windfields Farm, Cummington,
> Massachusetts

A quick cleanup for a tiled bathroom floor is to use a commercial, premoistened towelette or wipe.

> Ann and Clyne Long, Center Street
> Inn, Logan, Utah

Ceramic tiles can be cleaned easier with denatured alcohol. The alcohol is a fat solvent and cuts soap buildup.

Straight chlorine bleach kills mildew on tile grout. An application once a month beats the mildew.

> Marjorie and John Pratt, Inn on
> Cove Hill, Rockport, Massachusetts

To give a bathroom a fresh smell, dip a cotton ball in oil of citronella and hide it in a corner.

> Britt House Staff, San Diego,
> California

Toothpaste makes a wonderful substitute cleanser for scrubbing tubs or sinks.

A vinegar wash removes mildew stains from shower curtains.

> Barbara and Barry Lubao, Ellis
> River House, Jackson, New
> Hampshire

Liquid hand soap in bathrooms instead of messy bar soaps is not only sanitary but makes cleaning a whole lot easier.

> Honesty and Frank Buczek,
> Thompson Park House, Owego,
> New York

Shower stalls, claw-foot tubs, and whirlpools are much easier to clean if you extend your reach with a sponge mounted on a 24-by-30-inch handle. You can buy one in a hardware store or make your own with sponge, dowel, and glue.

> Denise Anderson and David
> Karpinski, Quill and Quilt, Cannon
> Falls, Minnesota

If you clean and scrub the bathtub after each use, it saves on backbreaking scrubbing later.

Nadine and Carl Glassman,
Wedgwood Inn, New Hope,
Pennsylvania

Our bath salts not only give guests a special treat, but the salts make cleaning the tub much easier. There's very little ring. Our recipe for bath salts:

4 pounds Epsom salts
2 cups Calgon water softener
2 cups baking soda

Combine all the ingredients and mix well. Store in an airtight container. Use one cup of the bath salts for each tub bath.

Joan and Dane Wells, Queen
Victoria, Cape May, New Jersey

What to Do with Soap Scraps

Slivers left from bar soaps can be salvaged and put to good use. We process them in the food processor, using the sharp blade. This makes a product only a little less fine than the famous, flaky, white laundry soap. Our scented soap slivers are treated differently. After being carefully washed, they are put into a tapered glass dish and softened in the microwave oven until soft enough to be compressed into a new cake for family use.

Carolyn and Arnold Westwood,
Windfields Farm, Cummington,
Massachusetts

Use leftover soap to keep dresser drawers from sticking. Rub the bar across the runners, and the drawers will move smoothly.

Marie and Dick Brophy, Isaiah Hall
B&B, Dennis, Massachusetts

I give our leftover soap to missionaries for third world countries and also to local charities.

> Beverley Roger Allison, Sleepy
> Hollow Farm, Gordonsville,
> Virginia

Cleaning Hardwood Floors

Raw wood floors can be cleaned with a mixture of clean bleach, sand, and salt. Let it dry and then vacuum it up.

> Korda Family, Historic Brookside
> Farms, Orwell, Vermont

To keep wood floors looking good, find the best floor refinisher in your area and have him spread on a long-lasting, nonshining sealer. We had that done eight years ago, and the floors still look great. We don't even have to buff them, just sponge any spots and use the dust mop.

> Pat Hardy, Glenborough Inn, Santa
> Barbara, California

Wide-plank flooring cleans and shines beautifully with a spray and wipe of commercial glass cleaner.

> Madeline and Don Mitchell, West
> Dover Inn, West Dover, Vermont

Our lovely Victorian inn is 102 years old and had many battle scars of modernization before we finally restored it. Fortunately, the beautiful, original red-pine floors were protected under layers of carpeting. We removed the carpeting, lightly sanded the floors, and put on a high-gloss varnish. Our guests always ask how we keep the floors so brightly polished. We explain: Once a week we damp-mop the floors with a dilution of Murphy Oil Soap and water. During the week we just dry-mop the floor with the same mop. A little of the oil adheres to the mop, which keeps the floors gleaming.

> Planaria Price and Murray Burns,
> Eastlake Inn, Los Angeles,
> California

Furniture polish sprayed on a dry mop keeps hardwood floors gleaming. Warn family and guests about slipping on them when walking around in stocking feet.

Marjorie and John Pratt, Inn on
Cove Hill, Rockport, Massachusetts

We have soiled oak-and-mahogany parquet floors. We started using paste wax to improve their condition but have found a more effective means. We now apply a liquid wax with a sheepskin mop. Now there is no buildup, and there is much less work. A good, old-fashioned dust mop, sprayed with Endust, works beautifully for daily touchups.

Ursel and Frank Walker, Gate
House Inn, Jackson, California

Stain Removal

When you drop an egg, scrape off as much of it as you can with a knife. Then sponge the spot with cold water. Wash in the usual manner. Never use hot water on an egg stain, because that will set the stain.

Libby and Jim Hopkins, Old Broad
Bay Inn, Waldoboro, Maine

Eggs that drop on the floor are messy and difficult to wipe up. A quick cleanup is to cover the egg completely with salt and let it sit for a couple of minutes. Then just wipe, and it comes right up.

Joanne and George Hardy, Hill
Farm Inn, Arlington, Vermont

Fabric stained with wine can be cleaned by stretching the stained portion over a bowl. Secure it with a rubber band. Sprinkle salt on the stain and pour hot water over it. This works pretty well.

Mustard can be removed from fabric by wetting the stain with hydrogen peroxide. Add a little ammonia. Let soak fifteen minutes, then flush with water.

We love our fresh blueberries and raspberries, but oh, do they stain! Try this: Sponge the area immediately with cold water, or soak it for about a half hour before the stain has a chance to set, or you will really have a problem. Ironing sets the stain further.

> Libby and Jim Hopkins, Old Broad
> Bay Inn, Waldoboro, Maine

Apply club soda quickly after coffee spills. Then blot dry with a towel.

> Beverly and Ray Compton, Spring
> Bank Inn, Frederick, Maryland

Lighter fluid removes candle wax from cloth.

> Shirley and Stephen Ramsey,
> Mayhurst B&B, Orange, Virginia

To remove wax from carpeting, lay a piece of tissue over the stain and place a hot iron on it for a second or two; the wax will come right up.

> Joanne Parker, assistant manager,
> Garnet Hill Lodge, North River,
> New York

Use an expired credit card to remove spilled candle wax, once it has cooled. This works particularly well on wood surfaces, provided you scrape in the direction of the woodgrain.

> Maureen and John Magee, Rabbit
> Hill Inn, Lower Waterford,
> Vermont

If you live in an area that has hard water, you've probably faced lime and mineral residue. We've found that ordinary household vinegar, used full strength, removes the residue from almost any surface and far more economically than specialty cleansers made for this purpose.

> Denise Anderson and David
> Karpinski, Quill and Quilt, Cannon
> Falls, Minnesota

Lye soap will get out tough stains that normal detergents will not. This old-fashioned method really works, but it's hard to find lye soap. We buy ours homemade from a local resident.

> Cathy Gartland and Debbie Barlow,
> McLean House, Bardstown,
> Kentucky

Hairspray will wipe out ink stains.

> Marie and Dick Brophy, Isaiah Hall
> B&B, Dennis, Massachusetts

To remove a grease stain, dampen it with cold water and cover with cornstarch. Let it dry. Brush off, and the stain is gone.
   Just rub baby oil over the paint-stained area and wipe it away.

> Ruthmary Jordan, Pride House,
> Jefferson, Texas

To remove "white stains" (such as water-glass rings or areas whitened by carelessly placed wet towels) from wooden antique pieces, gently rub mayonnaise onto the stain.

> Sharon and Scott Wright, Silver
> Maple Lodge, Fairlee, Vermont

Here's another variation on the mayonnaise idea: To remove rings from furniture, make a paste of mayonnaise and fine cigarette ashes. Rub with a soft cloth. Follow the treatment with Murphy Oil Soap. Then use lemon oil to restore the shine. It really works!

> Joanne Parker, assistant manager,
> Garnet Hill Lodge, North River,
> New York

Even the most careful guest will sometimes leave a water glass on a fine piece of wood. The spot can be removed by rubbing cigarette ashes mixed with walnut oil on the mark. It takes a lot of rubbing, but you can completely remove it.

> Ripley Hotch and Owen Sullivan,
> Boydville The Inn at Martinsburg,
> Martinsburg, West Virginia

A paste of toothpaste and baking powder rubbed on a white stain will remove it.

> Beverly and Ray Compton, Spring
> Bank Inn, Frederick, Maryland

Homemaking Improvements

Rugs and Carpets

Scatter rugs without a rubber backing are dangerous. To prevent slipping, you can purchase special pads from almost any carpet dealer, who can cut you an appropriate size and thickness.

> Maureen and John Magee, Rabbit
> Hill Inn, Lower Waterford,
> Vermont

Sometimes Persian rugs—and really almost any rugs with fringes that go awry—look unkempt. Yet the entire rug doesn't need vacuuming. Simply take a comb and comb the fringes straight.

> Joan and Sal Chandon, Doubleday
> Inn, Gettysburg, Pennsylvania

A mixture of one pound of baking soda and a few drops of your favorite scented oil sprinkled on rugs and vacuumed will freshen your room and your rug.

> Beverley Roger Allison, Sleepy
> Hollow Farm, Gordonsville,
> Virginia

If you live near a beach, do as we do in the summer. Place a rice-straw mat in several areas of the house. They are available for purchase at many import stores. These mats filter the sand, minimizing the tiny grains throughout the house and making cleanup easier.

> Elizabeth Gundry Hooper, Corner
> Cupboard Inn, Rehoboth, Delaware

Odor Removal

Get rid of cigarette smoke with a lit candle. When the smoker has gone, sprinkle baking soda on rugs and then vacuum.

> Marie and Dick Brophy, Isaiah Hall
> B&B, Dennis, Massachusetts

To remove refrigerator odors: Take pieces of charcoal and burned wood that has formed coals from your fire and put them into an open plastic bag. Leave the open bag in the refrigerator.

> Mary Louise and Ron Thorburn, Inn at Weathersfield, Weathersfield, Vermont

Undesirable smells on curtains or bedspreads can be removed without washing. Put the curtains or bedspreads into the clothes dryer. Pour liquid softener onto a washcloth and put it into the dryer. Set the dryer on cool and run for about twenty-five minutes.

> Daun Martin, Britt House, San Diego, California

 # Creative Housekeeping

We use freezer paper to line all our kitchen cabinets and dresser drawers. The paper is strong, easy to replace when soiled, and inexpensive.

> Pam Stewart, manager, Little River Inn, Aldie, Virginia

A blackboard in the kitchen by the telephone is helpful for writing messages, rather than using a piece of paper you can't find five minutes later.

> Amy Donohoe, manager, Barley Sheaf Farm, Holicong, Pennsylvania

Some mushrooms sold at supermarkets come in long straw baskets. When these containers are emptied, a little contact paper, ribbon, yarn, or cloth converts them for use in our bathrooms, for holding soap and toiletries.

> Joanne Parker, assistant manager, Garnet Hill Lodge, North River, New York

Author's Tip: If your grocer sells loose mushrooms, chances are they are shipped in similar wooden baskets. Ask the grocer to save them for you. They may be lined with colorful fabric. We decorate the baskets with Christmas holiday fabrics and served crackers and other goodies from them. They also make great holiday gift-giving containers. The outside of the basket can be painted or stenciled.

Small receptacles for little items such as rings you want to take off when doing the dishes, for example, can be attractive as well as functional and can cost little. I have painted dog-food cans (tuna cans will do) for presenting the check to our guests at the restaurant, and for carrying back their change. You can use the cans, decorated with contact paper, for example, by your kitchen sink.

> Hudson House, Cold Spring, New York

Organize pictures you want to store or show to friends. Arrange them according to subject and then turn them face down. Connect each one with a piece of tape running the width of the picture. Continue until they are all together. Now you can open them up accordian-style and show them off. You will have fewer fingerprints, and the pictures will always be in sequential viewing order.

> Kay Gill, Stephen Daniels House, Salem, Massachusetts

If you have the storage space, buy a year's supply of tissues, toilet paper, and paper towels at a wholesale shop. It saves money, and you don't need to buy as much on your weekly shopping trips. Look for such a place under paper products in the Yellow Pages.

> Mrs. W. B. Nottingham, Tokfarm Inn, Rindge, New Hampshire

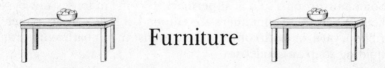

Furniture

The hub of summer activity is on the terrace, where tables take a lot of wear and tear. One all-weather solution: Cover the tables with painted ceramic tiles. Tile-top tables are easy to clean and are impervious to hot plates, pouring rain, and rust.

Beth and Franz Schober, Hopkins
Inn, New Preston, Connecticut

To clean wicker furniture, spray a clean paintbrush with furniture polish and dust as if painting.

Marie and Dick Brophy, Isaiah Hall
B&B, Dennis, Massachusetts

Author's Tip: When chair caning loosens (but is not broken) tighten it by wetting the cane with hot water. Soak the seat, and rub it gently with a mild detergent if the caning is soiled. As the caning dries, the seat will tighten.

For long-lasting polish/stain for furniture, use Kiwi light tan shoe polish (I learned this from a clockmaker who finished his cabinets this way).

Robina and Dick Conway, Almond
View Inn, Paso Robles, California

Sometimes I (Marie) have to move a piece of furniture by myself. I put a heavy, old towel or blanket under the legs, and then I can push the piece easily into place without marking the floor or overexerting myself.

Marie and Dick Brophy, Isaiah Hall
B&B, Dennis, Massachusetts

Author's Tip: If you or someone in your household owns a skateboard, place it under the furniture you want to move and roll your piece across the floor.

In a pinch, a squirt of hairspray stops a squeaky hinge.

Robin Brooks, Robins Nest, San
Andreas, California

 Laundry Care

Fold your newly cleaned towels in the manner in which you are going to hang them from a towel bar. This way you save the step of having to refold them to hang.

> Sally and Ken McWilliams, Main
> Street B&B, Madison, Indiana

Hang a small basket of cloth napkins by the laundry area. It's easier to wait for one load's worth and do them all at once.

> Diane and Al Johnson, Nauset
> House, East Orleans, Massachusetts

I did a cost analysis and discovered that it is cheaper for me to send out bed sheets and pillowcases than to do them at the inn. Now, most people won't take time to do such a study, so it sounds unbelievable. But it is true. It costs about two dollars a room to do the laundry, and it comes back pressed. There's nothing like pressed pillowcases! When you add up the cost of the water and detergent and the time it takes your help to wash and dry the sheets, it's cheaper to send them out. Even if you don't have hired help in your own home, your time may be valuable enough to make this option worthwhile, at least when you have guests.

> Cathy and Jim Bartaglia,
> Summerland Inn, Summerland,
> California

If you work from home with a computer, and you do the laundry, keep your computer close to the laundry area. I (Linda) catch up on business items and do other computer work while I do the wash (which is constant around here). I'm close at hand when the washer and dryer stop.

> Linda and Rob Castagna, Chestnut
> Hill on the Delaware, Milford, New
> Jersey

The lace-edged, linen pillowcases we use on guest beds have been washed and ironed a hundred times, and they still look great!

Old linens can be cleaned with a lot of bleach. Old cottons, for example, are tough materials and, unless they are edged with a very delicate lace, we soak them in a fairly strong bleach solution. For those mysterious rust stains on linens, we use a commercial stain remover.

> Helen and Gene Kirby, Horatio
> Johnson House, Belfast, Maine

To avoid ironing crocheted doilies, after laundering them, set them down on a flat surface while still wet.

> Pat Hardy, Glenborough Inn, Santa
> Barbara, California

We soak our antique linens for twenty-four hours or more in a mixture of detergent, gentle bleach, and water. They are then placed in the washing machine on a gentle spin. On nice days, they are dried flat on the grass in a sunny spot. This also bleaches them. When ironing, keep a spray bottle of water handy; for those linens needing more body, use a quick spray of starch. Never iron embroidered linens on their front side. Instead, lay a fluffy towel on the ironing board and iron on the back of the linen.

> Beverly and Ray Compton, Spring
> Bank Inn, Frederick, Maryland

Soak old, yellow-stained, linen-and-lace doilies in powdered dishwasher soap and water for several hours. Rinse. They should be as white or bright as the day your grandmother made them. For stubborn stains, soak them overnight and then rinse.

> Patricia W. and Donald R. Cornish,
> Palmer Inn, Noank, Connecticut

Don't want to iron now or don't have the time? In a plastic bag, mix damp items equally with dried ones. Refrigerate the bag to keep the items moist for easier ironing later. True procrastinators should place the bag in the freezer!

> Pat Hardy, Glenborough Inn, Santa
> Barbara, California

Cut down on ironing time and heat from the iron by placing aluminum foil, shiny side up, between the ironing board and its cover. It reflects heat.

Ripley Hotch and Owen Sullivan,
Boydville The Inn at Martinsburg,
Martinsburg, West Virginia

 # Bedding Control

If you're like most homeowners, you have trouble keeping sets of sheets together. We like to use many different patterns so that our inn is homey. But storage for three changes for seven different bedrooms is not easy. We fold the sheets in sets so that they can be found easily. Here's how:

1. *Top sheet:* Fold in half the long way, with the top of the sheet on the outside. Then fold in half again, then in half again—all the time keeping the top on the outside. You will have a rectangle. Fold it twice so that you have a long rectangle.

2. *Fitted bottom:* Fit the corners inside each other, and smooth the sheet to a rectangle. Fold the fitted part across, and then fold in thirds to the center. You will have a rectangle, slightly smaller than the folded top sheet.

3. Fold the pillowcases in thirds the long way, then in half and in half again, making small squares.

4. Put the bottom sheet on the top sheet with the fatter ends lined up. Then put the pillowcases on top and fold the top sheet over all. You will have a nice package of sheets that will stack easily.

We keep our linens in an old, stacking oak bookcase, such as those that used to be in lawyers' offices. And the bookcase is on the second-floor landing where all the guests can see the sheets.

Each room gets a shelf in the bookcase. The guests think this is both neat and amusing.

Ripley Hotch and Owen Sullivan,
Boydville The Inn at Martinsburg,
Martinsburg, West Virginia

Different colored linens are used for each bedroom and bath. This enables us to sort the laundry for the proper rooms more efficiently.

Marilyn and Gene Gundersen,
Pudding Creek Inn, Fort Bragg,
California

Goose-down duvets are on all of our beds as they save time in bed making. They are light, and the duvet cover matches the sheets and pillowcases. All of them can be washed easily.

Nan and Ian Aitchison, Over Look
Inn, Eastham, Massachusetts

Hospital-tucked corners really make a bed look nice after the comforter, quilt, or bedspread is turned down.

Hems of the pillowcase should be faced away from the center of the bed to the outside.

Turn your mattress frequently for longer life. Every three months is what is recommended. Turn it over and also reverse it from head to foot.

Beverley Roger Allison, Sleepy
Hollow Farm, Gordonsville,
Virginia

Front-Porch Philosophy

Words of Wisdom on the Front Porch and All around the Inn

America's inns have helped bring us back to the front porch, that embracing symbol of simpler times and family unity. Nearly every summer's eve in this country, inn guests swap tales above the gentle creaking of wicker rockers on the porch as they shield themselves from the descending sun. They exchange views on an endless repertoire of topics, mixing insightful thoughts with humor and personal anecdotes.

It seems fitting that the front porch, at least in warmer months, is the setting for uplifting conversation. Most people do not know it, but the porch attached to a house is claimed to be an American institution. The porch is not in the same vein as baseball and apple pie, but it is something America can call its own. Although the idea of a covered entry originated in Europe in the thirteenth century, it was designed for cathedrals only. The first house porch as we know it today was conceived and built in America during the Victorian era, which spanned 1837–1901 when Queen Victoria reigned in Great Britain.

The front porch became the gathering spot during good weather. Sitting in relaxation encouraged lighthearted conversation and exchanges of information. When the weather turned inclement, porches were vacated and family and friends often continued their outdoor chatter indoors.

It is much the same today at inns. Wherever there is a front porch, the old tradition of storytelling and news gathering continues. And when it gets cold outside, innkeepers coax the same scene in one of their home's many common rooms. Wouldn't it be nice to listen in on some of the conversations from inn porches and common rooms? Well, that is not possible. So I asked the innkeepers instead for some of their own personal philosophy. They gave me the following proverbial thoughts, which are displayed somewhere in their inn and reflect their outlooks. Guests often take these inspiring and sometimes just plain funny thoughts back home with them to ponder, perhaps relating them in front of their own hearths or on their own front porches.

A proverb on the wall:

> The hurrier I am, the behinder I get.
>
> Pride House, Jefferson, Texas

This is an interesting saying for those who like country decor. The motto is contained on a Danish cross-stitch sampler:

> Clocks, crocks, country chairs
> Calico curtains, patchwork squares
> Samplers, quilts, pewter and pine
> Friends for supper, chilled white wine
> Low-country crab boil, berry tarts
> Love, friendship, happy hearts.
>
> Laurel Hill Plantation,
> McClellanville, South Carolina

On the refrigerator door:

> Everything in the universe is subject to change
> —and everything is on schedule.
>
> Conyers House, Sperryville,
> Virginia

In the foyer:

> Stay overnight in my dwelling
> Wash thy feet in this place.
> Till morning seek what you will,
> Then onward your journey pursue.
>
> Ash Mill Farm, Holicong,
> Pennsylvania

In the small garden by the smokehouse, where daffodils and narcissus bloom profusely in the spring and herbs follow in the summer, this popular verse:

The kiss of the sun for pardon
The song of the birds for mirth
One is nearer God's heart in a garden
Than anywhere else on earth

> Spring Bank Inn, Frederick,
> Maryland

Embroidered on one pillowcase:
I slept and dreamt that life was beauty.
And on the other pillowcase:
I woke and found that life was duty.

> Borgman's B&B, Arrow Rock,
> Missouri

Just inside the front door and from Sarah Bernhardt:
It is in spending oneself that one becomes rich.

> Chestnut Hill on the Delaware,
> Milford, New Jersey

The Beauty of the House—is Order
The Blessing of the House—is Contentment
The Glory of the House—is Hospitality
The Crown of the House—is Godliness

> Chestnut Hill on the Delaware,
> Milford, New Jersey

From Robert Louis Stevenson: We are all travelers in the wilderness of this world and the best we can find in our travels is an honest friend.

> Kenniston Hill Inn, Boothbay,
> Maine

In our guest registry:
The register of a country inn is a treasury of the names of good people.

> Palmer House, Noank, Connecticut

Hand-embroidered and framed:
Guests you are welcome here. Be at your ease.
Get up when you're ready. Go to bed when you please.
Happy to share with you such as we've got.

The leak in the roof and soup in the pot.
You don't have to thank us or laugh at our jokes.
Sit deep and come often.
You're one of the folks.

> Covered Bridge Inn, Ephrata,
> Pennsylvania

Embedded in the stone fireplace:
Love Warms the Heart as Fire the Hearth.

> Northfield Country House,
> Northfield, Massachusetts

The only way to have a friend is to be one.

> Gilded Thistle, Galveston Island,
> Texas

Amish proverb:
It is pleasant and proper to be foolish once in a while.

> Isaiah Hall B&B, Dennis,
> Massachusetts

At our front door:
Whoe'er has travelled life's dull round
Where'er his stages might have been
May sigh to think he still has found
The warmest welcome at an inn.

> Old Yacht Club Inn, Santa Barbara,
> California

An embroidered picture, framed in the foyer:
Come in the evening
Come in the morning
Come when expected or
Come without warning.

> Six Water Street B&B, Sandwich,
> Massachusetts

A lovely old sampler hangs in our front hall. It was given to us by
some guests we helped out when their car broke down:

Let me live in the house by the side of the road and be a friend to man.

> Over Look Inn, Eastham,
> Massachusetts

This got us through some very difficult start-up times when people in our neighborhood, who knew nothing about bed-and-breakfast innkeeping, contended that we were not going to make one out of this house:

Eat a bullfrog first thing in the morning . . . and nothing worse can happen to you for the rest of the day.

> Almond View Farm, Paso Robles,
> California

Hanging in the dining room:

Sage maketh the lamp of life, so long as nature lets it burn, burn brightly.

> Sage Cottage, Trumansburg, New
> York

A handmade sampler proclaims:

All the flowers of all the tomorrows are in the seeds of today.

> Roaring Lion, Waldoboro, Maine

Two thoughts from innkeeper Gloria Belknap:

> Old, gentle things are best in furniture
> Real wood, real chairs, things that have
>   soft, elegant lines
> No reproductions can copy time.

> Terrace Townehouse, Boston,
> Massachusetts

Remember the house payment and smile.

> Terrace Townehouse, Boston,
> Massachusetts

In our office we have a sign:

Never put a guest in his place. Put yourself in his place.

> Governor's Inn, Ludlow, Vermont

We bought this framed quote by Abraham Lincoln in 1960. It has traveled with us through many years and many places. It's always one of the first things out when we move:

I like to see a man proud of the place in which he lives. I like
to see a man live so that his place will be proud of him.

Windward Inn, North East,
Pennsylvania

On a bookmark given to guests:

An Innkeeper's Thought
The
courteous traveler
passing at an Inn in the
country
on a detour
from the fret and fury of life
should receive:

A gentle welcome
A touch of history
A taste of Nature
A bit of farming
A portion of home cooking
A sense of quiet
A flow of private thought
A measure of informal comfort
A feeling of rest
A wealth of exploring
A moment of song
A stranger becoming a fireside friend
A regretful farewell
A memory worth havin'

Squire Tarbox Inn, Wiscasset,
Maine

In a hallway:

Friendship's a name too few confined
The offspring of a noble mind
A generous warmth that fills the breast
And better felt than expressed.

Glenborough Inn, Santa Barbara,
California

We think this hand-stitched picture in our entryway says it all:
   The blessing of this house is contentment.
>   Inn on Golden Pond, Holderness,
>   New Hampshire

On an antique sampler in our 1849 common room:
   Joy be with you while you stay.
   Peace be with you on your way.
>   Bramble Inn, Brewster,
>   Massachusetts

An antique sampler:
>   Make It Do
>   Wear It Out
>   Use It Up
>   Do Without
>   Bungay Jar, Easton, New
>   Hampshire

Hanging in our dining room:
   Ewe's not fat, just fluffy.
At our entryway:
   Give me a house to call my own. Family, friends to make it a
home.
>   Ellis River House, Jackson, New
>   Hampshire

On the lips of my sweet husband:
   How is it you never have time to do it right but always time to
do it over?
>   Gate House Inn, Jackson, California

Friendship is the comfort, the inexpressible comfort of feeling
safe with a person, having neither to weigh thoughts nor measure
words, but pouring all out just as they are, chaff and grain
together, certain that a beautiful, friendly hand will take and sift
them—keep what is worth keeping and with a breath of comfort,
blow the rest away.
>   Isaac Randall House, Freeport,
>   Maine

All guests make us happy . . . some by coming, some by going.

Middlebury Inn, Middlebury,
Vermont

A lovely cross-stitch from a former guest:
   Two old friends with a cup of tea, one of them you, one of them me.
On our refrigerator, a quote from Émile Zola:
   If you ask me what I came to do in this world as an artist, I will answer, "I came to live out loud."

Old Broad Bay Inn, Waldoboro,
Maine

On an old framed sampler:
   No matter where I place my guests, they seem to like my kitchen best.

Old Pioneer Garden, Unionville,
Nevada

We are not forgetful to entertain strangers: for thereby some have entertained angels unawares.

Sweetwater Farms, Glen Mills,
Pennsylvania

This hand-stitched sampler by my mother hangs in the dining room:

> Time goes so fast
> Life asks so much
> No wonder friends get out of touch.
> But in our hearts
> Deep, true, unseen
> Friendship stays forever green.

Betsy's B&B, Baltimore, Maryland

On a handmade sign:

> A stranger is a friend you have not yet met.

Tokfarm Inn, Rindge, New
Hampshire

According to Vermont tradition, house callers use the back door exclusively. Ours is no exception. "Back door friends are best" hangs in the kitchen.

Sunning Hill, Pittsford, Vermont

Victorians slept in shorter beds in a semireclining position, their heads and shoulders supported by mounded pillows. It was widely believed that it was unhealthy to sleep with one's head level with one's heart. The pillows propped against the headboard were covered during the day with a decorative cover that had a sentimental message embroidered by one of the ladies of the house. In our Rose Room, upon a massive, four-poster bed set very high off the floor and reached by a two-step ladder, one pillow says "Early to bed," and the other, "Early to rise."

Another motto is located on the fourth floor where two bedrooms share a sitting room between them:

Be not weary in well doing.

Red Castle Inn, Nevada City,
California

We're glad to have you as our guest
And hope you have a good night's rest
Tomorrow you again may roam
But while you're here—just feel at home.

Wildwood Inn, Ware, Massachusetts

Appendix

Inn Reference

The following list contains addresses and phone numbers of all of the inns that participated in this book. Tips, hints, ideas, philosophies, and recipes were submitted by the innkeepers or, in some cases, inn managers. Consult inn guidebooks for current names of the innkeepers, as the names listed with the tips may not include all of the innkeepers who own or operate the inn. Also, seek the guidebooks when making travel arrangements.

No inn paid to be in this book. The inns were included on the basis of their response to interviews and questionaires. They are not a reflection of the author's or the publisher's personal preferences.

ALABAMA

Vincent-Doan Home
1664 Springhill Avenue
Mobile, AL 36604
(205) 433–7121
An 1827 French-Creole house near historic attractions.

ALASKA

Glacier Bay Country Inn
Box 5
Gustavus, AK 99826
(907) 697–2288
Old-fashioned hospitality and scrumptious dinners.

ARIZONA

Graham's Bed and Breakfast Inn
150 Canyon Circle Drive, P.O.
  Box 912
Sedona, AZ 86336
(602) 284–1425
Designer home oozing with pleas-
antries.

ARKANSAS

Eton House
1485 Eton
Fayetteville, AR 72703
(501) 521–6344
Victorian ranch home with gracious
amenities.

The Hearthstone Inn
35 Kingshighway
Eureka Springs, AR 72632
(501) 253–8916
Victorian home with down-home
country comforts.

Williams House
420 Quapaw
Hot Springs National Park, AR
  71901
(501) 624–4275
Healthy, fresh seasonal foods served
here daily.

CALIFORNIA

Almond View Inn
912 Walnut Drive
Paso Robles, CA 93446
(805) 238–4220
Spanish facade and decorated in
eclectic fashion.

Annie Horan's
415 West Main Street
Grass Valley, CA 95945
(916) 272–2418
Family has been in hospitality business since 1940.

Beazley House
1910 First Street
Napa, CA 94559
(707) 257–1649
Wine-country mansion and carriage
house.

Bluebelle House
263 South State Highway 173,
  P.O. Box 2177
Lake Arrowhead, CA 92352
(714) 336–3292
Casual elegance with a European
flavor.

Britt House
406 Maple Street
San Diego, CA 92103
(619) 234–2926
Restored Queen Anne Victorian.

Carter House
1033 Third Street
Eureka CA 95501
(707) 445–1390
Gabled Victorian, featuring contemporary art.

Chateau Victorian
118 First Street
Santa Cruz, CA 95060
(408) 458–9458
Stately, turn-of-the-century home.

Coloma Country Inn
2 High Street, P.O. Box 502
Coloma, CA 95613
(916) 622–6919
Splendid decor in the heart of gold
rush country.

Eastlake Inn
1442 Kellam Avenue
Los Angeles, CA 90026
(213) 250–1620
A fine, circa-1887 bed-and-
breakfast.

Eiler's Inn
741 South Coast Highway
Laguna Beach, CA 92651
(714) 494–3004
Musical instruments and the ocean
are part of the decor.

Gate House Inn
1330 Jackson Gate Road
Jackson, CA 95642
(209) 223–3500
Victorian inn with great attention to
detail.

The Gingerbread Mansion
400 Berding Street
Ferndale, CA 95536
(707) 786–4000
Elegant, charming, and spacious
house dating from 1889.

The Glenborough Inn
1327 Bath Street
Santa Barbara, CA 93101
(805) 966–0589
Luxuriate in the garden hot tub, or
have breakfast in bed.

Healdsburg Inn on the Plaza
116 Matheson Street, P.O. Box
1196
Healdsburg, CA 95448
(707) 433–6991
Turn-of-the-century inn with rooftop gardens.

The Jabberwock
598 Laine Street
Monterey, CA 93940
(408) 372–4777
Takes you back to Alice in Wonderland.

La Maida House
11159 La Maida Street
North Hollywood, CA 91601
(818) 769–3857
Old-world villa filled with antiques
and artistry.

The Old Yacht Club Inn
431 Corona Del Mar Drive
Santa Barbara, CA 93103
(805) 962–1277
Turn-of-the-century charm by the
sea.

Pudding Creek Inn
700 North Main Street
Fort Bragg, CA 95437
(707) 964–9529
Former home of a Russian count.

Red Castle Inn
109 Prospect Street
Nevada City, CA 95959
(916) 265–5135
A fine Gothic inn.

The Robins Nest
Highway 49, P.O. Box 1408
San Andreas, CA 95249
(209) 754–1076
A fully restored 1895 home.

Summerland Inn
2161 Ortega Hill Road, P.O. Box
1209
Summerland, CA 93067
(805) 969–5225
New England charm on the West
Coast.

COLORADO

The Briar Rose
2151 Arapahoe Avenue
Boulder, CO 80302
(303) 442–3007
A 1904 residence that became an inn
in 1982.

Davidson's Country Inn
P.O. Box 87
Pagosa Springs, CO 81147
(303) 264–5863
Three-story log home, filled with
heirlooms.

Holden House 1902
1102 West Pikes Peak Avenue
Colorado Springs, CO 80904
(719) 471–3980
A restored, turn-of-the-century
home.

Queen Anne Inn
2147 Tremont Place
Denver, CO 80205
(303) 296–6666
One of ten top spots for a honey-
moon, says a bride's magazine.

Sweet Adeline's
949 F Street
Salida, CO 81201
(719) 539–4100
Two-story, delft-blue Victorian.

Wanek's Lodge
560 Ponderosa Drive
Estes Park, CO 80517
(303) 586–5851
Rustic, homey, and very relaxing.

CONNECTICUT

The Captain Stannard House
138 South Main Street
Westbrook, CT 06498
(203) 399–7565
A delightful inn, circa 1850.

Fowler House
P.O. Box 432
Moodus, CT 06469
(203) 873–8906
The landscape is part of the beauty
of this Queen Anne.

Greenwoods Gate
Greenwoods Road East, Route 44
Norfolk, CT 06058
(203) 542–5439
Elegant, country-style inn.

The Hopkins Inn
Hopkins Road
New Preston, CT 06777
(203) 868–7295
Austrian-Swiss cuisine is a hallmark
of the inn.

The Palmer Inn
25 Church Street
Noank, CT 06340
(203) 572–9000
Salty air in an old-fashioned seaside
haven.

Red Brook Inn
P.O. Box 237
Old Mystic, CT 06372
(203) 572–0349
Eighteenth-century dinners plus a
restored tavern.

Riverwind
209 Main Street
Deep River, CT 06417
(203) 526–2014
Sherry in the parlor, a vintage car in
the driveway.

DELAWARE

The Corner Cupboard Inn
50 Park Avenue
Rehoboth Beach, DE 19971
(302) 227–8553
Small, informal inn by the beach.

FLORIDA

Victorian House
11 Cadiz Street
St. Augustine, FL 32084
(904) 824–5214
Stenciling and much more at this
Victorian delight.

GEORGIA

The Forsyth Park Inn
102 West Hall Street
Savannah, GA 31401
(912) 233–6800
Be pampered circa nineteenth-
century southern style.

Shellmont Bed and Breakfast
  Lodge
821 Piedmont Avenue
Atlanta, GA 30308
(404) 872–9290
Victorian home with lovely stained-
glass windows.

HAWAII

Haikuleana
69 Haiku Road
Haiku, HA 96708
(808) 575–2890
A gentle rain falls nightly among the
pineapples. Ahhh!

IDAHO

Cricket on the Hearth
1521 Lakeside Avenue
Coeur d'Alene, ID 83814
(208) 664–6926
A kaleidoscope of theme dinners is a
highlight.

Greenbriar Inn
315 Wallace
Coeur d'Alene, ID 83814
(208) 667–9660
Gourmet breakfasts at this elegant,
romantic inn.

Heritage Inn
510 Lena Street
Salmon, ID 83467
(208) 756–3174
Eat breakfast in the circa-1888
glassed-in porch.

ILLINOIS

The Green Tree Inn
15 Mill Street, P.O. Box 96
Elsah, IL 62028
(618) 374–2821
Unusual 1840 house decorated in
three periods.

Hamilton House
500 West Main Street
Decatur, IL 62522
(217) 429–1669
Historic home with a Victorian and
Early American gift shop.

INDIANA

Cliff House
122 Fairmount Drive
Madison, IN 47250
(812) 265–5272
1885 Greek Revival home with marvelous portico and brick exterior.

Main Street Bed and Breakfast
739 West Main Street
Madison, IN 47250
(812) 265–3539
Impeccably decorated, nineteenth-
century, white-painted-brick
home.

IOWA

Hannah Marie Country Inn
RR 1, Highway 71 South
Spencer, IA 51301
(712) 262–1286
Brochure is right: ". . . home speaks
to guests from the heart."

Victorian Bed and Breakfast Inn
425 Walnut Street
Avoca, IA 51521
(712) 343–6336
Experience a true Victorian home.

KANSAS

Schoolhouse Inn
106 East Beck
Melvern, KS 66510
(913) 549–3473
1870 former schoolhouse, parson-
age, and town meeting hall.

KENTUCKY

McLean House
105 East Stephen Foster
Bardstown, KY 40004
(502) 348–4133
Local crafts and antiques abound.

LOUISIANA

The St. Francisville Inn
118 North Commerce, P.O.
  Drawer 1369
St. Francisville, LA 70775
(504) 635–6502
Twin-gabled, 1880 home with lovely
  front porch.

MAINE

Arcady Down East
South Street
Blue Hill, ME 04614
(207) 374–5576
Victorian mansion with fine arts and
  old-time crafts.

The Captain Jefferds Inn
Pearl Street, Box 691
Kennebunkport, ME 04046
(207) 967–2311
Old sea-captain's home with an-
  tiques from the Orient.

The Captain Lord Mansion
P.O. Box 800
Kennebunkport, ME 04046
(207) 967–3141
Seaside mansion in the grand old
  style.

The Chetwynd House
Chestnut Street, Box 130
Kennebunkport, ME 04046
(207) 967–2235
An elegant colonial dating from
  1840.

Dockside Guest Quarters
On the Harbor, P.O. Box 205
York, ME 03909
(207) 363–2868
Early Maine coastal homestead.

The Fairhaven Inn
RR2, Box 85, North Bath Road
Bath, ME 04530
(207) 443–4391
Gracious eighteen-room home from
  1790 with colonial tavern room.

The Horatio Johnson House
36 Church Street
Belfast, ME 04915
(207) 338–5153
1842 house in antiques haven of Belfast.

Isaac Randall House
Independence Drive
Freeport, ME 04032
(207) 865–9295
Antiques-studded, 1823 farm-
house.

Kenniston Hill Inn
Route 27, P.O. Box 125
Boothbay, ME 04537
(207) 633–2159
White-clapboard country-style
  home.

Melfair Farm
365 Wilson Road
Kittery, ME 03904
(207) 439–0320
1871 house in a town full of activities.

Old Broad Bay Inn
Main Street
Waldoboro, ME 04572
(207) 832–6668
Candlelight dinners, period fur-
  nishings, and gracious hosts.

Out-the-Inn-Door
P.O. Box 633
Freeport, ME 04032
(207) 865–3688
An inn-sitting service.

Pilgrim's Inn
Deer Isle, ME 04627
(207) 348–6615
Has been serving weary travelers for 200 years.

The Red House
Lincolnville Beach, ME 04849
(207) 236–4621
Cozy New England Cape Cod by the bay.

The Roaring Lion
75 Main Street, P.O. Box 756
Waldoboro, ME 04572
(207) 832–4038
1930 house featuring oak woodwork and tin ceilings.

Squire Tarbox Inn
RR 2, Box 620
Wiscasset, ME 04578
(207) 882–7693
1763, New England homestead in pastoral setting.

The Wild Rose of York
78 Long Sands Road
York, ME 03909
(207) 363–2532
1814 sea-captain's house near the beach.

MARYLAND

Betsy's Bed and Breakfast
1428 Park Avenue
Baltimore, MD 21217
(301) 383–1274
Historic townhouse-style inn.

The Inn at Buckeystown
Buckeystown, MD 21717
(301) 874–5755
Lovingly restored Victorian mansion.

The Inn at Mitchell House
Box 329, RD 2 (Tolchester Estates)
Chestertown, MD 21620
(301) 778–6500
Charm and grace in a historic area to explore.

Spring Bank Inn
7945 Worman's Mill Road
Frederick, MD 21701
(301) 694–0440
A grand landmark house.

Strawberry Inn
17 Main Street, P.O. Box 237
New Market, MD 21774
(301) 865–3318
Beautiful restoration in an old-town setting.

MASSACHUSETTS

The Bramble Inn
Route 6A
Brewster, MA 02631
(508) 896–7644
Dinners and rooms are discriminatingly appointed.

Captain Dexter House
100 Main Street, P.O. Box 2457
Vineyard Haven, MA 02568
(508) 693–6564
Eighteenth-century home on historic Martha's Vineyard.

The Captain's House
371 Old Harbor Road
Chatham, MA 02633
(508) 945–0127
Colonial-style country inn in picturesque setting.

Charles Hinckley House
Route 6A and Scudder Lane
Barnstable, MA 02630
(508) 362–9924.
Rustic house with flourishing wildflower garden.

Cobb's Cove
Barnstable Village, MA 02630
(508) 362–9356
View of Cape Cod Bay is mesmerizing.

The Four Chimneys
38 Orange Street
Nantucket, MA 02554
(508) 228–1912
Built in 1835, during Nantucket's whaling days.

The Gingerbread House
141 Division Street
West Harwich, MA 02671
(508) 432–1901
Victorian house known for its real British teatime.

Historic Merrell Tavern Inn
Main Street, Route 102
South Lee, MA 01260
(413) 243–1794
Received a historic preservation award in 1982.

The Inn on Cove Hill
37 Mount Pleasant Street
Rockport, MA 01966
(508) 546–2701
Built with pirate's gold in 1791.

Isaiah Hall Bed and Breakfast Inn
152 Whig Street
Dennis, MA 02638
(508) 385–9928
House's first owner patented the cranberry transport barrel.

The Marlborough Inn
320 Woods Hole Road
Woods Hole, MA 02543
(508) 548–6218
Cape Cod–reproduction filled with antiques.

The Nauset House
Beach Road, P.O. Box 774
East Orleans, MA 02643
(508) 255–2195
1900s-style conservatory blooms with books and flowers.

Northfield Country House
School Street
Northfield, MA 01360
(413) 498–2692
Romantic setting for an inn with an evangelical past.

The Over Look Inn
Route 6, P.O. Box 771
Eastham, MA 02642
(508) 255–1886
Victorian parlor, extensive library, antique billiards.

The Palmer House
81 Palmer Avenue
Falmouth, MA 02540
(508) 548–1230
1901 house noted for its gourmet breakfasts.

Six Water Street Bed and
    Breakfast
6 Water Street, Box 1295
Sandwich, MA 02563
(508) 888–6808
Sandpipers and breeze-blown dunes come to mind about this inn.

The Stephen Daniels House
One Daniels Street
Salem, MA 01970
(508) 744–5709
Primitive American architecture and decor at its warmest.

The Terrace Townehouse
60 Chandler Street
Boston, MA 02116
(617) 350–6520
Circa 1870 house with wonderful antiques.

Thomas Huckins House
2701 Main Street, Route 6A
Barnstable, MA 02630
(508) 362–6379
1705 house where canopy beds
reign.

The Weathervane Inn
Route 23
South Egremont, MA 01258
(413) 528–9580
1785 farmhouse in the rolling green
Berkshires.

The Wildwood Inn
121 Church Street
Ware, MA 01082
(413) 967–7798
Heirloom quilts, eyelet curtains
equal old-fashioned warmth.

Windfields Farm
RR #1, Box 170
Cummington, MA 01026
(413) 684–3786
Organic gardening here, and maple
syrup a specialty.

MICHIGAN

The Park House
888 Holland Street
Saugatuck, MI 49453
(616) 857–4535
Restored 1857 house where herbs
grow abundantly.

MINNESOTA

Bluff Creek Inn
1161 Bluff Creek Drive
Chaska, MN 55318
(612) 445–2735
A fine inn in the heart of the Minnesota River valley.

Historic Taylors Falls Jail
102 Government Road
Taylors Falls, MN 55084
(612) 465–3112
Century-old jail cell is now a guest
room.

The Hutchinson House
305 NW Second Street
Fairbault, MN 55021
(507) 332–7519
Splendid Victorian with fun-loving
innkeeper.

Quill and Quilt
615 West Hoffman Street
Cannon Falls, MN 55009
(507) 263–5507
Quilts, four-poster beds, whirlpool,
stenciling, much more.

MISSISSIPPI

Weymouth Hall
1 Cemetery Road, P.O. Box 1091
Natchez, MS 39120
(601) 445–2304
Plantation breakfasts along the Mississippi.

MISSOURI

Benner House
645 Main Street
Weston, MO 64098
(816) 386–2616
1898 steamboat-gothic architecture.

Borgman's Bed and Breakfast
Arrow Rock, MO 65320
(816) 837–3350
A quiet, relaxing, 100-year-old trea-
sure.

Zachariah Foss Guest House
4 Lafayette Street
Washington, MO 63090
(314) 239–6499
Restored, enchanting guest cottage.

MONTANA

O'Duach'ain Country Inn
675 Ferndale Drive
Bigfork, MT 59911
(406) 837–6851
Lodge-style home with gourmet
fare.

NEBRASKA

Bundy's Bed and Breakfast
RR2, Box 39
Gretna, NE 68028
(402) 332–3616
Primitives and crystal find harmony
here, too.

NEVADA

Old Pioneer Garden Country Inn
No. 79
Unionville, NV 89418
(702) 538–7585
Snuggle under handmade quilts in
front of a fire.

Winters Creek Inn
1201 U.S. 395 North
Carson City, NV 89701
(702) 849–1020
Snow-crusted mountains dwarf this
lovely inn.

NEW HAMPSHIRE

Amos A. Parker House
Route 119 West
Fitzwilliam, NH 03447
(603) 585–6540
1780 home in the Monadnock re-
gion.

The Beal House
247 West Main Street
Littleton, NH 03561
(603) 444–2661
Federal-style home with antiques
and cookie-jar collection.

The Birchwood Inn
Route 45
Temple, NH 03084
(603) 878–3285
Henry David Thoreau once stayed
here.

Bungay Jar
Route 116 (P.O. Box 15,
Franconia)
Easton, NH 03580
(603) 823–7775
Restored barn is part of the inn's
quarters.

Ellis River House
Route 16, Box 656
Jackson, NH 03846
(603) 383–9339
Warm, homey atmosphere in the
heart of the White Mountains.

Freedom House Bed 'n Breakfast
1 Maple Street
Freedom, NH 03836
(603) 539–4815
New England house near a mill-
pond.

The Hilltop Inn
Main Street, Route 117
Sugar Hill, NH 03585
(603) 823–5695
1895 house with panoramic views.

The Inn on Golden Pond
Route 3, P.O. Box 126
Holderness, NH 03245
(603) 968–7269
Fifty-five wooded acres for cross-
country skiers.

The Inn at Thorn Hill
Thorn Hill Road, Box A
Jackson Village, NH 03846
(603) 383–4242
Classic inn from a romantic era.

The Jefferson Inn
Route 2
Jefferson, NH 03583
(603) 586–7998
1897 beauty overlooking the White
Mountains.

The Lyme Inn
Lyme, NH 03768
(603) 795–2222
1809 inn specializing in fresh seafood.

Partridge Brook Inn
Hatt Road, P.O. Box 151
Westmoreland, NH 03467
(603) 399–4994
Elegant inn with a delightful cook-
ing hearth.

Province Inn
P.O. Box 309
Bow Lake, Strafford, NH 03884
(603) 664–2457
A romantic, eighteenth-century co-
lonial.

The Steele Homestead Inn
RR 1, Box 78
Antrim, NH 03440
(603) 588–6772
Fireside breakfasts at this 1810 inn.

Thatcher Hill Inn
Thatcher Hill Road
Marlborough, NH 03455
(603) 876–3361
Rambling farmhouse was a parson-
age in 1794.

Tokfarm Inn
Wood Avenue, Box 229
Rindge, NH 03461
(603) 899–6646
Lovely, 150-year-old farmhouse.

White Goose Inn
Route 10, P.O. Box 17
Orford, NH 03777
(603) 353–4812
Ponds and woodlands surround this
elegant Victorian.

NEW JERSEY

Alexander's Inn
653 Washington Street
Cape May, NJ 08204
(609) 884–2555
1883 home with time and place for
afternoon tea.

The Brass Bed
719 Columbia Avenue
Cape May, NJ 08204
(609) 884–8075
1872 charming seaside retreat.

Chestnut Hill on the Delaware
63 Church Street
Milford, NJ 08848
(201) 995–9761
The Delaware is reflected in this gracious Victorian.

The Manor House
612 Hughes Street
Cape May, NJ 08204
(609) 884–4710
Turn-of-the-century American architecture.

The Mason Cottage
625 Columbia Avenue
Cape May, NJ 08204
(609) 884–3358
1871 home catches seaside breezes
on verandas.

The Queen Victoria
102 Ocean Street
Cape May, NJ 08204
(609) 884–8702
Classic inn with an annual Dickens
extravaganza.

The Summer Cottage
613 Columbia Avenue
Cape May, NJ 08204
(609) 884–4948
Nineteenth-century holiday traditions abound.

NEW MEXICO

Grant Corner Inn
122 Grant Avenue
Santa Fe, NM 87501
(505) 983–6678
Charming, lovely home in a Southwest setting.

Inn of the Arts
618 South Alameda
Las Cruces, NM 88005
(505) 526–3327
Century-old house with an affinity
for famous artists.

NEW YORK

The Butternut Inn
Route 16 and Genesee Road
Chaffee, NY 14030
(716) 496–8987
1930s, family-oriented farmhouse.

The Edge of Thyme
6 Main Street
Candor, NY 13743
(607) 659–5155
Stately Georgian where Rockefellers once lived.

The 1819 Red Brick Inn
2081 Route 230
Dundee, NY 14837
(607) 243–8844
Rooms are accented in wine varieties! Wine-tastings, too.

Garnet Hill Lodge
North River, NY 12856
(518) 251–2821
Resort inn in the mountains.

Gates Hill Homestead
Brookfield, NY 13314
(315) 899–5837
Replica of 1793 homestead built by
the innkeepers.

Glendale Farms
224 Bostwick Road
Ithaca, NY 14850
(607) 272–8756
Breakfast in the Finger Lakes in this
1865 home.

Hudson House
2 Main Street
Cold Spring, NY 10516
(914) 265–9355
Country inn on the Hudson across
from West Point.

The Lamplight Inn
2129 Lake Avenue (Route 9N)
Lake Luzerne, NY 12846
(518) 696–5294
1890 Gothic in the Adirondack
Mountains.

The Maidstone Arms
207 Main Street
East Hampton, NY 11937
(516) 324–5006
Home is steeped in history from the
1600s.

Rosewood Inn
134 East First Street
Corning, NY 14830
(607) 962–3253
Gracious home filled with fine antiques and country comfort.

Sage Cottage
112 East Main Street, Box 121
Trumansburg, NY 14886
(607) 387–6449
130-year-old Gothic Revival topped
with gingerbread.

Simmons' Way Village Inn
Main Street
Millerton, NY 12546
(518) 789–6235
A pleasant escape in a town that time
forgot.

Summerport Bed and Breakfast
17 South Avenue
Schroon Lake, NY 12870
(518) 532–9339
A turn of the century gem with enthusiastic innkeepers.

Thompson Park House
118 Front Street
Owego, NY 13827
(607) 687–4323
1866 Victorian on the Susquehanna River

Troutbeck
P.O. Box 26
Amenia, NY 12501
(914) 373–9681
Tudor-style estate on 400 acres in the Berkshires.

Two Brooks
Route 42
Shandaken, NY 12480
(914) 688–7101
Learn fly-fishing and explore collection of old postcards.

Ujjala's Bed and Breakfast
2 Forest Glen
New Paltz, NY 12561
(914) 255–6360
1910 home nestled among fruit trees.

NORTH CAROLINA

Leftwich House
215 East Harden Street
Graham, NC 27253
(919) 226–5978
Southern hospitality in the European tradition.

The Lord Proprietors' Inn
300 North Broad Street
Edenton, NC 27932
(919) 482–3641
Elegant accommodations in a historic setting.

Mill Farm Inn
P.O. Box 1251
Tryon, NC 28782
(704) 859–6992
Small, cozy, help-yourself inn.

Randolph House
Fryemont Road, P.O. Box 816
Bryson City, NC 28713
(704) 488–3472
1895 country inn with a friendly atmosphere.

NORTH DAKOTA

The Triple T Ranch
Route 1, Box 93
Stanley, ND 58784
(701) 628–2418
Rustic ranch home with nearby fishing holes.

OHIO

Blossom Tyme
P.O. Box 54
Gambier, OH 43022
(614) 427–3300
Thirty-five-year-old home decorated in Early American style.

Locust Hill
1659 East U.S. 22–3
Morrow, OH 45152
(513) 899–2749
Victorian in the midst of antiques and nature.

OKLAHOMA

Clayton Country Inn
Route 1, Box 8, Highway 271
Clayton, OK 74536
(918) 569–4165
Rustic inn with down-home cooking and lots of fishing.

OREGON

The Pringle House
114 NE Seventh Street, P.O. Box
   578
Oakland, OR 97462
(503) 459–5038
1893 home features a doll collection.

PENNSYLVANIA

Academy Street Bed and
   Breakfast
528 Academy Street
Hawley, PA 18428
(717) 226–3430
Historic Civil War home in the Po-
cono Mountains.

Ash Mill Farm
Route 202, P.O. Box 202
Holicong, PA 18928
(215) 794–5373
Eighteenth-century,   sophisticated
   country home in Bucks County.

Barley Sheaf Farm
Route 202, Box 10
Holicong, PA 18928
(215) 794–5104
1700s elegant farmhouse. Sheep
   graze and raspberries grow.

The Bechtel Mansion Inn
400 West King Street
East Berlin, PA 17316
(717) 259–7760
Queen Anne house encourages romance and adventure.

The Bodine House
307 South Main Street
Muncy, PA 17756
(717) 546–8949
Collections of many kinds abound
   here.

The Brafferton Inn
44–46 York Street
Gettysburg, PA 17325
(717) 337–3423
History was made where you sleep at
   this eighteenth-century inn.

Churchtown Inn
Route 23
Churchtown, PA 17555
(215) 445–7794
Stone-faced, eighteenth-century
   home near Amish country.

Covered Bridge Inn
990 Rettew Mill Road
Ephrata, PA 17522
(717) 733–1592
1814 limestone farmhouse recalls
   horse-and-buggy days.

The Decoy
958 Eisenberger Road
Strasburg, PA 17579
(717) 687–8585
The clip-clop of an Amish buggy
   may be heard from a window.

The Doubleday Inn
104 Doubleday Avenue
Gettysburg, PA 17325
(717) 334–9119
Historic home is on the Gettysburg
   Battlefield.

The Harry Packer Mansion
Packer Hill
Jim Thorpe, PA 18229
(717) 325–8566
A spirited 1874 home built as a wed-
   ding gift.

Historic Smithton Inn
900 West Main Street
Ephrata, PA 17522
(717) 733–6094
1763 stone-faced colonial in Pennsylvania Dutch country.

The Inn at Starlight Lake
Starlight, PA 18461
(717) 798–2519
Resort-style country inn on a lake.

The Mercersburg Inn
405 South Main Street
Mercersburg, PA 17236
(717) 328–5231
Red-brick mansion furnished with
antiques.

The Pelham Inn
30 Pelham Road
Philadelphia, PA 19119
(215) 844–3727
English manor house was a wedding
gift and then a convent.

Pineapple Hill
1324 River Road
New Hope, PA 18938
(215) 862–9608
Charming inn on the Delaware.

Red Willow Farm
224 East Street Road
Kennett Square, PA 19348
(215) 444–0518
1710 farmhouse with lots of land to
explore.

Spring House
Muddy Creek Forks
Airville, PA 17302
(717) 927–6906
Elegant farm home where tasteful
antiques abound.

Sweetwater Farm
Sweetwater Road, Box 86
Glen Mills, PA 19342
(215) 459–4711
Nineteenth-century farmhouse
bursting with hospitality.

Tyler Hill Bed and Breakfast
Route 371, P.O. Box 62
Tyler Hill, PA 18469
(717) 224–6418
1847 farmhouse featuring homegrown specialties.

The Wedgwood Inn
111 West Bridge Street
New Hope, PA 18938
(215) 862–2570
Inn school is often held in this 1870
Victorian.

Windward Inn
51 Freeport Road
North East, PA 16428
(814) 725–5336
1929 Colonial Revival with formal
rose garden.

RHODE ISLAND

Ilverthorpe Cottage
41 Robinson Street
Narragansett, RI 02882
(401) 789–2392
Walk to the beach from this 1896
inn.

SOUTH CAROLINA

Laurel Hill Plantation
P.O. Box 182
McClellanville, SC 29458
(803) 887–3708
Plantation home on the National
Register of Historic Places.

The Shaw House
8 Cyprus Court
Georgetown, SC 29440
(803) 546–9663
Breakfasts and hospitality are
hearty.

SOUTH DAKOTA

Audrie's Cranbury Corner
RR 8, Box 2400
Rapid City, SD 57702
(605) 342–7788
A creatively decorated bed-and-
breakfast.

TENNESSEE

Hannah's House
Route 3, Middle Creek Road
Pigeon Forge, TN 37863
(615) 428–2192
Gourmet picnics among the berry patches.

TEXAS

The Gilded Thistle
1805 Broadway
Galveston Island, TX 77550
(409) 763–0194
Late nineteenth-century house with award-winning landscaping.

High Cotton
214 South Live Oak
Bellville, TX 77418
(409) 865–9796
1906 house built by a cotton broker. Lots of antiques.

Pride House
409 East Broadway
Jefferson, TX 75657
(214) 665–2675
Victorian, Eastlake, and country primitive furnishings.

The White House Inn
203 North Commercial
Goliad, TX 77963
(512) 645–2701
Inn done in art deco and English and American antiques.

UTAH

Center Street Inn
169 East Center
Logan, UT 84321
(801) 752–3443
Century-old mansion and carriage house with exotic rooms.

VERMONT

The Black Lantern
Route 118
Montgomery Village, VT 05470
(802) 326–4507
Dust-swirling stagecoaches dropped off travelers in 1803.

Blueberry Hill
Goshen, VT 05733
(802) 247–6735
1813 farmhouse and skier's paradise.

The Churchill House Inn
Route 73 East, Box WB7
Brandon, VT 05733
(802) 247–3300
Gourmet country cooking in an 1871 farmhouse.

Dorset Inn
Church and Main streets
Dorset, VT 05251
(802) 867–5500
200-year-old home that serves fresh country dinners.

Emersons' Guest House
82 Main Street
Vergennes, VT 05491
(802) 877–3293
Lovely Victorian home in the Champlain Valley.

The Four Columns Inn
230 West Street
Newfane, VT 05345
(802) 365–7713
Stately inn accented by four gracious Greek columns.

The Governor's Inn
86 Main Street
Ludlow, VT 05149
(802) 228–8830
Prize-winning chefs cook. Stars have dined here.

Greenhurst Inn
Bethel, VT 05032
(802) 234–9474
Extensive library in this late-Victorian gem.

Hill Farm Inn
RR 2, Box 2015
Arlington, VT 05250
(802) 375–2269
Restored eighteenth-century farmhouse.

Historic Brookside Farms
Highway 22A
Orwell, VT 05760
(802) 948–2727
Working farm, afternoon tea, musician/writer innkeepers.

The Inn on the Common
Craftsbury Common, VT 05827
(802) 586–9619
New England classic and charming getaway.

1830 Inn on the Green
Route 100, Box 104
Weston, VT 05161
(802) 824–6789
English gardens are the innkeeper's passion.

The Inn at Weathersfield
Route 106, Box 165
Weathersfield, VT 05151
(802) 263–9217
Live in the eighteenth-century for a few days.

Kedron Valley Inn
Route 106
South Woodstock, VT 05071
(802) 457–1473
Breakfast on the porch. Gorgeous quilts abound.

Knoll Farm Country Inn
Bragg Hill Road
Waitsfield, VT 05673
(802) 496–3939
Simple country living the way it used to be.

The Middlebury Inn
14 Courthouse Square
Middlebury, VT 05753
(802) 388–4961
A lovingly restored, 1827 inn in a campus town.

Mill Brook Bed and Breakfast
Route 44, P.O. Box 410
Brownsville, VT 05037
(802) 484–7283
Once a boarding house for local mill loggers.

Rabbit Hill Inn
Lower Waterford, VT 05848
(802) 748–5168
Music, candlelight, and antiquity add up to pampered guests.

The Reluctant Panther
West Road, Box 678
Manchester, VT 05254
(802) 362–2568
Cozy lodge-style rooms and flickering fireplaces.

Shire Inn
P.O. Box 37
Chelsea, VT 05038
(802) 685–3031
Antiques abound in this picturesque inn and setting.

Silas Griffith House
RR 1, Box 66F
Danby, VT 05739
(802) 293–5567
Vermont's first millionaire would still love his place.

Silver Maple Lodge
South Main Street
Fairlee, VT 05045
(802) 333–4326
A 1925 home with a wraparound
colonial porch.

Sunning Hill
Arch Street
Pittsford, VT 05763
(802) 483–9402
Antique plans helped restoration
down to the moldings.

Tulip Tree Inn
Chittenden Dam Road
Chittenden, VT 05737
(802) 483–6213
Spellbinding, romantic, friendly,
adventurous.

The Vermont Inn
Route 4
Killington, VT 05751
(802) 773–9847
Country inn with swimming pool
and exercise room.

Vermont Marble Inn
On the Town Green
Fairhaven, VT 05743
(802) 265–8383
1867 inn believed built by member
of the Ethan Allen family.

West Dover Inn
Route 100
West Dover, VT 05356
(802) 464–5207
Warm, sprawling home with many,
cozy, country accents.

VIRGINIA

Balcony Downs
P.O. Box 563
Glasgow, VA 24555
(703) 258–2100
1802 home in cheerful environment.

The Conyers House
Slate Mills Road, Route 707
Sperryville, VA 22740
(703) 987–8025
So much tradition and splendor in
this 1770 country house.

The Inn at Gristmill Square
P.O. Box 359
Warm Springs, VA 24484
(703) 839–2231
Inn surrounded by art gallery and
much more to explore.

La Vista Plantation
Route 3, Box 1255
Fredericksburg, VA 22401
(703) 898–8444
1857 house reflects a classic revival
style.

Little River Inn
Box 116
Aldie, VA 22001
(703) 327–6742
Rustic home dates to mid-1860s,
plus one-room log cabin.

Mayhurst Bed and Breakfast
P.O. Box 707
Orange, VA 22960
(703) 672–5597
Rooftop gazebo highlights this ele-
gant Victorian.

Sleepy Hollow Farm
Route 3, Box 43
Gordonsville, VA 22942
(703) 832–5555
Old farmhouse filled with the home-
made and the homespun.

Trillium House
P.O. Box 280
Nellysford, VA 22958
(804) 325–9126
Country inn, plus plenty to see and
do nearby.

The Widow Kip's
Route 698
Mt. Jackson, VA 22842
(703) 477–2400
Stately 1830 homestead.

WASHINGTON

Cedarym: A Colonial Bed and
    Breakfast
1011 240th Avenue Northeast
Redmond, VA 98053
(206) 868–4159
Reproduction colonial home with
    gardens.

WEST VIRGINIA

Boydville The Inn at Martinsburg
601 South Queen Street
Martinsburg, WV 25401
(304) 263–1448
1812 home filled with Civil War history.

Countryside Bed and Breakfast
Box 57
Summit Point, WV 25446
(304) 725–2614
Small inn in a quaint village setting.

Folkestone Bed and Breakfast
Martinsburg Road
Berkeley Springs, WV 25411
(304) 258–3743
English-style residence adjacent to a
historic spa.

WISCONSIN

Wisconsin House
2105 East Main
Hazel Green, WI 53811
(608) 854–2233
Circa-1846 home highlighted by
yards of stenciling.

WYOMING

Annie Moore's Guest House
819 University
Laramie, WY 82070
(307) 721–4177
Don't miss the innkeeper's photog-
raphy.

Index

A

Almond Snowballs, 136–37
Amaretto Bread Pudding, 96
Amaretto Cordial, 80
Anise Cakes, 131–32
Antiques
    buying and caring for, 247–51
    using, 227–47
Apothecary jar, 245–46
Appetizers
    Artichoke Dip, Hot, 72
    Beef Pasties, 141
    Brie and Bread, 72
    Clam Spread, 76
    Cucumber Sandwiches, 138
    Greek Hummus Dip, 77
    Green Chili Pie, 75
    Hot Ryes, 74–75
    Meatballs for a Santa Watch, 73–74
    Mexican Roll-Ups, 76
    Mushroom Strudel, The Governor's Inn, 72–73
    Red or Green Pepper Jelly, 71–72
    Sausage Biscuits, 77–78
    Sesame Cheese Sticks, 70–71
    Shrimp Appetizer, 75–76
    Teriyaki Nuts, 71
Apple(s)
    for aroma, 17–18
    for candle holders, 157
    cider, hot spiced, 17–18, 79
    Flan, Cheesy, 135–36
    Glazed Sausage and, 64
    Muffins, Dutch, 127
    Muffins, Skyline, 50
    Pancakes, Baked, 61
    for pectin, 78
    in pie, 100
    for welcome, 22
Applesauce, in muffins, 56
Apricot Glaze French Toast, Churchtown Inn's, 59–60
Armoire, 15, 213–14, 241
Artichoke(s), 92
    with Crabmeat Ravigote, Baby, 90
    Dip, Hot, 72
    Soup, Delicate Cream of, 82–83
Auction, 250

B

Bacon, Canadian, and Eggs, 66–67
Bagels, 157
Baked Apple Pancakes, 61
Baking center, adjustable, 26–27
Bali H'ai Muffins, 53
Balloon, for first aid, 22
Banana
    in muffins, 57
    and Nut Muffins, 54–55, 56
    Pancakes, 61–62
Bangles, cut-crystal, 156
Baskets, 6, 13, 14, 15, 40, 212, 249, 254, 289–90
Bathrobe, 15
Bathroom
    adding, 170
    cleaning advice, 281–83
    decorating, 210, 215–17, 233–35

Bathroom (*cont.*)
 preparing for guests, 13–15
 restoring and renovating,
  182–84
 stenciling, 202
Bath salts, 283
Bathtub, decorating, 183, 202,
 210
Bed, 10, 247–48
 headboard, 195, 200, 235–
  36, 248
Bedding, 9–10, 292–95, 304
Bedroom
 decorating, 199, 217–19,
  235–36
 preparing for guests, 8–13
Beef
 in Meatballs for a Santa
  Watch, ground, 73–74
 Pasties, 141
 Stuffed Tenderloin of, 86
Bellows, 237
Berries, freezing, 50
Beverages
 alcoholic, 79–81
 breakfast, 48–49
 coffee, 45–46
 cranberry juice cocktail, 81
 hot cider, 79
 teatime, 104–7, 113–16
Birch log, 158
Bird cage, 245
Bird feeders and identification,
 7
Biscuit(s)
 crate, 230
 Sausage, 77–78
 Treats, Spring, 139–40
Blackberry Cobbler, 134–35
Block-and-tackle pulley, 230
Blooming Bloody Marys, 81

Blueberry Bread, Whole
 Wheat Wild Maine, 123–
 24
Boiler, copper, 270
Bookcase, 213
Books, 11, 222
 cleaning, 249
 covers, 200
Bottles, 231, 232, 246
Bouquet garni, 91
Braised Leeks, Wild
 Mushrooms, and Roasted
 Red Peppers, 90–91
Brass
 polishing, 280
 removing paint from, 199
Bread
 Brie and, 72
 Coffee Mug, 55–56
 Country Corn, 83
 Dill and Cheese, 83–84
 freezing, 56, 84
 Lemon Cashew, 121
 Lemon Yogurt, 123
 Pumpkin-Raisin Bundt, 122–
 23
 Squire Tarbox Nut Loaf,
  138–39
 Strawberry, 124
 Tropical Tea, 121–22
 Whole Wheat Wild Maine
  Blueberry Bread, 123–24
Breakfast Egg Casserole, 64–65
Breakfast Parfait, 51
Breakfast Quiche, 65
Bricks, 230, 247
Brie and Bread, 72
Broccoli, 92
Bronze, polishing, 280
Brownies, Benner House, 94–
 95

Bugle, 234
Butter, 58–59
Butter churn, 227

C

Cabbage, 42
Cabinets, kitchen, 184–86, 229, 289
Cake pedestal, 29–30
Cake (*See also* Tea Cakes)
  Anise, 131–32
  in Britt House Favorite Trifle, 130–31
  Cappuccino Cheesecake, 137–38
  Cranberry Cheesecake Bars, 132–33
  decorating, 100
  on holidays, 150, 162
  Prize-Winning Spice, 95
  Raisin Harvest Coffee, 124–25
  Spiced Jam Bars, 133
  Squire Tarbox Inn Pound, 131
  Torte Turnaround, 99
Candle(s), 25, 30–31, 108, 192, 211
  holders, 28, 157, 158, 211, 243, 244
  wax, 30–31, 207, 286
Candy, 6, 100
  molds, 58
Cappuccino Cheesecake, 137–38
Carpentry tools and supplies, 180–81
Carrots
  in Bird's Nest Side Dish, 91
Cast-iron, 199

Ceilings, 181, 183, 212
Centerpieces, 28–30, 149, 157–58, 163, 165, 167
Chair rail, 199, 212, 215
Chalkboard, child's, 7
Champagne, chilling, 46
Chard, Swiss, 42
Cheese, 78
  Apple Flan, 135–36
  Brie and Bread, 72
  and Ham Sandwich Puff, 66
  in Hot Ryes, Swiss, 74–75
  Sticks, Sesame, 70–71
Chestnuts, 274
Chicken pot pie, 39
Chili peppers, 75
  in Green Chili Pie, 75
  in Hot Artichoke Dip, 72
Chimney, 169
China, 38, 231
Chocolate
  Bread Pudding with Brandied Apricots and Pears, 97
  butter, 113
  Coeur à la Crème, White, 93–94
  Crust, 137–38
  leaves, 101
  Lemonade, 116
  melting, 100
  mints, 100
  shaving, 100
Christmas, 153–161
  Plum Pudding, Eastlake Inn, 97–99
Cider, hot spiced, 17–18, 79
Cigar box, 228
Citrus Vinaigrette, 86
Clam Spread, 76
Cleaning advice, 7, 275–87

Clothes tree, 9
Clothes wringer, 235
Clothing, decorating with, 214, 238, 242–43
Clothing, storage, 218, 250
Coconut, 39
    Tea Cakes, 120
Coffee, 45–46, 233
    Viennese Mocha, 116
Coffee grinder, 230
Coffee Mug Bread, 55–56
Collections, 194–95, 206, 219–21
Cookie cutters, 37, 42, 112, 142, 156
Cookies, 23, 146
    Almond Snowballs, 136–37
Copper, polishing, 280
Cornish Game Hens with Orange Sauce, Stuffed, 87
Cornstalks, 151
Country Corn Bread, 83
Coupe Toblerone, 96
Crab
    Brunch Squares with Red-Pepper Cream Sauce, 69–70
    Ravigote, 90
    soft-shell, 92
Cradle, 241
Cranberry(ies)
    barrel, 140
    Cheesecake Bars, 132–33
    Cordial, 80
    in Cranbury Corner Muffins, 126
    juice cocktail, 81
    Juice Sparkler, 49
    and Orange Sauce, 152
    scoop, 240

Cream
    clotted, 103, 118–19
    whipped, 84, 99, 100
Crock, 106, 216, 234, 240
Crystal, 38, 231, 232
Cucumber Sandwiches, 138, 143
Cupboard doors, 185
Curtains and draperies, 206–8
Cutting board, 229, 280

D

Decorating, 189–226
    with antiques, 227–47
    basics, 191–97
Deed box, 230
Desk, 218, 236, 239, 244
Desserts, 93–101, 130–38
    Almond Snowballs, 136–137
    Amaretto Bread Pudding, 96
    Anise Cakes, 131–32
    Blackberry Cobbler, 134–35
    Brownies, Benner House, 94–95
    Cappuccino Cheesecake, 137–38
    Cheesy Apple Flan, 135–36
    Chocolate Bread Pudding with Brandied Apricots and Pears, 97
    Christmas Plum Pudding, Eastlake Inn, 97–99
    Coupe Toblerone, 96
    Cranberry Cheesecake Bars, 132–33
    English Lemon Curd, 137
    Leftover Pudding Surprise, 99
    Pound Cake, Squire Tarbox Inn, 131

Sour Cream (or Yogurt) Raisin Pie, 130
Spice Cake, Prize-Winning, 95
Spiced Jam Bars, 133
Torte Turnaround, 99
Trifle, Britt House Favorite, 130–31
Walnut Pie, 133–34
White Chocolate Coeur à la Crème, 93–94
Devils on Horseback, Hannah Marie's, 140–41
Dill and Cheese Bread, 83
Dishcloth, 36
Doilies, 28, 34, 35, 165, 218–19, 224, 237, 293
Doll carriage, 237
Doll clothing, 242
Doors, 179, 212
Doorstop, 228, 239
Dresser, 234, 289
Drier rack, 237
Dyes, 148–49

E

Easel, 222
Easter, 147–49
Easy Spud Breakfast, 64
Eggcup, 38, 68
Eggs, 64–68
in Breakfast Quiche, 65
Canadian-Baconed, 66–67
Casserole, Breakfast, 64–65
on Easter, 147–49
in Easy Spud Breakfast, 64
in Green Chili Pie, 75
on Halloween, 150–51
in Ham and Cheese Sandwich Puff, 66

for One, Shaw House, 65–66
on Saint Patrick's Day, 147
on Valentine's Day, 147
Electrifying house, 172–73
Entertaining etiquette, 41
Entertaining preparations, 27–28
Entrees and side dishes, 86–92
Eucalyptus, 16

F

Fabric (*See also* Sheets)
car-seat, 213
stain removal, 285–87, 293
stenciling on, 203–4
on walls, 200
on windows, 207
Face masks, 218
Fan, ceiling, 13
Fan, decorative, 206
Financing, home, 174
Fingerbowl, 35
Fingernail polishing, 19
Fire
extinguisher, 238
starting, 266–69
Fireplace decor, 269–79
First aid remedies, 22
Fish, 92–93, (*See also* Crab, Lobster, Shrimp)
Flags, decorating with, 145
Flan, Cheesy Apple, 135–36
Flashlight, 5
Flatware, 184
Floor plan, 175
Floors, hardwood
cleaning, 219, 284–85
painting, 219
restoring, 181–82
stenciling, 204
Flower bricks, 216

Flowerpot, 39, 256, 257, 258
Flowers, dried, 16–17, 32, 246, 255
Flowers, fresh, 30
  arranging, 30, 253–56
  displaying, 245–47, 256, 258
  drying, 18
  as garnishes, 43–44, 45
  growing, 247, 255, 262, 263
  in tea, 114
Flowers, silk, 222, 231
Foot warmers, 109, 239
Foyer, 213
Framing, 224, 225–26, 250
French toast, 59–61, 63, 150
Fruit(s), 48–51
  in bread, 129
  in Breakfast Parfait, 51
  butter, 58
  Crisp, Stu's Quick, 63–64
  in Eastlake Inn Christmas
    Plum Pudding, 97–99
  frosted, 159
  as garnishes, 43, 44–45, 50, 84, 92
  Hot Curried, 49–50
  and milk drinks, 48–49
  salad, frozen, 50
  toppings for, 50
  and yogurt, 50
Frying pans, 232
Furniture
  cleaning, 290–91
  oil, 180–81

G

Game, glue gun, 162
Gardening, 257–63
Garlic Butter, 88–89
Garnishes, 41–45, 84, 92

Gazpacho, White, 82
General's Toast, 60
Ghost stories, 270–72
Gift giving, 112, 146
Gingerbread house, 158–59
Ginger Muffins, 125
Ginger root, 93
Glazed Sausage and Apples, 64
Golf bag, 261
Granola, Homemade, 51–52
  in Breakfast Parfait, 51
Grapefruit
  Salad of Endive, Radicchio,
    and, 85
  Sorbet, 88
Grater, 211
Gravy boat, 246
Greek Hummus Dip, 77
Greeting cards, 224–25
Guest book, 22–23

H

Halloween, 150–51
Ham and Cheese Sandwich
  Puff, 66
Hamper, 10
Handkerchiefs, 36
Hangers, 12
Hats, 167, 242
Hearth cooking, 152, 161, 272–74
Herb(s)
  for aroma, 6, 16–17
  in bouquet garni, 91
  for garnishes, 43, 44, 84
  growing, 263–64
  on Saint Patrick's Day, 147
  in tea, 108, 114–15
  vinegar, 85
  wreath, 151

Holidays, celebrating, 145–62
Home, old
    restoring, 175–82
    shopping for, 170–75
    turning into inn, 173, 174
Honeymooners, 22
Honeysuckle, 17
Hosting guests, 18–22
Hot Buttered Wedgwood, 79
Hot Curried Fruit, 49–50
Hot dogs, 65–66, 93
Hot tub, 242, 260
Hot water bottle, 11
Humidor, 236

I

Ice bucket, 46, 243
Ice cubes and sculpture, 43, 81
Icing, royal, 159
Independence Day, 150
Ironing, 10, 292–94
Ironing board, 12, 228

J

Japanese dinner, 164
Jelly, Red or Green Pepper,
    71–72
Jewelry box, 242
Juice, 39, 49 (*See also* Beverages)

K

Kahlua, Kim's Homemade, 79–
    80
Ketchup container, 101
Kissing ball, 155
Kitchen
    cleaning advice, 278, 280–81

decorating, 215, 228–33
renovation, 26–27, 184–86
tips, 26–27, 289–90
Knife rest, 232

L

Lace, 155, 157, 219
Ladder, 40, 213, 229–30
Ladle, 231, 239
Lamp, 211, 238
    shade, 228, 237–38
Laundry care, 292–95
Lemon
    Cashew Bread, 121
    Curd, English, 137
    Yogurt Bread, 123
Lemonade
    Chocolate, 116
    Freshly Squeezed, 115–16
Lettuce, 85–86 (*See also* Salad)
Light-bulb ring, 18
Lighting, 210–12
Lobster, 93
Luggage rack, 236
Lumber, cost, 174

M

Magazines, 11, 241
Mailbox, 230
Mannequin, 234, 238
Mantel, 218, 269
Maple-sugar bucket, 240, 244–
    45
Meatballs for a Santa Watch,
    73–74
Memorial Day, 150
Menus, 164
Meringue Mushrooms, 142
Mexican Roll-Ups, 76

Mildew, removing, 187, 282
Milk can, 231, 246
Milk, scalding, 130
Millet, 86
Mint Tea, Churchtown's, 115
Mirror, 34–35, 214
Mocha, Viennese, 116
Molding, 177, 212, 214, 215
Morning Glory Muffins, 54
Mortar, testing, 172
Moth bag, 16
Muffins, 52–57, 125–29
  Bali H'Ai, 53
  Banana Nut, 54–55
  in baskets, 40
  Cranbury Corner, 126
  Dutch Apple, 127
  freezing, 56, 57
  and fruit butter, 58
  Ginger, 125
  Morning Glory, 54
  Orange, 126–27
  Peach Cobbler, 128
  Pineapple, 53–54
  Quick Mix, 55
  Skyline Apple, 52
Mushroom, 73
  Aztec, 42
  Strudel, Governor's Inn, 72–73

N

Naming rooms and house, 190, 195
Napkins, 34–38, 145
Napkin rings and holders, 37, 145, 158, 164, 165, 167, 228
Nasturtium sandwiches, 142
New Year's Eve, 161–62

Nightlight, 14, 210, 211
Nightshirt, 11–12
Nostalgia, 224–26
Note cards, 22
Nut Loaf, Squire Tarbox, 138–39
Nuts, Teriyaki, 71

O

Odor removal, 288–89
Onions, 92
Orange
  and Cranberry Sauce, 152
  Frappé, Grant Corner Inn, 48–49
  Muffins, 126–27
  Sauce, 87

P

Paint
  in bathroom, 183
  calcimine, 181
  marine, 187
  removing, 198, 199
Painting, 192, 197–99
  glass globe, 211
  iron, 248
  paneling, 178–79
Pancakes, 61–62, 63
Paneling, 178–79, 183, 216
Parasol, 7
Parties, 145–67
Pasta Primavera, Chef Michael Myers', 88–89
Pasties, Beef, 141
Peach Cobbler Muffins, 128
Pear, for garnish, 44–45
Pectin, 78
Peg rail, 14

Pepper Jelly, Red or Green, 71–72
Pests, animal and insect, 256, 259, 260, 263
Pew, 237
Piano legs, 233
Picnics, 47–48
Pie (*See also* Cobbler, Flan, Quiche)
  Green Chili, 75
  Sour Cream (or Yogurt) Raisin, 130
  Walnut, 133–34
Pie safe, 185–86, 228
Pillows, 145, 218–19
Pillow shams and cases, 208, 292–93
Pineapple
  for decorating, 20–21, 157–58
  Muffins, 53–54
  serving, 51
  Spice Scones, 117–18
Pinecones
  for decorations, 154–55, 158
  for fires, 267
Place cards, 31–32
Place mats, 33–35
Plants
  displaying, 28, 29, 211, 230, 244–45, 256
  growing, 256–58, 262
Plaster, 179, 200–201
Plastic pails, 39
Plum Pudding, Eastlake Inn Christmas, 97–99
Pomander, 16, 272
Pond, digging, 259–60
Popovers, 57
Porch, 188

Post cards, 22
Potato
  in Bird's Nest Side Dish, 91
  in Easy Spud Breakfast, 64
Potpourri, 18, 246
Press cupboard, 241
Pulpit, 237
Pumpkin, 150, 152
  and Raisin Bundt Bread, 122–23

Q

Quail, Stuffed Brace of, 87–88
Quiche, Breakfast, 65
Quick Fruit Crisp, Stu's, 63–64
Quick Muffin Mix, 55
Quilt, 32, 179, 214, 223–24, 247

R

Radiator, 215
Radish, 92
Raisin
  Harvest Coffee Cake, 124–25
  Pie, Sour Cream (or Yogurt), 130
  and Pumpkin Bundt Bread, 122–23
  to soften, 129
Rake, 223–24
Raspberry vinegar, 85
Recipe cards, 23
Roof, 187
Rosemary Tea, 114
Rose petals, for fragrance, 18
Rugs and carpets, 219, 288
  stenciling, 204–5

S

Sachet, 16
Sad iron, 228
Saint Patrick's Day, 147
Salad, 42, 85–86
    as centerpiece, 163
    of Endive, Radicchio, and
        Grapefruit with Citrus
        Vinaigrette, 85
Salt containers, 231, 232,
    240
Salt-free diet, 92
Sandwich(es), 142–43
    Cucumber, 138
    giant submarine, 162
    Puff, Ham and Cheese, 66
    Spring Bank, 140
Sauce
    Crabmeat Ravigote, 90
    Cran-orange, 152
    cream, 70
    freezing, 91
    Hard, 98–99
    for Meatballs, 74
    Nutmeg, 134–35
    Orange, 87
    pouring, 101
    Red-Pepper Cream, 69
Sausage, 69
    and Apples, Glazed, 64
    Biscuits, 77–78
    in Breakfast Egg Casserole,
        64–65
    in Breakfast Quiche, 65
    in Shaw House Egg for One,
        65
Sausage stuffer, 230
Scales, 244, 256
Scent-sational ideas, 6, 16–18,
    161, 282

Scones
    Pineapple Spice, 117–18
    Tea, 117
Scoop, 211, 239–40
Seashells, 32, 38
Serving dishes, 38–45
Sesame Cheese Sticks, 70–71
Sewing machine, 228, 241
Sewing supplies, 10, 240, 243–
    44
Sheets, 9–10, 196, 292, 294–
    95
    as curtains, 207
    decorating with, 208–10
    folding, 294
    as tablecloths, 33
Shoes, button-top, 239, 245
Shopping, 27–28, 290
Shortening, measuring, 70
Shrimp
    Appetizer, 75–76
    Spread, 77
Sifter, 229
Sightseeing information, 21
Silver
    goblets, 39
    polishing, 280
Sketch, house, 22
Sleep bags, 17
Sleigh, 154, 245
Slipcovers, 210
Soap, 14, 260, 283–84
Sorbet, Grapefruit, 88
Soup, 82–84, 109
    Delicate Cream of Artichoke,
        82–83
    garnishes for, 84
    serving, 39
    White Gazpacho, 82
Sour Cream Raisin Pie, 130
Souvenirs, 22, 23

Special occasions, 21–22, 110–13, 144–67
Spiced Jam Bars, 133
Spice rack, 230
Squash, 41–42, 152, 167
Stain removal, 285–87
Stairway, 214, 279
    painting, 169, 219
    stenciling, 204
Stenciling, 201–5, 243, 244
Stereo, concealing, 241
Stereopticon, 241
Stove, 233
Strawberry
    boxes, 246
    Bread, 124
    as garnish, 45, 50
    Tea Cakes, 119–20
Stuffed Brace of Quail, 87–88
Stuffed Cornish Game Hens
    with Orange Sauce, 87
Stuffed Tenderloin of Beef,
    86
Sugar, 63
Sun screen, 187–8
Syrup, 63, 129

T

Tablecloth, 32–33, 145
    for beds, 217
    for curtains, 207, 208
Table, 11, 228, 236
    coffee, 228, 237
    dining, 29, 34, 40
Table setting, 28–45, 145, 149
Tea(s)
    Churchtown's Mint, 115
    iced, 106–7, 113–14
    making, 23, 104–7

Rosemary, 114–15
    serving, 102–4, 107–10
    Sun, 115
    theme, 110–13
Tea Cakes
    Coconut, 120
    French, 119
    Strawberry, 119–20
Teacups, 18, 246, 257
Teakettle, cleaning, 111
Teapot, 104, 108, 110, 257
Television, hiding, 241
Teriyaki Nuts, 71
Thanksgiving, 151–52
Tiles, 38–39, 282, 290–91
Tin, punched, 185–86
Tins, 38, 240
Toast caddy, 228
Toaster, 228
Toiletries, 6, 14
Tomato rose, 42
Tongs, 229
Tool caddy, 261, 276–77
Tools, carpentry, 177, 180–81,
    234
Towel racks and holders, 15,
    229, 234–35
Towels, 10, 15, 34, 35, 215,
    292
Toys, 10, 226
Travel information, 21
Tray, 230, 236
Tricycle, 247
Trifle, Britt House Favorite,
    130–31
Tropical Tea Bread, 121–22
Trunk, 235, 243

U

Utility bills, 171

V

Valentine's Day, 146–47
Vanilla, 100
Vase, 30, 38, 145, 245–46,
    253, 254
Vegetables, 90–92
    in Chef Michael Myers' Pasta
        Primavera, 88–89
    with Garlic Butter, 88–89
    as garnishes, 41–43
Ventilation, 13, 179–80
Violets, 110

W

Waffles, 62
Wainscoting, 178, 183–84
Wallcoverings, 199–201, 208–
    10
Wall hangings, 216, 221–26
Walls
    corners, 178
    in old house, 178–79, 201
    paneled, 178–79, 216
Walnut Pie, 133–34
Washboard, 225–26, 235
Washcloth, 36
Wassail, 160
    Churchtown Inn's Favorite,
        80–81

Wastebasket, 240
Water, drinking, 12, 45, 105,
    111, 286
Wheelbarrow, 258
Whiskey barrel, 258
White Chocolate Coeur à la
    Crème, 93–94
Wicker, 291
Window cleaning, 279
Window treatments, 203, 206–
    8
Wine, 21, 46–47
    stains, 285
    storage, 213–14, 239
Wood (*See also* Floors)
    cleaning, 280, 287
    polishing, 248, 291
    refinishing, 248
    repairing, 181, 187
    unvarnished, 180–81
Wreath, 145, 151, 206

Y

Yarn, 213
    winder, 244
Yogurt
    and fish, 93
    and fruit, 50, 51
    and oatmeal, 93
    Raisin Pie, 130